# The Sales Bible

# The Sales Bible

## The Ultimate Sales Resource

### Revised Edition

# Jeffrey Gitomer

John Wiley & Sons, Inc.

Published by John Wiley & Sons, Inc., Hoboken, New Jersey.
Published simultaneously in Canada.

For general information on our other products and services please contact our Customer Care Department within the United States at (800) 762-2974, outside the United States at (317) 572-3993 or fax (317) 572-4002.

Wiley also publishes its books in a variety of electronic formats. Some content that appears in print may not be available in electronic books. For more information about Wiley products, visit our web site at www.wiley.com.

Library of Congress Cataloging-in-Publication Data:

Gitomer, Jeffrey
 The sales bible, the ultimate sales resource / Jeffrey Gitomer
  p. cm.
Includes index.
 ISBN 0-471-45629-2 (pbk.)
 1. Selling--Study and teaching. I. Title.
 HF5438.2.G58 2003
 658.85--dc21

2003001696

Printed in the United States of America
30  29  28  27  26  25

I want to
dedicate this book
and issue a special
*"Thank you"*
to every buyer
and prospect
who ever told me,
"No."

# I just made a sale!

You are my new customer. Thank you for your business. I appreciate your support and your patronage.

With all the customers I serve through my consulting practice, speaking engagements, volunteer activities, and through writing *Sales Moves* and *The Sales Bible*, I have three goals:

1. To help people.
2. To establish long-term relationships.
3. To have fun.

My goal in writing this book was to make it so helpful to you that you would tell (refer) ten of your co-workers and friends to buy one. Please let me know if I reach my goal with you.

Because of you, and all my other valued customers,
I have the opportunity to do what I love to do …
sell, write, speak, and teach.

# Thank You!

# About the Author

Jeffrey Gitomer is the best sales trainer in the world. He gives seminars, runs annual sales meetings, and conducts internet training programs on selling and customer service. He can be reached at 704/333-1112 or e-mail salesman@gitomer.com.

## What real salespeople say about *The Sales Bible*

*"Jeffrey Gitomer's* Sales Bible *is overflowing with creative tips, tools, and techniques that'll make you GIT off your butt, GIT out the door, and GIT some SALES!!!"*
Don "The Idea Guy" Snyder
www.DonTheIdeaGuy.com

*"Sales Bible? More like sales commandments. Jeffrey's no-nonsense approach to sales in this book has put money in my and my salespeople's pockets."*
Chris Rohland
Business Development Director
Greenspun Media Group

*"Jeffrey Gitomer's* Sales Bible *is, by far, the most effective sales tool I have seen in my 23 years in the profession. Please stop selling these books before the competition catches on."*
Greg Gillis
Outside Sales (Foodservice Equipment)
Loubat Equipment Co.

*"Jeffrey is right. It does take an investment to make more money selling. I used up three highlighters on this book."*
Dan Seidman,
SalesAutopsy.com
Author of *The Death of 20th Century Selling*

*"I have read a number of articles and books about sales, this was the first time I felt a book was written to me. I have a feeling my sales people will feel the same as I do."*
Jim Horvath
Bates Container

*"Every business person is in Sales regardless of your title. This is a must 'read and apply' for everyone in business, from the CEO to the shipping clerk."*
Ron Shelton
Sales Engineer
TelCove

# 49.5 More Reasons You Should Own One …

*"The Sales Bible is a book that belongs on the bookshelf – make that next to the phone of every sales professional. Whether you're looking for a new idea, fresh approach, or a good old-fashioned kick in the butt, Gitomer delivers."*

Jenifer Lambert
VP Business Development
TERRA Resource Group

*"The Sales Bible doesn't belong on your shelf. It should be opened, in your hands, where it makes you money!"*

Dan Seidman,
SalesAutopsy.com
Author of *The Death of 20th Century Selling*

*"Thanks to this book I make a lot of money. I should send Gitomer a commission check every week (but I won't)."*

Sheri Horoshko
Sales Rep
Rockwell Transportation Services, Inc.

*"This book is second only to the* Holy Bible *for providing you the tools you need to succeed."*

Stuart H. Lowe
Project Sales Engineer
John W. Danforth Service Company, Inc.

*"Pure Dynamite! In my almost thirty years of sales training, I've never before found such a common sense how-to approach to sales inside the covers of a book. Jeffrey's* Sales Bible *is required reading for every salesperson in our organization!"*

Alan Risener
Market Manager
Results Radio Group
Rolla, MO

"The Sales Bible *exudes an attitude that is contagious. The faster you get the attitude, the more successful you'll be.*"

Mike Kelly
Director of Strategic Sales Development
Muzak, LLC

"The Sales Bible *has been and continues to be the most productive, fruitful seed in my sales library.*"

Lori Ward
Vehicle Tracking Sales Consultant
Locarta Technologies, Inc.

*"Absolutely one of the top five sales books I've ever read. It's the basics – sales is not rocket science but doing the right things over and over – Jeffrey knows the right things – and is willing to share."*

Cyndi Caldwell
Account Executive
WKHX WYAY WDWD
ABC RADIO ATLANTA

*"It's the multi-tool of sales books. When you have this one, all the others become redundant. Just one page in this book made it all worthwhile."*

Andrew Risner
The Big Man with Huge Solutions
London, U.K.

*"The advice & wisdom found in* The Sales Bible *has not only made me successful, but has contributed to the success of every member of my team.* The Sales Bible *is required reading in our office!"*

Eric Flannery
District Manager
Arch Wireless

*"I am 24 years old and have no education beyond high school. Jeffrey gave me the drive and the knowledge to not only be the most successful sales and marketing person on our staff, but also the courage to start and run my own company. Not bad for 24. Gitomer for life!"*

Dave Warner
Sales/Marketing
Micro Manufacturing, Inc.

*"Bookmark this site ... why-didn't-I-read-gitomers-sales-bible-5-years-ago.com"*
Joe Norwood
Sales Manager
York Simpson Underwood Neighborhood Marketing Services

*"Wait! The material in this book is only priceless if you choose apply it. Don't even think of opening this book ... until you're ready to become a success."*
Mike Tischer
New Business Development
Tailored Solutions, Inc.

*In the beginning, there were lackluster sales. Jeffrey Gitomer said, "Let there be WOW!"*
Jason Damron
Sales Rep
Video Products Distributors, Inc.

*"Your book* The Sales Bible *has given me a FIRE inside that only you can understand! I love your book! Thank you! It makes me want to be a better person in sales and also in my personal life. It has now been three months since I sent you this E-mail. I am happy to say that my sales have been at 100%, I repeat 100% success. I am a changed man in every aspect of my life!"*
Harold Lockwood
President
Advanced Tool

*"This book is soooo ... good, that I used the invaluable information in it to sell Jeffrey Gitomer on putting my testimonial in this book!!"*
Al Garza, P.E.
Director of Engineering Sales
Alamo Controls, Inc.

*"I still refer to my first edition of* The Sales Bible *to get myself and my sales staff back to the basics of Jeffrey's stellar sales techniques and customer service philosophies. I was unemployed when I bought* The Sales Bible *in 1994 ... I now run one of the largest business brokerages in the country. Jeffrey's no-nonsense approach to sales justified and solidified my own 'value first business style' that enabled me to get to the top ... the right way."*

Andrew R. Cagnetta CBI, CFBI
President
Transworld Business Brokers, LLC.

*"Jeffrey Gitomer's book* The Sales Bible *could have led Moses out of the wilderness and surely can lead any fumbling sales rep to glory! He puts the pedal to the metal, the tire to the road, the butter on the bread with words from the mouths of babes and if you have a shred of lifeforce, this book is the #1 absolutely essential volume that must be on your bookshelf, close at hand at all times."*

Peter Hupp
Sacramento, Ca.

*"Our sales are double what they were last year at this time, while our industry is reporting a new excuse weekly for their poor performance. I use your weekly Sales Caffeine and TrainOne sessions as the road map for our sales success."*

George Armstrong
Sales Manager, Partner
Media Capital Associates, LLC

*"Just reading a few pages of* The Sales Bible *each day jump-started me on the road to increased sales and more income. Jeffrey Gitomer is my pick for sales motivator of 2003."*

Tim Soldan
Account Executive, PAX-TV

*"I highly recommend* The Sales Bible *to anyone who is in sales. Starting a business isn't easy but with the help of Jeffrey, I had a crash class in selling. I refer to it before every sales call. I stayed up all night and read it before my first big presentation. I made the sale!"*

Christina Sutton
Partner
InDesign Creative Studios

*"I started in sales with a family-owned business in January 2003. Following Jeffrey's advice about closing sales on Monday to start off the week, I am happy to report that 7 out of the last 8 Mondays I closed new business to get the week off to a good start. Thanks, Jeffrey!"*

Paul Pescitelli
Phoenix Designs

"The Sales Bible *is an incredible resource. I use it every day."*
Tim Haraden
Branch Manager
G&K Services

*"Not only do I practice the lessons of* The Sales Bible, *as a speaker/trainer in the recruiting industry, I'm always referencing the lessons from Jeffrey's books. I actually read this one cover to cover, which says a lot for a sales personality."*

Candy Bradford CPC,CTS
President
Bradford Group, LLC

*"I am an Account Executive for Oakwood Corporate Housing and have been in the sales industry for 10+ years.* The Sales Bible *is literally my bible. It has given me fresh and effective sales tools to utilize in a tumultuous economy. I doubled my sales in less than 3 months after reading* The Sales Bible."

Malia Johnson
Account Executive
Oakwood Worldwide

*"After only being in sales for eight months, my company gave me the title 'salesman,' but Jeffrey's book,* The Sales Bible, *made me a great 'Sales Man.'"*

Aaron Sabartinelli
Independent Dealer
Aqua Solutions

*"Jeffrey Gitomer delivers a heaping dish of the 'necessary' for every salesperson: Know and understand your client, their business, and their needs. Be honest about YOUR product/services and, for gosh sakes, be decent, respectable human beings in the process. Jeffrey Gitomer captures some very mysterious truths for the sales public: Be Knowledgeable, Be Honest, Be Helpful, Be FUN!! My sales team has profited professionally and personally from his writings and teachings. Jeffrey never fails to blatantly tell sales people the good, the bad, and the ugly. Should be required reading for any individual striving to transform their 'sales selves' into a true professional."*

Jackie Hoofring
Vice President, Operations
On Assignment Lab Support


*"Just like the* Holy Bible, The Sales Bible *is an inspirational must read for anyone selling anything. I regularly re-read and analyze chapters. It's a book you'll come back to for a refresher long after the first reading."*

Chris Stephenson
Chief of Creative Ideas
SPI (sunrise promotions, inc.)


*"Jeffrey's work in sales is among the best there is. His original writing was instrumental and significant research for my master's thesis, 'An Analysis of the Use of Humor in Sales.'"*

Bob Pontius
General Manager
The Vitamin Shoppe


*"Jeffrey's* Sales Bible *is a must read for every independent contractor; it has changed the way I run my business. Thanks, Jeffrey!"*

Crystal Chappell
Thomas Publishing Company

"Outrageous ... that's what prospects, clients, and friends say about my voice mail message on my mobile phone! However I get more people leaving messages and WANTING to speak with me because of it! Thanks for sharing this winning idea from your Sales Bible Jeffrey ... I never let it out of my sight! Oh by the way, I really do get people calling me up ... just to listen to my message and they tell others about it too which has led to heaps of profitable business relationships!"

Gary Outrageous
The World Famous Business Hypnotist!
Gary Foster & Associates

"I take the time to read this book prior to every sales meeting or training I walk into. Quite simply, it reminds me that sales is an ever changing industry where a positive attitude and a personal commitment allow for success."

John D. Simpson
Regional Manager
GSM Wireless

"I have been a sales professional for nearly a decade, which means I knew it all; then I read The Sales Bible. After reading The Sales Bible and applying the principles found within, my professional relationships improved, my sales increased, my competitors found it more difficult to gain an audience with my clients, and most importantly, I learned that as a sales professional you can always learn more. This was a very good read, this book never leaves my side."

Dean Forcucci
Sales Engineer
Experian–Scorex

"Jeffrey Gitomer's The Sales Bible is your 15 minutes of reading a day for sales success!"

Peter Radizeski
RAD-INFO, Inc.

"The Sales Bible was not only informative but exciting to read! I could not put it down! I am grateful that it was available during my transition to a new entry level sales position."

James Wickfall
ProxyMed, formerly MEDUNITE

*"The primary thing I have learned from Jeffrey is that differences sell. From the first call to picking up the check, I have learned how Jeffrey's insights make me different from every other person in my industry, and my success is clear evidence of Jeffrey's influence."*

Marc J. Lewyn
Financial Advisor
GV Financial Advisors, Inc.
GV Capital Management, Inc.

*"More sales are made because of friendship and you have more fun along the way. And when people laugh they remember more of what you have said, so being outrageous is a good sales technique."*

Sheila Long Armstrong
author of *Never Drink Coffee From Your Saucer and Other Tips on Socially Correct Dining*
published by Andrews & McMeel

*"If there's a better book on sales out there, I have yet to find it. Jeffrey's insight goes far beyond the sales process and reaches deep into the heart of the matter – building the relationship that creates sales."*

Mark Meyer
VP – Sales
Marketing & Technical Materials, Inc.

*"Holy-Moly! The Prophet (Profit?) Gitomer has collected the most sacred of lessons into one very 'good book' on creating real relationships that lead to real business. Jeffrey turns on the light when he says, 'Let there be sales' – And sales are good."*

Don (The Idea Guy) Snyder
www.DonTheIdeaGuy.com

*"The Sales Bible has been terrific at keeping me focused, teaching me new approaches, and frankly, keeping my sales gun full of more yes bullets than my buyers have no's. I'd have cheated myself if I didn't read it, and refer to it regularly."*

Mark Weniger
Vice President of Sales and Acquisitions
Vision Management Services

"The Sales Bible *is an incredibly useful marketing tool. An easy read packed with tips and information for success. I purchased five copies, one for each of my sales associates and one for me. It's a must have book."*

Nancie Cameron
President
Creative Cakes, Inc.

*"I have used* The Sales Bible *as an integral part of my coaching since February of 1997. Gitomer provides tacit strategies that remove the subjective components of managing sales executives and driving revenue. His work provides an objective sales GPS system that removes excuses and provides real life methodologies to drive goals, follow-up, and execution. Personally, I still refer to it at least weekly after 6 years and provide copies of both his books to all my new sales executives."*

Terence Healy
Director of Sales and Marketing
Abacus Communications

*"Ever since reading* The Sales Bible, *my eyes have been opened to just how much I was missing and how good I THOUGHT I was. Now I use Jeffrey's rock-solid advice daily and have realized successes way beyond my expectations!"*

Chris Moline
Owner
CarpetFactory.com

*"You can either go through life 'working' a job or enjoy life by doing what you love. In every sense of the word* The Sales Bible *shows you how to both enjoy and love having your customers 'buy' from you."*

Brian Spears
Market Director
McLeodUSA

*"I can honestly say I'm past the nausea of the sales roller coaster, and am now just enjoying the ride. Being consistent is what will get you to this end."*

Jennifer Stanley
AT&T Wireless
Austin Texas

*"Jeffrey opened my eyes on how to develop lasting and mutually rewarding business relationships with my prospects, built on dedication, commitment, and creativity."*

István Préda
Managing Director
Magánbankár Buyout Advisory Kft.

*"Since I began to end conversations with my customers with the statement 'Thanks for being my customer,' I have garnished more comments and positive results than any other single thing I have done in the past year. Instant results."*

Christopher Frey
V.P. CGM Industries Inc.
CGM Industries Inc.
CGM Transportation, Inc.

*"Innovative, Inspiring, and Creative!* The Sales Bible *gave us a new outlook to not only compete and win in today's fighting economy, but to make ourselves memorable to our customers in the process!"*

Julie Carey
Director of Marketing & Business Development
SWM Printing & Promotions

*"You can't afford to not read this book! When I stray from the positive elements and paths that lead to success and achievement, I pick up* The Sales Bible *to get back on track!"*

Larry Tiberio
Hamilton Sundstrand

## And reason 49.5 you should own *The Sales Bible* --

*"So we get to go to college."*

*Julia Caplen
Claudia Grodowsky
Morgan Grodowsky
Jeffrey's granddaughters*

# The Sales Bible

## Table of Contents

Practical sales information you can read daily and use immediately.

**Read it from cover to cover ... or ...**
**Open it anywhere and learn what you need for the moment ... and ...**
**Use it the minute you read it.**

# Part 3 Please Allow Me to Introduce Myself

# Part 4 Making a Great Presentation

# Part 5 Objections, Closing and Follow-up ... Getting to *YES*

# The Sales Bible

## THE SALES BIBLE

**Part 1**
**The Rules, the Secrets, the Fun**

# Genesis

# Begin Now!

Everyone wants to succeed at sales. Most people don't.

It's not that they can't. It's just that they don't know how.

*The Sales Bible* is a success tool. A place where you can get insight about all facets of sales.

There are also rules. To succeed at sales you must:
• Know the rules
• Learn the rules
• Take ownership of the rules
• Live by the rules

The Book of Genesis reveals a story of the new way of sales, talks about a few of the basic rules, and presents a surefire way to achieve any rule, sales goal, or career goal ...

Don't just read it.
Use it. Go for it.

*"If you think you can,*
*or if you think you can't,*
*you're right either way."*
Henry Ford

1.1

# *The Sales Bible,*
# The Second Decade

What makes sales books endure? Why do salespeople read sales books? Reason: Salespeople are looking for **answers**. *The Sales Bible* is 110% answers. I love to give answers.

This is the second decade of *The Sales Bible*. The book has endured and will continue to endure, because it gives easy-to-implement, real-world answers that you can take out onto the street a minute after you read it, and turn the ideas into money.

Over the years, some of the articles have been revised and updated. They are still what I believe to be true about sales. Most of the revised articles relate to technology as it applies today. Ten years ago, there was no such thing as e-mail.

Time flies – but not as fast as technology.

Ten years ago, laptops had memories of 30 megabytes. Ten years ago, you could receive something via 2,400 KB modems. I was a lot poorer 10 years ago than I am today, thanks to this book.

So here is *The Sales Bible*, the second decade.

I will report back again in ten years.

Jeffrey Gitomer

# Introduction

# "It'll never happen."

## *Where did this book come from?*

As with most sales, it started when I got turned down. An article published about me and my sales skills in the *Charlotte Observer* in the spring of 1992 made my phone ring off the hook. I went running back to the paper to offer my services. "I want to write a weekly article on sales," I trumpeted. Not only did they turn me down, they said, "It'll never happen." I said, "No, it'll never happen here." That same morning – 1 hour later – I struck a deal with the *Charlotte Business Journal* to publish a weekly column on selling skills. I called it *Sales Moves*.

## Next time someone tells you "never," remember that means "not for at least 1 hour."

Hey, my name is Jeffrey Gitomer and I'm a salesman. I don't have a Ph.D. I'm a college dropout. I don't live in an ivory tower, I live in Charlotte, North Carolina. I learned to sell in New Jersey and New York, where I grew up. I was in multilevel marketing when it was called pyramiding. I have cold called every office in downtown Charlotte, and I've cold called Fortune 500 company presidents and made the sale. I've made $1 sales and I've made $1,000,000 sales. I'm a salesman who has been on the street for almost 30 years. Sometimes face up, sometimes face down. I love to sell.

*Sales Moves* first appeared in *The Business Journal* in Charlotte on March 23, 1992. The column was an instant success. It soon found its way to Dallas, Atlanta, Denver, Princeton, and a number of other cities.

Mark Ethridge, publisher of *The Business Journal*, Pulitzer Prize-winning journalist, and my good friend and supporter, said that publishing *Sales Moves* was his most impactful marketing decision of 1992. WOW.

People began to call, and still do every day, from all over the country. Papers wanting to publish the column, readers thanking me for helping them make sales. I found out that salespeople were hanging my weekly article on the wall in their offices. They were copying the column and passing it around. They were mailing it to friends and co-workers in other cities. They were using the column to lead sales meetings.

My daughter, Stacey, bought a car in Charlotte. Everyone in the dealership reads my article. When she got to the closing room (alone), they said, "We're giving you the best deal of the year because we don't want your dad to write anything bad about us."

The first day I wrote an article, I knew I would write a book. It was a natural progression. My good friend and mentor Ty Boyd suggested the same thing. Encouragement means a lot to a salesman. I'm grateful for his; I'm grateful for yours.

The material I use is mine. I'm drawing on my 30 years of selling experience, 16 of which have been in consulting. I have listened to thousands of hours of tapes, read everything I could find, and went to every seminar that time would permit. My mission is to learn as I teach. I seek to learn something new every day.

I will continue to write my weekly column to provide you with information that you can use to make more sales out there in the trenches … today. I know what you're up against. I know how hard you work. I know how frustrating it can be. I will help you.

I began the construction of this book in August 1993. After countless late hours in the office, a week at Beech Mountain, NC, and a week at Hilton Head Island, SC, with my Macintosh; my ace critic, editor, and friend, Rod Smith; and my cat, Lito, I was done. I thought it would be a snap. Seven hundred man-hours later – snap.

Here's *The Sales Bible*. I hope it makes you as much money as it will me.

# 8.5 ways to use this book.

**Salespeople are constantly searching for new ideas.**
**Salespeople need a constant source of motivation.**
**Salespeople need immediate answers.**
**Salespeople are looking to make more sales … today.**

Salespeople have lots of problems all at once. **In the same day they cold call, follow-up ten prospects, go to a networking event, make three presentations, send five letters, get turned down six times, and make one sale.** That's a regular day! Salespeople need a dependable reference with real-world answers to their immediate questions, stumbling blocks, or challenges. They need *The Sales Bible*.

*The Sales Bible* is not a "method" of selling. It's a series of real-world observations, techniques, and philosophies that you can modify to your style of selling. You use what you need to make the sale today. You use what you need to prepare for the sale tomorrow. You acquire the knowledge you need to achieve your sales goals.

*The Sales Bible* is a real-world resource. These lessons aren't a bunch of highbrow, Ph.D., clinical research. They're a result of 30 years of success and failure in some of the toughest selling environments the business world has to offer. They're based on actual experiences of mine that I know work because I worked 'em. They are simple, pragmatic solutions, and they make sense where it counts – in your sales environment. They will help in your real world. Try a few and see.

## Use this book! …

**1. As a resource** … To expand and strengthen your knowledge and expertise with the selling process and daily sales challenges.

**2. For a daily lesson** … As part of your daily rededication to be the best.

**3. In a study group** … To grow and develop as a professional salesperson.

**4. To lead a meeting** … Most chapters are an ideal length to use as a guide for a sales training or brainstorming meeting.

**5. To solve a problem** … When you're out of ideas and need an answer now.

**6. To prepare for a sale** … To gain a competitive advantage.

**7. To close a sale** … The solutions and answers are indexed for fast access.

**8. In the heat of the battle** … Take it with you as you work your sales day and reach for it as the doors begin to slam in your face, as the important contacts need to be made, when that hot prospect won't return the voice-mail message you left for the third time. (*Read on to find way 8.5.*)

## One great way to abuse this book …

**As you read it** … Read with a yellow highlighter and a red pen. Highlight the areas that pertain to the knowledge you seek. Write your thoughts, action plans, and ideas in the margins.

## One great way to learn from this book …

**Try it now** … For maximum benefit, use the information you read as soon as you can. On a prospect or customer. As soon as you use it, you own it. One new technique per day is 220 new techniques per year. In 5 years, you'll have more than 1,000 techniques at your command. WOW. Carry this book with you … Use it as a resource and a reference. Read a chapter at lunch. Discuss a point with your co-workers. But most of all, use it to make a sale. Lots of sales.

## The spirit of sales!

Each chapter has a quote at the top that's designed to capture the spirit of its content. Spirit plays a major role in *The Sales Bible*. The spirit in which the information is offered and the spirit in which it's received – and used. Each lesson stands on its own. Each lesson evolves to the next. Each lesson interacts with the others. Each lesson reflects the whole. Each lesson contributes to the whole.

Read the chapter titled *Post-It Note*™ *your way to achievement* found in *Genesis*. Use this method to chart your progress through this book. It will be good practice, and it will ensure that you get the maximum benefit. Set goals for chapters you'll read each day. Set specific goals for enacting what you've learned. Set goals for improving your attitude. Set goals for having fun in your career. Then set goals for big sales.

The accompanying flashcards, available online, contain crucial support information from *The Sales Bible*. You can carry them with you on sales calls, to networking events, or to the trade show for quick reference under fire. The flashcards will reinforce the principles of sales. They will help you gain mastery of the selling process. Go to www.gitomer.com, register if you are a first-time user, and enter "FLASHCARDS" in the GitBit Box.

# 8.5 Double your money!

I have created an income-doubling plan. It is outlined in *The Book of Numbers*. I did it because so many salespeople have unharnessed talent. I challenge you to double your income. I have given you the tools to do it. Now it's up to you to prove it to yourself. Can you develop the discipline needed to do it?

# So, what's in it for you?

**Your reward** will be the achievement of the loftiest goals you've ever entertained for your sales career.

**Your reward** will be the recognition you'll get as a superior salesperson.

**Your reward** will be the personal satisfaction of being the best salesperson you believe you can be. And you did it yourself.

**Your reward** will be more sales.

I have designed this book to help you
in every facet of your everyday sales tasks
by providing practical real-world solutions
to your real-world selling situations and problems.
A real-world reference. A resource.
A bible.

Before you begin this book, ask yourself the following questions:

- How well do I think I sell?
- How do I practice my skills every day?
- How much time do I spend learning new sales skills?
- How many new techniques do I put into practice daily?
- How dedicated and committed to success am I?

Sales is a discipline. Not a militaristic kind of discipline ("do it or peel potatoes"), but a personal dedication to achievement that can only occur when discipline is present. It's control that comes from within, not rules of law from without. Not the drudgery of discipline, the joy of it. Discipline is the everyday process of focusing on what you want. And striving for it relentlessly until you get it.

I don't want to sound religious, but that's the closest comparative discipline there is. If you pray or meditate every day, that's the discipline, the ritual, you need to succeed at sales. *In sales, you get to make your own miracle.*

# As a salesperson you're the most important person in the world of business!

*Nothing happens in business **until someone sells something**.*

*You sell so that the factory can produce the orders, so that the product can be delivered, so that the administrative salaries can be paid, and so that the new computer system needed for the bean-counting department can be purchased.*

*Selling even occurs when you want the bank to loan you money or extend your line of credit. You must sell your banker or vendor on your ability to perform and repay.*

## *And a sale is always made!*

# Either you sell the customer on YES or he sells you on NO!

# The old way of selling doesn't work anymore ... sort of.

It went out with leisure suits and bell-bottoms. We still wear clothing, just in a different fashion. The same in sales. We must change the way we sell in this decade, or we will not make enough sales to break even, much less to meet our goals and dreams.

The recession of the 1990s forced a change in the sales process that will benefit the world of business forever. To succeed as a sales professional, you must be able to sell someone twice. Or sell to someone who will go out of his or her way to refer you to someone else.

The new way uses the old way; **you must still be a master of every sales technique** – *just employ them in a different way ... a friendly way, a sincere way, a way that emphasizes serving first and selling second.* It always grates me when someone says selling is an art. Baloney. Selling is a science. It is a response-triggered, repeatable set of words, phrases, and techniques that convince the prospect to buy. Like science it requires experimentation to determine what works best or what theories have practical application.

*The new rules of the game are simple, and you can apply them today. Your challenge is not just to use them, but to master them. Here are 7.5 of them to ponder, but there are hundreds in the pages that follow ...*

**1. Say it (sell it) in terms of what the customer wants, needs, and understands** ... Not in terms of what you've got to offer.

**2. Gather personal information** ... And learn how to use it.

**3. Build friendships** ... People want to buy from friends, not salesmen.

**4. Build a relationship shield that no competitor can pierce** ... My competitors call on my clients from time to time. My clients have actually given them my number and told the competitor to call me and get my opinion of their services. They say, "Call Jeffrey Gitomer and explain it to him. If he thinks it's OK, he'll tell us." Will your clients do that if your competitor calls them? What are you doing to ensure it?

**5. Establish common ground** ... If we both like golf or have kids, we've got issues and things in common that will draw us closer.

**6. Gain confidence** ... Once you motivate them to act, you'd better have built enough confidence to buy, or they'll buy from someone else.

**7. Have fun and be funny** ... It ain't brain cancer, it's your career. *Have a great time*. If you can make prospects laugh, you can make them buy. Laughter is tacit approval. Tacit approval leads to contractual approval.

**7.5 Never get caught selling** ... It makes me mad when a salesperson sounds like a salesperson. Learn the science and convert it to an art.

These and hundreds of other rules, guidelines, and techniques contained in these pages are dedicated to the science of selling, so you can turn selling into an art. **Your challenge is to learn to use these techniques and principles daily to succeed in the real world ... your world.**

If you read one lesson in this book every day and practice it as soon as you read it, you will have more than 100 lessons and more than 1,050 techniques in less than 6 months.

Hey, want to learn the best, easiest surefire way to sell everyone you meet? Try reading *Grimm's Fairy Tales* – You won't sell everyone. But you can sell more than you're selling now, much more. **There is an easy way. And it's fun.**

When you read *The Sales Bible,* you gain new knowledge and implement it daily. Learning from the daily experience of its implementation leads to sales mastery. If you don't follow the process, sales will remain a mystery. You may not fail, but you won't succeed. Not the way you want to.

Selling is fun, selling is lucrative, but only if you're willing to get serious about your commitment to being the best you can be at it.

To succeed at selling, you must realize that there is not just one way to sell; there are thousands. You learn a little from everyone and combine it with your experience and adapt it to your personality to develop your style.

The one thing I have found after selling and studying sales for 30 years that is the absolute truth – the best salespeople are the ones with the best attitude, the best product knowledge, and who give the best service.

I have come to an understanding about sales and how sales are made. I came to that understanding after years of making and not making sales. After cold calling and getting hung up on, and after cold calling Fortune 500 presidents and making the sale. My objective is to share that understanding with you so that you can use it to make more sales. Lots more.

# Selling successfully in a down economy.
## What's new new?
## The economy and the rules.

Welcome to the New New Economy. That's the economy that's coming right after the New Economy's bubble finishes bursting.

The new economy is over. Some of it worked; some of it bombed, or should I say, dot.bombed. And many businesses – dot or not – are experiencing their first dose of tight times in 10 years.

Why did the dot.com economy fail? It failed because people forgot to sell something. They tried (unsuccessfully) to combine their business idea with the philosophy of the movie *Field of Dreams*. *If you build it, they will come*. One problem. They came, but they didn't buy.

For a year or so, America marveled at how some kid could come to work in flip-flops and raise a ton of money to "staff-up," advertise, give everyone stock options and Beemers, then do ostensibly nothing, other than have an idea and a (very expensive) business plan (also called "model") that he thought might work. Wow, how did he do that? Well, it turns out he couldn't … he failed at it. And because that greed bandwagon has come to an abrupt halt, we are now back to business as usual – dog-eat-dog. Or, in their case, mouse eat mouse.

Then came the tragedy of 9.11 and the economy has fallen further. We are now in a 9.12 economy, and in spite of the news, we're going to stay that way for a while.

In my travels I ask everyone "how's business?" In Vegas I ask the cab drivers. They say, "It's picking back up" – that means it still sucks, but it doesn't suck as bad as it did a few months ago.

The pinch is upon us. And if it ain't you yet, don't be too sure it won't be after big companies do their new budgets, and you get cut.

As the old "New Economy" tightens down a bit, and its replacement, the "New New Economy," cranks up, some people will be in panic mode. Many (maybe even you) have never experienced a slowing of sales. I was in

Charlotte, NC, for the last one ('89, '90, '91), and that's how I began to build my successful business here – selling and networking while others were whining.

## Want to know what to do?

I have just the formula. BUT it will require a different (than last year's) work ethic to make it happen. I'll tell you what to do, but you gotta do it, baby. Here's a hint in a nutshell – Get Ready! These are the strategies and formulas for converting from the dot.bombed, rose-colored "New Economy" to the emerging, not as robust, "New New Economy," where things ain't so rosy, or are at the very least uncertain.

## 24.5 sales and personal strategies needed to succeed in these new new times, and a new new question at the end of each strategy to test your reality:

**1. Guard your present customers with your life.** Others will be eyeing your customers like a hungry tiger ready to hunt fresh prey. Now is the time to invest time and money in relationship. **New new question:** What would happen if you lost two of your top 10 customers to your competition? What's your plan to be CERTAIN that doesn't happen? Ouch!

**2. It's the relationship, not the price.** When business isn't expanding, everyone will be trying to steal your customers with a lower price. Your biggest opportunity is to build relationships with value (help customers build their business, give them ideas they can use for their profit). Your biggest vulnerability is to ignore your present customers in quest of additional customers. **New new question:** What new ways have you created to build relationships?

**3. It's now time to do the things you didn't do (or put off) when you were fat and happy.** Start here. Train yourself to be the best. Train your people to be the best. Now is the time to invest in your people with the best possible training both in sales and service, and now is the time to encourage your people to invest in their own time to study.
**New new question:** What is your training budget? What is your training discipline each week?

**4. Review your quality, and eliminate anything that isn't BEST.** Elevate everything you do or have anything to do with to BEST. Take a quality inventory, and compare your products and services with your competitors and your market. If you're not in first place, you will lose ground to someone who is. Lexus and Mercedes will continue to sell cars. Lower-quality car dealerships will drop like flies. **New new question:** When was your last internal quality review of everything and everyone? What are you BEST at?

**5. Network more than you have ever networked.** It is the single best way to build existing relationships and find new ones. Rededicate yourself to the networking process. If you're not networking 4 to 6 hours a week, you will lose to someone who does. Networking is the ideal way to build relationships, whether it's a golf outing, a trade association meeting, or just a lunch with two or three customers and two or three prospects that you bring to the table for them. *NOTE WELL*: The good ole boys network is alive and well. Don't curse it; embrace it. Join it. Y'ever been good ole boy'ed? Sure you have. Somebody else had an inside track or a better relationship than you did, and got the business. And it's most interesting to note that Billy Bob doesn't have the lowest price; he just has the best relationship. **New new question:** Do you have a written 1-year networking plan to get in front of more customers and prospects?

**6. Position yourself as a person of value by being seen and known in the community.** If you become known as a person of value, people will seek you out for answers (not brochures). This is a combination of networking, industry and community leadership, and reputation. In this economy (more than ever before) it's not who you know, it's who knows you. **New new question:** What do the top 10 people in your industry know about you? Do they call you?

**7. Everyone else will be scrambling, too, and may not have time to hear a bunch of crap about you.** But customers and prospects ALWAYS have time for valuable information and new ideas to help them build THEIR business. Think about it this way. Do your customers need another one of your brochures or product sheets? Or would they rather have a hot sales lead? Why not make a list of 10 things that you can begin to give your customers that are low in cost, like sales leads, but high in value. And begin to make daily or weekly communication to strengthen your present status and earn future orders. You better have bulletproof customers, because your competition is packing heat. **New new question:** Have you identified five areas where you can give value? What value do you give now?

**8. Build your reputation, because that's what you will become known for.** The actions you have taken over the past few years have molded your present reputation. How is it? The biggest challenge in slow times is: Do everything you can to build an impeccable reputation.

P.S. Not everybody will like you ... get over it. But your best chance for success over the next few years is to have lots of customers who LOVE you. **New new question:** What do people say about you when you're not there?

## 9. Make decisions based on who you want to become -- not simply on the basis of your monthly quota.
Eventually this mess will be over – where will you be AS the smoke clears? Please note that I did not say "when" the smoke clears. Because when the smoke clears, it's too late. Your reputation, based on your words, deeds, and actions, will be a legacy that you leave for yourself. If you heed the words of Dr. Paul Homoly, who preaches, "Make all decisions based on the person you want to become, rather than on your present situation," then all of your actions will be directed toward long-term relationships rather than short-term quotas. **New new question:** When you make a sale, are you making short-term compromise or long-term commitments?

## 10. Spend more time figuring out solutions than whining about problems.
"You can't be a winner if you're a whiner, wiener." That's a famous quote said in 1993 by me after I observed who came out of the recession of '91 and who didn't. This is a time to prepare and be your best, and you can't do that if you're whining. The good news is, most people will be whining. This leaves plenty of room for you to succeed. **Note well:** People will still be buying during this period of time. They just won't be buying as much. Business (sales) will go to the prepared. **New new question:** What are you whining about? What solutions make you a winner?

## 11. Study attitude; don't just think you have a good one.
Spend 15 minutes a day reading. The best time is in the morning, before you start your day. Read happy, positive thoughts, even if it's just a re-read of a Dr. Seuss book. (The best one for salespeople is *Green Eggs and Ham*.) **New new question:** What are you reading every morning? Or are you just watching TV?

## 12. Invest, don't spend
(in money, in time, in business, in anything that you do). Now is the time to guard your assets (and perhaps the abbreviated form of the word). It's real easy to put your head in the sand and think that everything will return to the way it was. The reality is, dig in, but use your assets to build a fortress of positive thought, new information, and strategic appearances at networking events to ensure business victory. **New new question:** What is your time investment in yourself each day?

## 13. Create a REAL (and perceived) difference between you and everyone else.
Work on differentiation in new ways. Change EVERYTHING ordinary to memorable. Greetings, literature, proposals, messages, and you. **New new question:** What is memorable about you? What is different about you?

**14. The new new rules include the Internet and e-commerce.** For speed, ease of doing business, the appearance of 24.7.365, ease of communication, scheduling, inventory availability, AND information that helps others build THEIR business, your web presence must border on dominance. If you didn't invest in the Web when you had the money, bite the bullet and do it now. Or prepare to lose to someone who does. **New new question:** What is WOW about your Web site?

**15. Study creativity.** Upgrade everything you say, every action you take, and every customer communication (brochure, fax cover sheet, business card, invoice) to WOW! **New new question:** What book on creativity have you read in the past 3 months?

**16. Learn the joy of rejection.** Practice by making more cold calls. More people will be saying "No" to you. Get over it. **New new question:** What do you say when someone tells you "No"? What should you (could you) say?

**17. Work while others sleep.** The earlier you rise, the better chance you have of bettering yourself and beating the competition. My column has existed and thrived for 11 years. Written early in the morning and late at night. I owe my success to the fact that I'm willing to do more than most other people are willing to do. Much more. Look at "balance" a new way – if you're not working out of balance, your checkbook will be. **New new question:** What are your work hours? What are your TV hours?

**18. Become a morning person, not an evening person.** After 43 years, I finally discovered that my thoughts are better and clearer in the morning. If you're reading this and think, "You've got it all wrong, Jeffrey. I'm an evening person," you're incorrect. The reason most people don't think of themselves as morning people is because they're so screwed up the night before, they can't function in the morning. **New new question:** What do you do with your early morning hours? What else could you be doing?

**19. What you do off the job will determine your success on the job.** Invest your money in books and training, not beer (*re-read number 15*). **New new question:** What are you doing in the evening that's keeping you from being a morning person? Ouch!

**20. Put your goals in front of your face and say them twice a day.** The formula for achieving goals may differ, but the universal truth of "out of sight, out of mind" still remains valid. Write your goals on Post-It Notes on your bathroom mirror and read them twice a day until they're accomplished. Then post them on your bedroom mirror. **New new question:** What goals are you not even working on?

**21. Figure out the daily dose and do that no matter what.** Part 2 of goal achievement is to break the goal down into daily actions. Save $1,000 at $3 a day. Make 30 sales with five appointments a day. If you figure out and can consistently achieve the smallest bit each day, any goal is within your grasp. **New new question:** What small bit could you do each day toward your biggest goal?

**22. Bet on yourself -- and get in shape to do it or you won't win the race.** You better be a lean, mean, selling machine. This is a time to invest in your mental self, not in your material self. **New new question:** What can you do to get "leaner and meaner"? How much are you investing in you?

**23. It is, and always has been your attitude.** If someone asks you, "How ya doin'?" you respond with, "Cashin' checks!" **New new question:** What do you say when people ask you, "How's it going?"

**24. It's not up to your company. It's up to you.** Take responsibility and ownership of your job, your work habits, your customers, and yourself. **New new question:** Who are you blaming for things you should be taking responsibility for?

**24.5 Regain the tenacity you had as a 4-year-old in the grocery store asking your mom for a candy bar, and not taking "no" for an answer.** How often did you make that sale? As often as you're making sales now? How tenacious were you then? Now? If you need help in this area, take your child shopping. **New new question:** Giving up too soon? What could you be fighting harder for?

# Wow -- that's a list.

All you have to do is master each strategy and the market share will remain yours.

Business Summary? Sure. There's less (but lots) of business, but don't be looking too hard and look past your biggest asset – present customers and vendors. (Yes, vendors.) Do all you can to keep your customers loyal, because your foxy competition is hungry and looking for food in your hen house. Take new new steps to keep your customers loyal.

Personal Summary? Sure. *The new new economy will be shaped and determined by the dedication to the new new you!*

Well, now what? **TWO THINGS:** Easy answers, hard work. And I'll be in there fighting myself to keep my share of my market. Once again, I'll be selling while others are whining. You?

*You will look at those Post-it Note™goals*
*until you are sick of looking at them …*
*and then you'll begin to accomplish them.*

# Post-It Note™ your way to achievement.

**Goal:** I want to be a success.

**Challenge:** Easier thought than done.

**Thought:** Success means achieve goals.

**Wrong thought:** Many people are afraid of success.

**Reality:** People are not afraid of achieving success; they just don't know how to do it.

**Bigger reality:** It's that time of the year again – no, no, not Christmas time. Goal time. Resolution time. Achievement time. Rats.

**Biggest reality:** Last year's resolutions (goals) never made it through February.

**Depression starter:** It's now March and you haven't accomplished squat.

**Idea:** Go purchase a pad of Post-it Notes, and you'll be on the path to success!

A resolution is really a goal. You have several goals you want to achieve, but they're not written down *in plain sight*. They just sit on a piece of paper in a drawer or on the back page of a daytimer, or pop up in your head every once in a while, only to be buried in a black hole of procrastination, excuses and guilt. Take heart – I found a way to beat the system: Post-it Notes.

Want to achieve your goals? Want your resolutions to become a reality? Here are all the tools necessary to achieve the success that has eluded you so far:

- Post-it Notes
- Bathroom mirror
- Bedroom mirror
- Felt-tip pen

# And here's the tested and proven method ...

**1. Write down big ones** ... On 3 x 3 yellow Post-it Notes, write down your prime goals in short words (get funding for business; win salesman of the year award; new client: First Citizens Bank).

**2. Write down small ones** ... Use three more notes and write down your secondary goals in short words (read about attitude 15 minutes a day; read book – Dale Carnegie; organize desk; build new closet).

**3. Put them in front of your face** ... Post them on your *bathroom* mirror, where you are forced to look at them – and yourself – every morning and evening.

**4. Say them aloud each time you look at them** ... Look AND say doubles the affirmation.

**5. Keep looking and talking until you act** ... You will look at them until you are sick of looking at them and will begin to take action – achievement action – and accomplish them.

**6. Seeing the note there every day makes you think about acting on it every day.** Once you start acting, the note triggers a "What do I have to do today to keep the achievement on target?" The note forces you to act. To achieve your goal.

By posting the goal in the bathroom, you are consciously reminded of your goals at least two times a day. From there your subconscious gets into the act, gnawing away at your soul until you are driven to take positive action. Achievement actions.

And when you get to the top of the mountain – when you achieve what you've been working for – at last you can say the magic words. Scream them – I DID IT! (Screaming positive things always feels wonderful.)

**6.5 Revisit your success every day** ... Here comes the best part – after your goal is achieved, *take the Post-it Note off the bathroom mirror and triumphantly post it on your bedroom mirror*. Now, every day when you check out "how you look for the day," you also get to see your success.

# WOW!

Not only does it feel great, but you are able to set the tone for a successful day, every day, first thing in the morning by looking at (goal) success, remembering how good it felt, and thinking about what it took to do it. Plus – it gets you motivated to keep achieving more.

- The program is simple.
- The program works.
- The results will change your attitude.
- The results will change your life.
- The results will change your outlook about your capability of success achievement.

By the time you have your bedroom mirror full of achieved Post-it Note goals, you'll have enough money to go out and buy a bigger mirror – and the house to put it in.

### Post it. Post haste.

### Get your Post-It Note goal achiever starter kit. Want a preprinted pad of Post-it Notes to get started? I'd love to send you one in appreciation of your continued support and readership. **Send $1 to cover postage** to BuyGitomer, 310 Arlington Ave., Loft 329, Charlotte, NC 28203.

# The Book of Rules

**1.2**

## "This Rules!"
*-- Beavis & Butt-head*

Rules ...
And the guidelines that
turn them into sales.

How do you turn a
prospect into a customer?

Let me count the ways.
There are 39.5 ways.

Read them and you'll say,
"Aha!"

Follow them and you'll say,
"Thanks for the order."

Sales rule!

*Following the fundamental
rules of selling will lead to
sales success faster than any
high pressure sales technique.*

# 39.5 rules of sales success

People aren't afraid of failure; they just don't know how to succeed.

In 1960, I met a college basketball coach on the court and asked him for his best, niftiest pointer. He took the ball, walked under the basket, and shot an easy layup. "See that shot," he said gruffly; "99% of all basketball games are won with that shot; don't miss it," and he walked away. I felt cheated that day, but 20 years later I realized it was the best sales lesson I ever got. Concentrate on the fundamentals: 99% of all sales are made that way.

We are each responsible for our own success (or failure). Winning at a career in sales is no exception. To ensure a win, you must take a proactive approach. Prevention of failure is an important part of that process. If you find yourself saying, *"I'm not cut out for sales," "I'm not pushy enough," "I hate cold calling," "I can't take the rejection," "My boss is a jerk,"* or *"My boss is a real jerk,"* you're heading down the wrong path.

Here are 39.5 recurring characteristics and traits of successful salespeople. How many of these apply to you? How many of these guidelines can you honestly say you follow? If you are serious about achieving sales success, I recommend you post this list someplace where you can see it every day. Read it and practice these principles until they become a way of life.

**1. Establish and maintain a positive attitude** … The first rule of life. Your commitment to a positive attitude will put you on a path to success that will be unstoppable. If you doubt it, you don't have a positive attitude. A positive attitude is not just a thought process, it's a daily commitment. Get one.

**2. Believe in yourself** … If you don't think you can do it, who will? You control the most important tool in selling: your mind.

**3. Set and achieve goals. Make a plan** ... Define and achieve specific long-term (what you want) and short-term (how you're going to get what you want) goals. Goals are the road map that will direct you to success.

**4. Learn and execute the fundamentals of sales** ... Never stop learning how to sell. Read, listen to tapes, attend seminars, and practice what you've just learned. Learn something new every day and combine it with hands-on experience. Knowing the fundamentals gives you a choice in a sales call. Even in a relationship or partnership, sometimes a technique is needed.

**5. Understand the customer and meet his or her needs** ... Question and listen to the prospect and uncover true needs. Don't prejudge prospects.

**6. Sell to help** ... Don't be greedy, it will show. Sell to help customers; don't sell for commissions.

**7. Establish long-term relationships** ... Be sincere and treat others the way you want to be treated. If you get to know your customer and concentrate on his best interest, you'll earn much more than a commission.

**8. Believe in your company and product** ... Believe your product or service is the best and it will show. Your conviction is evident to a buyer and manifests itself in your sales numbers. If you don't believe in your product, your prospect won't either.

**9. Be prepared** ... Your self-motivation and preparation are the lifeblood of your outreach. You must be eager and ready to sell, or you won't. Be ready to make the sale with a sales kit, sales tools, openers, questions, statements, and answers. Your creative preparation will determine your outcome.

**10. Be sincere** ... If you are sincere about helping, it will show, and vice versa.

**11. Qualify the buyer** ... Don't waste time with someone who can't decide.

**12. Be on time for the appointment** ... Lateness says, "I don't respect your time." There is no excuse for lateness. If it can't be avoided, call before the appointed time, apologize, and continue with the sale.

**13. Look professional** ... If you look sharp, it's a positive reflection on you, your company, and your product.

**14. Establish rapport and buyer confidence** ... Get to know the prospect and his company; establish confidence early. Don't start your pitch until you do.

**15. Use humor** ... It's the best tool for relationship sales I have found. Have fun at what you do. Laughing is tacit approval. Make the prospect laugh.

**16. Master the total knowledge of your product** ... Know your product cold. Know how your product is used to benefit your customers. Total product knowledge gives you the mental freedom to concentrate on selling. You may not always use the knowledge in the sales presentation, but it gives you confidence to make the sale.

**17. Sell benefits, not features** ... The customer doesn't want to know how it works as much as he wants to know how it will help him.

**18. Tell the truth** ... Never be at a loss to remember what you said.

**19. If you make a promise, keep it** ... The best way to turn a sale into a relationship is to deliver as promised. Failure to do what you say you're going to do, either for your company or your customer, is a disaster from which you may never recover. If you do it often, the word gets out about you.

**20. Don't down the competition** ... If you have nothing nice to say, say nothing. This is a tempting rule to break. The sirens are sweetly singing. Set yourself apart from them with preparation and creativity – don't slam them.

**21. Use testimonials** ... The strongest salesman on your team is a reference from a satisfied customer. Testimonials are proof.

**22. Listen for buying signals** ... The prospect will often tell you when he is ready to buy – if you're paying attention. Listening is as important as talking.

**23. Anticipate objections** ... Rehearse answers to standard objections.

**24. Get down to the real objection** ... Customers are not always truthful; they often won't tell you the true objection(s) at first.

**25. Overcome objections** ... This is a complex issue – it's not just an answer, it's an understanding of the situation. Listen to the prospect, and think in terms of solution. You must create an atmosphere of confidence and trust strong enough to cause (effect) a sale. The sale begins when the customer says no.

**26. Ask for the sale** ... Sounds too simple, but it works.

**27. When you ask a closing question, SHUT UP** ... The first rule of sales.

**28. If you don't make the sale, make a firm appointment to return** ... If you don't make the next appointment when you're face-to-face, it may be a long, hard road to the next one. Make some form of sale each time you call.

**29. Follow up, follow up, follow up** ... If it takes between 5 and 10 exposures to a prospect before a sale is made, be prepared to do whatever it takes to get to the 10th meeting.

**30. Redefine rejection** ... They're not rejecting you; they're just rejecting the offer you're making them.

**31. Anticipate and be comfortable with change** ... A big part of sales is change. Change in products, tactics, and markets. Roll with it to succeed. Fight it and fail.

**32. Follow rules** ... Salespeople often think rules are made for others. Think they're not for you? Think again. Broken rules will only get you fired.

**33. Get along with others (co-workers and customers)** ... Sales is never a solo effort. Team up with your co-workers and partner with your customers.

**34. Understand that hard work makes luck** ... Take a close look at the people you think are lucky. Either they or someone in their family put in years of hard work to create that luck. You can get just as lucky.

**35. Don't blame others when the fault (or responsibility) is yours** ... Accepting responsibility is the fulcrum point for succeeding at anything. Doing something about it is the criterion. Execution is the reward (not the money – money is just the by-product of perfect execution).

**36. Harness the power of persistence** ... Are you willing to take *no* for an answer and just accept it without a fight? Can you take *no* as a challenge instead of a rejection? Are you willing to persist through the 5 to 10 exposures it takes to make the sale? If you can, then you have begun to understand the power.

**37. Find your success formula through numbers** ... By determining how many leads, calls, proposals, appointments, presentations, and follow-ups it takes to get to the sale. And then following the formula.

**38. Do it passionately** ... Do it the best it's ever been done.

**39. Be memorable** ... In a creative way. In a positive way. In a professional way. What will they say about you when you leave? You always create a memory. Sometimes dim, sometimes bright. Sometimes positive, sometimes not. You choose the memory you leave. You are responsible for the memory you leave.

*The 39.5 characteristic is the most important of them all – **Have fun!*** *You will succeed far greater at something you love to do.* *Doing something you enjoy will also bring joy to others.* *Happiness is contagious.*

Not following the rules leads to slow but sure failure. It doesn't happen all at once – there are degrees of failing. Here are five of them. What degree are you?

1. Failing to do your best.
2. Failing to learn the science of selling.
3. Failing to accept responsibility.
4. Failing to meet quota or pre-set goals.
5. Failing to have a positive attitude.

Success is a level of performance and a self-confidence brought about by winning experiences. **Failure is not about insecurity. It's about lack of execution.** There's no such thing as a total failure. Zig Ziglar has an answer: "Failure is an event, not a person." Vince Lombardi said it better: "The will to win is nothing without the will to prepare to win."

The guy who won the 100-meter dash in the last Olympics did it in just under 10 seconds. Ten seconds isn't too long to run in a race, but how long did it take him to prepare to run it? Do you have the same will to win? I hope so.

## Sales Success Formula ...

# Aha!™

## Attitude -- Humor -- Action

This is a combination of elements I have found to be effective for sales achievement. It's simple on the surface and even simpler in practice. Each element contributes to the whole and is vitally linked to the other two. They are useful by themselves, but together they make sales magic.

Here's how it breaks down:

**Attitude --** Your positive mental attitude is your driving force to success in every endeavor of your life. Positive attitude is not just a thought process; it's a discipline and a commitment. Each day you wake to a rededication to being positive, thinking positive, and speaking positive. It's not something that comes and goes. It's all-consuming. It makes you feel good all the time on the inside, no matter what the circumstance is on the outside. All the time.

**Humor --** Humor is not just being funny. It's how you see things. Humor is a perspective for effective living and a successful career in sales. It's your sense of humor AND your ability to find and create humor. Making others laugh and feel good in your presence, making others smile. Hearing "I like talking to you. You make me laugh," or "You just made my day." That's what humor does. It makes others look forward to talking to you instead of ducking your call. It's medicine, sales medicine.

**Action --** Walking your talk. Waking up in the morning to a clearly defined set of goals. Having a daily agenda that you're totally prepared for. Making the last call. Following your own game plan for success. Doing more than anyone else you know. Doing enough to make yourself proud. WOW.

*The combination of these three elements provides the pathway to success.*

I challenge you
to master each element,
then combine them
in your own way
to suit your own personality.
The monetary results will astound you,
but the personal reward
is way beyond money.
Follow them to the letter
and you'll say ...

*Aha!*

# The Book of Secrets

## Mystery Mastery

Secrets ...

Listen. (Tu-da-lu)
Do you want to know
a secret?

In order to master a trade,
you must know its secrets.

Knowledge of sales secrets
can save you years of
frustration and wasted
effort.

Learn these sales secrets
and ... master the mystery.

1.3

*50% of success is believing you can.*
*Simply put, you become what you think about.*

# Why do salespeople fail?

Because they think they will.

Do you have a positive attitude? Everyone will say yes, but less than 1 in 1,000 actually do! One-tenth of 1%. Are you really in that small percentile? All you have to do is pass this simple test.

Yes No
☐ ☐  I watch the news for about 1 hour per day.
☐ ☐  I read the paper every day.
☐ ☐  I read a news magazine every week.
☐ ☐  I sometimes have a bad day, all day.
☐ ☐  My job is a drag.
☐ ☐  I get angry for an hour or more.
☐ ☐  I talk to and commiserate with negative people.
☐ ☐  I look to blame others when something goes wrong.
☐ ☐  When something goes wrong or bad, I tell others.
☐ ☐  I get angry at my spouse and don't talk for more than 4 hours.
☐ ☐  I bring personal problems to work and discuss them.
☐ ☐  I expect and plan for the worst.
☐ ☐  I'm affected by bad weather (too cold, too hot, rain)
          enough to talk about it.

**0-2 *yes* answers:** You have a positive attitude.
**3-6 *yes* answers:** You have a negative attitude.
**7 or more *yes* answers:** You have a problem attitude. Serious problem.

More than 4 *yes* answers? Go out and invest in the books, tapes, and courses of Dale Carnegie, Norman Vincent Peale, Ken Blanchard, W. Clement Stone, Napoleon Hill, Earl Nightingale, Wayne Dyer, Tony Robbins, and Denis Waitley. These people tell you how you *can*, not why you *can't*.

**The plot thickens.** Several national tests have revealed the following startling statistics about why salespeople fail:

> 15% Improper training – both product and sales skills.
> 20% Poor verbal and written communication skills.
> 15% Poor or problematic boss or management.
> 50% Attitude.

Sounds almost impossible, doesn't it? Salespeople (or anyone else) could succeed 50% more if they just change the way they think. Earl Nightingale in his legendary tape, The Strangest Secret, reveals the secret of a positive attitude: *We become what we think about.* But it's a dedicated discipline that must be practiced ... every day.

Want to begin to change your attitude? It will miraculously affect your success (and income). Live these thoughts and exercises:

✔ When something goes wrong, remember it's no one's fault but yours.

✔ You always have (and have had) a choice.

✔ If you think it's OK, it is ... if you think it's not OK, it's not.

✔ Ignore the junk news – work on a worthwhile project, make a plan, or do something to enhance your life.

✔ For 1 year, read only positive books and material.

✔ When you face an obstacle or something goes wrong, look for the opportunity.

✔ Listen to attitude tapes, attend seminars, and take courses.

✔ Ignore people who tell you that "You can't" or try to discourage you.

✔ Check your language. Is it half full or half empty, partly cloudy or partly sunny? Avoid *why, can't, won't.*

✔ Say why you like things, people, job, and family. Not why you don't.

✔ Help others without expectation or measuring (keeping score). If you say, "I'm not 'cause he's not,'" who loses? If you say, "Why should I, when he only ...," who loses?

✔ Visit a children's hospital or find someone in a wheelchair.

✔ How long do you stay in a bad mood? If more than 5 minutes, something's wrong.

✔ Count your blessings every day.

If you take the hour a day that you currently waste watching the news and convert it into positive action or learning for yourself, your business or your family, at the end of 1 year you will have captured more than 15 full 24-hour days. Which will help your success more – 15 days a year watching the news or 15 days a year building your future? You have a choice.

# When Vince Lombardi said, "Winning isn't everything, it's the only thing," he should have substituted the word *attitude* for *winning* to get closer to the truth.

*Selling is a learned skill*
*acquired by people with the*
*attitude, aptitude, fortitude, desire,*
*and persistence to succeed.*

# Are you born to sell?
# No, you learn to earn!

You've heard it; you've probably said it: "That guy's a born salesman."
Baloney! That is one of the biggest fallacies in sales. Selling is a science.
An acquired skill. The salesperson who you thought was born to sell
painstakingly developed the traits and characteristics to do so, then went
about learning and applying the science of selling.

Are you in sales and not performing the way you want to, or thinking of
getting into sales and wanting to have some idea if you'll succeed?

Take this personal inventory test. These are 21 traits and characteristics of
great salespeople. How many do you have? (IMPORTANT NOTE: There is a
middle ground between *yes* and *no* for salespeople called "working on it."
You're better off marking it *no* until you achieve that characteristic.)

Yes No

☐ ☐ I have set my goals in writing.

☐ ☐ I have good self-discipline.

☐ ☐ I am self-motivated.

☐ ☐ I want to be more knowledgeable.

☐ ☐ I want to build relationships.

☐ ☐ I am self-confident.

☐ ☐ I like myself.

☐ ☐ I love people.

☐ ☐ I love a challenge.

Yes No

☐ ☐ I love to win.

☐ ☐ I can accept rejection with a positive attitude.

☐ ☐ I can handle the details.

☐ ☐ I am loyal.

☐ ☐ I am enthusiastic.

☐ ☐ I am observant.

☐ ☐ I am a good listener.

☐ ☐ I am perceptive.

☐ ☐ I am a skillful communicator.

☐ ☐ I am a hard worker.

☐ ☐ I want to be financially secure.

☐ ☐ I am persistent.

Answer over 15 with an HONEST yes and you've got what it takes. Between 10 and 14, it could go either way (better chance if you answered yes to knowledge, enthusiasm, self-confident, perceptive, self-motivated, and persistent). Under 10, don't do it even if it would mean world peace, an end to disease, and helping the space program.

• **Note well that none of the above statements said anything about closing sales or overcoming objections.**

• **The science of selling can be learned and applied easily if you embody the above traits.**

• **All you have to do is believe you can do it, commit yourself to doing it, and live up to your commitment.**

*Are you missing opportunities because
you are too focused on obstacles?*

# Do you have a self-imposed
# mental handicap?

People with physical disabilities regularly overcome their challenges
(handicaps) in a way that inspires their non-handicapped counterparts.
People with self-imposed mental handicaps need help. Self-help. **What is a
mental handicap?** See if these excuses sound familiar:

- I can't get him on the phone.
- She won't return my calls.
- He won't give me an appointment.
- I overslept. I forgot. I didn't write it down.
  No one told me.
- She didn't show for our appointment.
- I can't get him to commit.

*Wait a second while I go get my violin. Wah, wah, wah. Woe is you.* Is it
brain cancer that can't be operated on, or was it just a problem getting a
customer or prospect to return your call? Big deal. **It seems to me that it's
actually harder to invent excuses than it is to get the sale.**

The answer to mentally handicapped salespeople lies in their ability to be
or not to be **FOCUSED**.

**Focus leads you in the direction of the sale.** It creates intensity, desire, and
commitment. Focused energy provides the drive you need to follow
through and win (make the sale) in a competitive market. Face it – the days
of the easy sale are gone. Competition is so fierce sometimes that it can
cause you to rethink your career or position.

Here are seven things you can do to keep the focus, intensity, drive, and commitment necessary to change your direction from *woe is me* to *whoa, what a sale!*

### 1. Stop blaming circumstances for your situation. It's not the rain, or the car, or the phone, or the product – it's YOU. You have a choice in everything you do. Choose a better way. Don't blame the path, change the path. Don't blame the situation, change the situation.

### 2. Stop blaming other people for your situation. Take responsibility for yourself and your actions. Here's the rule of thumb: If you are consistently blaming other people, guess what, Bubba – it ain't them.

### 3. Get to know your customer or prospect better every day. It is just as powerful to prevent problems as it is to handle them. If you can't get the prospect on the phone, it's your fault for not knowing the best time to reach him. Know the right time to call; know when a decision is to be made. Double confirm every commitment.

### 4. Persist until you gain an answer. A prospect will respect a tenacious salesperson. If it takes 5 to 10 exposures to make a sale, do you have what it takes to hang in there? Even if it's "no," at least you know where you stand.

### 5. Know where you are, or where you should be. Manage your time. Lunch a customer, not a friend. Keep perfect records. Know enough about your prospect or customer that follow-up becomes easy and fun. Are you organized enough to get to the 10th exposure and make the sale?

### 6. Work on your skills every day. Tapes, books, seminars. You can never read enough books or listen to enough tapes. I challenge you to do it for an hour a day. One hour a day, seven days a week, for one year is equal to more than nine full weeks of work. Think about what you could be doing to improve your focus and knowledge base the next time you mindlessly turn on the TV.

### 7. Become solution oriented. Instead of griping or wallowing in your problems, why not spend the same amount of time working on solutions? I have found that being solution oriented has done more for me and my path to success than any single philosophy. Every obstacle presents an opportunity – if you're looking for it. If you're too busy concentrating on the problem, the opportunity will pass you by.

You have been given a bag of cement
and a bucket of water.
You can either build a stepping stone
or a stumbling block.

*The choice is (and always has been) yours.*

*Don't use a bunch of time-worn*
*sales techniques to pressure me*
*to buy when I don't want to.*

# How the customer wants to be treated, honestly.

To be the best salesperson in the world (and I hope you think you are), you must recognize *listening* as the first commandment of sales. So, I started calling people who buy and asked them what they want salespeople to do. How they want salespeople to act. What they want salespeople to say (or not say). I listened, and I wrote.

**Unless you're an order taker, the way you treat (handle) a prospect will determine how often you get the order.** And a sale is always made – either you sell the prospect on yes or the prospect sells you on no.

*Here is a list of what customers want from salespeople – direct from their mouths.* In a nutshell they are saying, "Here's how I want to be sold." How many items on this list can you say you fulfill each time you present your product or service? These customer requests will help you to get yes more often. If you use them in combination, you will have more power to build a relationship and close a sale.

Here's what *your customers* have to say about how they want you to act:

• **Just give me the facts** – I don't want a long, drawn-out spiel. After you get to know me a little, get to the point.

• **Tell me the truth, and don't use the word *honestly*. It makes me nervous** – If you say something I doubt or I know not to be true, you're out.

• **I want an ethical salesperson** – Did someone say honest lawyer? Salespeople often get bum raps because of a few without ethics. Your actions will prove your ethics, not your words. (The salespeople who talk ethics usually are without them.)

• **Give me a good reason why this product/service is perfect for me** – If I need what you're selling, I need to understand how it benefits me to buy it.

• **Show me some proof** – I'm more likely to buy if you can prove what you say. Show me an article in print reinforcing my confidence, or confirming my decision. (The buyer is saying, "I don't believe most salespeople. They lie just like we do.")

• **Show me I'm not alone. Tell me about a similar situation where someone like me succeeded** – I don't want to be the first or the only. I need to know how it (or you) has worked elsewhere. I will have a lot more confidence if I know of someone else like me or with the same situation as me who purchased and likes it or did well with it.

• **Show me a letter from a satisfied customer** – One testimonial has more strength than 100 presentations.

• **Tell me and show me you will serve me after you sell me** – I have bought a lot of empty service promises in the past.

• **Tell me and show me the price is fair** – I want reassurance the price I'm paying is fair for what I'm buying. Make me feel like I'm getting a deal.

• **Show me the best way to pay** – If I can't afford to pay, but I want what you've got, give me alternatives.

• **Give me a choice and let me decide, but make a consultive recommendation** – Tell me what you would *honestly* (Hey, if I can't say it, neither can you.) do if it was *your* money.

• **Reinforce my choice** – I may be nervous I'll make the wrong choice. Help me reinforce my choice with facts that will benefit me and make me feel more confident to buy.

• **Don't argue with me** – Even if I'm wrong, I don't want some smartass salesman telling me (or trying to prove) I am. He may win the argument, but he'll lose the sale.

• **Don't confuse me** – The more complicated it is, the less likely I am to buy.

• **Don't tell me negative things** – I want everything to be great. Don't say bad things about someone else (especially competition), about yourself, your company, or me.

• **Don't talk down to me** – Salespeople think they know everything and think I'm stupid. Don't tell me what *you* think I want to hear. I'm so dumb, I think I'll buy from someone else.

• **Don't tell me what I bought or did is wrong** – I want to feel smart and good about what I did. Be tactful if I goofed; show me how others goofed, too.

• **Listen to me when I talk** – I'm trying to tell you what I want to buy, and you're too busy trying to sell me what you've got. Shut up and listen.

• **Make me feel special** – If I'm going to spend my money, I want to feel good about it. It all hinges on your words and actions.

• **Make me laugh** – Put me in a good mood and I'm more likely to buy. Making me laugh means I agree with you, and you need my agreement to make a sale.

• **Take an interest in what I do** – It may not be important to you, but it's everything to me.

• **Be sincere when you tell me things** – I can tell if you're being phony just to get my money.

• **Don't use a bunch of time-worn sales techniques to pressure me to buy when I don't want to** – Don't sound like a salesman. Sound like a friend. Someone trying to help me.

• **Deliver me what you sell me -- when you say you will** – If I give you my business and you disappoint me, it's unlikely I'll do business with you again.

• **Help me buy -- don't sell me** – I hate being sold, but I love to buy.

I have given you 25 statements made by buyers about how they like to be sold. Take another 10 minutes to review how many you incorporate into your sales presentation and philosophy of selling.

The buyer has the ultimate weapon against your sales technique – he or she can *just say no*. They also have the ultimate weapon for doing it right – *their pen*.

Imagine the nerve of our customers and prospects
wanting all this stuff. Don't they know we're busy?
And why don't they return our phone call anyway?

*Return my phone call.*

# How a salesperson wants to be treated, honestly.

Salespeople have feelings too. If you're a buyer, company owner, or CEO, I ask you – how do you treat salespeople? Would you like to know how they want to be treated?

I have talked to thousands of salespeople who talk about what they wish buyers and prospects would do (or not do). If you're a decision maker for your company, how many of the items below can you *honestly* (there goes that word again) say you do in your relationship with a salesperson?

*Important note* ... This section is not about a bunch of whiny salespeople moaning about how they're being mistreated. Rather it's a series of statements about what salespeople need to build relationships with you – their customers.

If you have ever asked yourself the question, "What do salespeople want?" here are the answers:

• **Return my phone call.** The number one gripe of salespeople, especially if you've got the dreaded *voice mail*. Why can't you take 2 minutes of your time and return someone's call? Don't you want your call returned?

• **Take my call if you're in -- If you screen my call, don't screen me out.** The other day I called Dick Kittle, president of Associated Mailing, the largest mailing house in the Charlotte area. I said, "Is Dick there?" Next thing I know, a voice says, "Dick Kittle." I said, "Dick, no screen on your calls?" He said, "I don't want to miss any opportunities." And I'll bet he misses darn few.

• **Don't have your gatekeeper say, "Mr. Johnson doesn't see anyone without an appointment."** At least have the courtesy of telling Johnson I'm here and giving him the choice. Jerk.

• **Tell me the truth.** I'd rather know the truth than have you string me along, or lie about the situation. Have the guts to be truthful. You want it from me, don't you?

- **If you don't decide (or aren't the only decision maker), tell me, and tell me who (or who else) does.** Don't waste my time or yours. I like you, but I want to talk to (all) the decision makers – in person.

- **Tell me how you feel while I'm presenting.** If I'm doing something right or wrong, I want to know so I can help serve you better.

- **Give me your undivided attention during my presentation.** No phone calls or people running in and out or reading your mail. Thanks.

- **Tell me your real objection.** If you do, it will help us both. Your true objection will shorten the sales cycle and make us both more productive. You won't hurt my feelings – I really want to know the truth.

- **Do what you say you will do.** *Example*: If you tell me a decision will be made by Wednesday, take my call on the appointed day and tell me the answer. *Example*: You tell me to call you on Friday to set up a meeting. I call. Your secretary says, "Oh, he's out of town and won't be back until Tuesday." Common courtesy. Do what you say. That's not too much to ask. Is it?

- **Don't tell me you want to think about it.** We hate that. Tell me the real objection or how you really feel. Admit it – you've already decided.

- **Don't tell me it's not in the budget or you spent your budget for the year.** Tell me how you feel about my product or service and if you want to buy it now, next year, or never.

- **If you don't have the money and you want to buy, tell me, so I can help you find a way to buy.** Don't let pride or ego get in the way of the selling process. Salespeople run into people without money all the time (too much of the time, actually), and we want to help.

- **Don't play games.** Don't say, "I can get it for $500 less. Will you match the price?" or "I'm going to shop around to see if your deal is the best, then I might call you back." Be straight up with me. Put your cards on the table if you want a long-term relationship (like I do).

- **Respect me.** Often common courtesy will do more to enhance our relationship than anything (besides a big order).

- **If you must meet with others to get a final decision, let me be there too.** So I can answer questions about my product or service that are sure to arise.

- **Be on time for our appointment.** I don't want to wait. It's not fair to appoint me at 10 and take me at 10:30 and say, "I'm sorry. I got tied up." I'll say, "That's OK," but it ain't what I'm thinking. Be as timely as you would want me to be.

- **Show up for your appointment.** Sometimes you say, "Oh, it's just a salesman. What's the difference?" The difference is common courtesy. Show me you're as dependable as you want me to be.

- **Decide now.** You already know the answer. Why don't you just tell me?
- **Give me the sale when I ask for it.** Even though this is a fantasy request, I couldn't resist putting it in a list of things salespeople want.

And hey, Mr. CEO who has no time for – is rude to – won't return the calls of salesmen and saleswomen, I ask you this – Do you have salespeople? Are you treating salespeople the same way you want your salespeople treated in a selling situation? Think about it the next time you don't return a phone call from a salesperson.

It's amazing to me how simple the sales process would be
if buyers just followed one rule --
*The Golden Rule.*

Maybe if we revised it for sales and gave it to CEOs and decision makers, it would have an impact. Here it is for the first time ...

### *The Golden Rule of Sales for CEOs ...*

# Do unto salespeople as you would have buyers and decision makers do unto *your* salespeople.

*The hot button is a bridge that can get you
from the presentation to the sale.*

# The elusive hot button ...
# How do you find it?

All sales training includes this line: *If you want to make the sale, be sure to
push his hot button.* Great, where's that? It's within plain sight; it's within
asking distance; it's within listening distance. All you have to do is be alert.

*Pushing the hot button only works if you can find it. Here are some
ways to discover or uncover a personal or business hot button in a
conversation (NOTE WELL: personal is hotter than business):*

• **Ask questions about status and situation** – Where he vacationed,
where his kid goes to college. Where the business stands at the moment,
where it came from (history).

• **Ask questions about issues of pride** – Biggest success in business.
Biggest goal this year.

• **Ask questions about personal interests** – What does he do with
most of his free time? What sports or what hobbies does he pursue?

• **Ask what he would do if he didn't have to work** – What are his real
dreams and ambitions?

• **Ask goal-related questions** – What is the prime objective of his
company this year? How is he going to meet that objective? What does he
see as his biggest barrier to the goal?

• **Look at everything in the office** – Look for something outstanding.
Something framed apart from others, or looking bigger, more prominent.
Look for pictures and awards. Ask how he got them.

Asking and looking are the easy parts. Listening is the hard part. Listening is the important part. *The hot button is in the answer!*

**1. Listen to the first thing said or alluded to** – What is first said in response to a question is what is foremost in the mind of the respondent. The thing most on your mind is usually what you talk about first. It may not be the actual hot button – but it will provide insights to it.

**2. Listen for the tone of first responses** – The tone will depict the urgency or importance. His gestures and loudness will indicate passion.

**3. Listen for immediate, emphatic responses** – Knee-jerk reactions are hot subjects. Absolute agreement.

**4. Listen for a long, drawn-out explanation or story** – Something told in detail is usually compelling (and hot).

**5. Listen to repeated statements** – Something said twice is at the front of the mind.

**6. Look for emotional responses** – Something said with passion or in a different tone.

OK, you think you found it. Now, let's push it.

*Here are 4.5 button-pushing techniques:*

**1. Ask questions about importance or significance.** *What's the importance of that to you?* or *How will that impact you?* will help you understand the situation better.

**2. Ask questions about the area you think is hot.** If you have taken notes, there are some areas to probe that will generate heat.

**3. Ask questions in a subtle way.** Work them into the pitch as a part of the conversation, and watch the reaction. If you believe it's a *hot button*, offer solutions that satisfy that circumstance.

**4. Don't be afraid to bring up the *hot button* throughout the presentation.** Reconfirm it and listen for emphasis of response from the prospect.

**4.5 Use "If I** *(offer a solution)* **..., would you** *(commit or buy)* **...?" and variations. Try "There's a way ..."** This type of question or statement gets a true response because it consists of a possible solution that hits the button.

*Words of caution:*

• **The *hot button* is sometimes a very sensitive issue.** It may have other ramifications that the prospect is not willing to divulge. Your job is to uncover the button and use it to make the sale. Use your best judgment. If you sense the issue is touchy, don't push too hard.

• **The *hot button* is elusive.** But you can find it with a question or observation. The *hot button* is a prize you can win if you listen to the prospect with care. The *hot button* is a bridge that can get you from the presentation to the sale.

• **The *hot button* is an elevator.** It will go all the way to the top floor (the sale). But it only works if you push the button.

The hot button is a bridge that can get you from the presentation to the sale. All you gotta do is find it. How do you find it? Elementary, my dear Watson ... In 1888, Sherlock Holmes said, "It is a capital offense to theorize before one has data." You gotta be a detective to find the hot button.

# Listening is the hard part.

# Listening is the important part.

*The "hot button" is in the prospect's response!*

# The Book of BIG Secrets

## Eh, Confidentially, Doc

Big Secrets ...

Ok, Ok. We've established the fact that I can't keep a secret.

I knew that! But neither can you, loose lips.

Here are some deep, dark ones. A treasure map that will lead you to El Dorado.

Well, not actually, but if you follow these secrets, you can buy an Eldorado.

> *Your best competitor couldn't blast*
> *you away from a customer*
> *who is also a friend.*

# More sales are made with friendship than salesmanship.

Your mom said it best. As a child, when you were fighting or arguing with a sibling or friend, your mom would say, "Billy, you know better than that! **Now you make friends with Johnny.**"Your mother never told you to use the alternative-of-choice close or the sharp-angle close on Johnny. She never said to quote Johnny with our policy. She just said make friends. That may have been one of the most powerful sales and service lessons you ever got.

There's an old business adage that says, "All things being equal, people want to do business with their friends. And all things being NOT so equal, people STILL want to do business with their friends." It is estimated that more than 50% of sales are made and business relationships are kept because of friendship.

In the South it's called "the good old boy network"; in the North they say it's "who you know," but it's really just friendship selling.

If you think you're going to make the sale because you have the best product, best service, or best price, dream on, Bubba. You're not even half right. If 50% of sales are made on a friendly basis, and you haven't made friends with your prospect (or customer), you're missing 50% of your market.

**And the best part is that friends don't need to sell friends by using sales techniques.** Think about it. You don't need sales techniques when you ask a friend out or ask for a favor – you just ask.

Looking to make more sales? *You don't need more sales techniques; you need more friends.*

Think about your best customers. How did they get that way? Don't you have great relationships with them? If you're friends with your best customer, it will often eliminate the need for price checking, price negotiating, and delivery time demands. You can even *occasionally* give bad service and still keep the customer.

There's another huge bonus to being friends – competition is eliminated. **Your best competitor couldn't blast you away from a customer who is also a friend.**

Most salespeople think that unless they are calling a customer to sell something, it's a wasted call. Nothing could be farther from the truth. People don't like to be sold – but they love to buy.

How do you start? Slowly. **It takes time to develop a relationship; it takes time to build a friendship.** (If you are reading this and thinking, "I don't have time for this relationship stuff. I'm too busy making sales" – find a new profession. This one won't last long.)

Here are a few places to meet or take your customer. The biggest mistake salespeople make is giving away tickets and not going WITH the customer. You can learn a lot (and give value to a relationship) by spending a few quality hours with the people who provide the money to your company. A different venue than the office will begin building friendships and relationships. Here are a few to ponder:

- A ball game.
- The theater.
- A concert.
- A gallery crawl.
- A Chamber after hours event.
- A community help project.
- A breakfast, a lunch, a dinner.
- A seminar given by your company.
- If your customer has kids, get a few tickets to an I-Max theater. Go on the weekend. Talk about solidifying a relationship. An I-Max movie is great fun, and it ain't just for kids.

**Join a business association and get involved.** I belong to the Metrolina Business Council. MBC is a 17-year-old group of business owners and managers whose main objective is to do business with one another and help members get business. But MBC is not just about business, it's about relationships and friendships – ask any member.

CAUTION: This does not eliminate your need to be a master salesman. You must know sales techniques to capture the other half of the market. So keep reading books and listening to those tapes in your car.

Having moved from the North (Cherry Hill, NJ) to the South (Charlotte, NC) has helped me understand the value of business friends. They are much easier to establish in the South. And more loyal.

I'm often in conversations where someone is lamenting the fact they can't get into or around the so-called "good old boy" network. That is the biggest bunch of baloney and lamest sales excuse I've heard. All the salesperson is saying is that he has failed to bring anything of value to the table and failed to establish a relationship or make a friend – *AND SOMEONE ELSE HAS*.

# You can only earn a commission using a sales technique, but you can earn a fortune building friendships and relationships.

*If you make a sale, you earn a commission.*
*If you make a friend, you can earn a fortune.*

*Your present customer has a history of buying,*
*has credit terms, likes your product, and likes you …*
***What are you waiting for?***

# Your best new prospects are your present customers.

Looking for new prospects? Who isn't! It may interest you to know that you have hundreds of HOT prospects you're not paying attention to – your present customers.

Consider these 10.5 assets already in your favor:

1. They know you.
2. They like you.
3. You have established rapport.
4. Confidence and trust have been built.
5. You have a history of delivery and satisfaction.
6. They respect you.
7. They use (and like) your product or service.
8. They will return your call.
9. They will be more receptive to your presentation and product offering.
10. They have credit and have paid you in the past.
10.5 They don't have to be sold – they will buy.

Think about this for a second. You're a farmer, and you need milk. You wake up and decide to go milk your neighbor's cows. You walk by your barn where the cows are full of milk – udders so full that they're begging even for a set of cold hands – but you just pass them by and head for some unknown neighbor in search of milk. Sales is the same.

Why go out and cold call or prospect when your present customer base is ready to milk? They're waiting for you, dripping with business. I don't think you could ask for much more than that. It beats a cold call by 1,000 to 1.

*Here are some ideas to get your present customers to buy more – now:*

**Sell them something new.** People love to buy new things. Your enthusiasm will set the tone. Create excitement about how your new (better) product will be exactly what will serve better or produce more. Sell sizzle; sell appointments – then let them buy.

**Sell them an upgrade or an enhancement.** Bigger, better, faster. Enhancements and upgrades have kept the computer software industry profitable since its inception. Up-selling has built fortunes – just ask any fast-food business. (The question, "Do you want cheese on that?" sells more than one billion pieces of cheese annually.)

**Sell them more of the same in a different place.** Look for other uses, other departments, growth or expansion of the customer's company, or replacement due to wear and tear. You may have to dig a little, but the soil is softer at a present customer's place of business than the pile of rocks you usually face at a new prospect's company.

**Sell them additional products and services.** Your company may sell multiple products or offer varied services, and very few of your customers carry your full line. Sometimes a customer will say, "Oh, I didn't know you sold that." When you hear a customer say that, DON'T BLAME THE SALESPERSON – blame the salesperson's trainer.

**Get your customers to meet you for lunch.** If you can get the customer out of the office environment, you can often uncover more opportunities to sell (ask them to bring a referral along). Build the relationship, and you build sales.

**Get them to give you one referral a month.** This is the true report card on the job your product or service has done in performing for your customers, as well as a report card on your ability to gain enough buyer confidence that they will refer you to a friend or business associate.

**Give them one referral a month.** Getting your customer business will create new thought patterns in the way the customers perceive you. If you get them business, they will find new ways and new people to do the same for you.

**NOTE: No matter whether you make a sale or not, continuing to be in front of your customer builds relationship and goodwill.**

If you can't call on your present customers, or if you come up with some lame excuse like, "I've sold them everything I can sell them," what this really means is …

- You have failed to establish enough rapport with the customer.

- You have probably not followed up well (or at all) after the sale.

- Your customer had some problem and you're reluctant to call and open a can of worms.

- You're in need of more sales and creativity training.

And the big one …

- You have not developed a proper relationship with the customer.

Most salespeople think that unless they are calling a customer to sell something, it's a wasted call. Nothing could be farther from the truth.

I'm amazed at the salespeople who make a sale and move on to the next prospect. I challenge you to carefully (and honestly) look at your customer list. I'll bet there are hundreds of opportunities to sell something.

# I would rather have 100 satisfied customers to do business with than 1,000 prospects.

*The secret to a great week is to use Monday
as a springboard. Schedule your hottest
prospect for Monday morning.*

# Make a sale on Monday ...
## It does wonders for your week.

I'm often asked if there is some secret for consistent sales performance.
The answer is simple. Have a great Monday. Have a great Friday.

If you're looking for consistency in selling performance, try these 8.5 steps.
You won't believe how lucky you start to get.

1. Make a sale on Monday morning to start the week.
2. Listen to a sales training tape on Monday morning (mental weight lifting).
3. Make enough (at least five) appointments on Monday to ensure a
   productive week.
4. Work like hell all week.
5. Listen to a sales training tape on Friday morning.
6. Make a sale on Friday afternoon to end the week.
7. Confirm and solidify your Monday appointment on Friday.
8. Make five appointments on Friday for next week.
8.5 Keep your pipeline full. Have enough qualified prospects in the bank so
   that a Monday sale isn't a major barrier. PREPARE for your success or it
   won't occur.

**Monday. How you do on the first day of the week sets the tone for
the rest of it. And how you do on Monday is based entirely on how
smart you worked last week.** If you are disciplined enough to follow
these methods, you won't believe the difference it will make in your week
and your productivity.

**1. *Make a sale first thing Monday morning* ...** Set an appointment
for early Monday morning you are confident will buy. It makes you feel great
to capture a sale to start your week. Sets you in motion and gives you a
mental boost to work harder (and make another one).

NOTE WELL: Since there are a lot of companies having sales meetings on Monday A.M., you're as productive as you can be with an appointment. You can start making sales calls after 10 A.M. (If time permits, you can also try a few calls before 8 A.M. Lots of decision makers are early risers.)

**2. *Learn something new* ...** Pop a training or motivational tape into your car or home stereo (or both), and instead of listening to the same old news or music, try to feed your head with new knowledge that will help you make that first sale. When you learn a new technique on the way to an appointment, you can try it out in minutes.

**3. *Make at least five appointments for the rest of the week* ...** Why not have a Monday full of success and positive anticipation? It's up to you. Pick up the phone and work at it.

**4. *Work like hell all week* ...**

**Friday.** How you do on the last day sets the tone for the next week. Most people slack off. If you work intensely on Friday, it will ensure success next week and give you good reason to have a great weekend.

**5. *Learn something new* ...** Continuing your sales education throughout the week on a regularly scheduled basis is as important to your success as any other aspect of sales, but make sure you listen on Friday morning.

**6. *Make a sale on Friday afternoon* ...** Schedule a close for Friday afternoon ... nothing like ending the week on a positive note.

**7. *Confirm and solidify your Monday appointment on Friday* ...** If you worked hard the last 4 days, you've already set your Monday A.M. make-a-sale appointment. Call the prospect on Friday and confirm it.

**8. *Make at least five appointments for next week* ...** Why not guarantee yourself a full schedule next week? Spend your weekend relaxing instead of worrying about how few appointments you have. Make this commitment to yourself: I won't leave work on Friday until I have five appointments and I've set my Monday appointment/sale.

**8.5 *The secret to a great week is to use Monday as a springboard.*** The bigger secret is to trigger it by making a sale call on Monday. The biggest secret is you having enough qualified prospects in your pipeline to make that Monday sale possible. Keep your sales pipeline full.

Sounds simple. Make appointments, listen to tapes, make sales. It is simple. It just isn't easy. But if you work intensely, you can do it. I can make one promise to you ... follow these guidelines and you'll have sales consistency (you'll also earn money).

Now you know the secret. I've given you the answer. The question is what will you DO with the answer.

*In every company there is one person you are
certain can make a decision: The CEO.
Why start anyplace else?*

*The power of being introduced by the CEO
down to the decision maker is better than a Christmas
where Santa brings you everything on your list.*

# Easiest way to make a sale?
# Top-Down Selling™!

What does the Guggenheim Museum (a classic modern art museum in
NYC housed in a building designed by Frank Lloyd Wright) have in
common with sales success? They recommend that you *start at the top.*

The building is one big circular ramp. You take an elevator to the top floor
and casually walk down eight inspiring floors. It's the same in sales. Why
start at the bottom and fight your way up through people who can't
decide and who'll use their ounce of power to make your life miserable?
*Take the elevator and start at the top. Don't walk uphill!*

Where do you start? How high up the ladder do you dare go when making
an initial approach to a prospect? The rule is … **The higher you start,
the more success you're likely to meet.**

Getting there properly can be tricky. If you just ask for the president, the
owner, the boss, or the fearless leader, you may get through, but it will pay
you to prepare before making a call to the CEO, especially if the prospect
represents an important sale to you.

Here is a four-step plan for contacting and scoring a CEO appointment:

## 1. Get ready before you start. You only have one shot at it; make it your best one.

- *Have a written game plan* – Target 1 to 10 companies and define in writing what you want to accomplish and what it will take to get what you want.

- *Be totally prepared to sell before you make the call* – Have everything (sales pitch, concept, samples, daily planner) prepared and in front of you before you make the first call.

- *Identify the leader (by name) and get as much information and as many characteristics as you can* – Make calls to underlings, associates, and associations to get pertinent information before you make the big call.

## 2. Use the right tactics when getting to and getting through ...

- ASK FOR HELP.

- If you get the president's secretary, get her name and use it.

- Be polite, but firm.

- Be professional.

- Persist – you can't take the first no or rebuff.

- Get his name – You can try "how do you spell his last name?" but it's embarrassing to hear J-O-N-E-S.

- If they won't put you through the first time ...

    ➤ Get his extension number.

    ➤ Get the best time to call.

    ➤ Find out when he usually arrives.

    ➤ Find out when he takes lunch.

    ➤ Find out who sets his calendar.

    ➤ Find out if he leaves the building at lunch.

    ➤ Find out when he leaves for the day.

Example: You call; the secretary says, "Mr. Jones is on vacation." You say, "Wow, that's great, Sally. Where did he go?"

- Get anything personal you can (golf, sales meeting time, staff meeting time, important new product) and refer to it subtly when you get him or her on the phone.

- Make sure the person closest to the boss likes you.

- Take a chance on humor. Try this line: *I know you actually run the company, but could I speak to the person who thinks they do?*

### 3. When you get him or her on the phone, shoot quickly.

- Have your opening line.
- Get right to the point.
- Make it compelling (the best Power Question and statement of your life).
- Ask for no more than 5 minutes (offer to be thrown out if you go past 5).
- Have five comebacks if you are initially rebuffed.

*Notes about the CEO and the process ...*

- CEOs are hard to get to, harder to appoint, and easiest to sell.
- If the CEO is interested, he or she will take you by the hand and introduce you to the team member (underling) who will actually do the deal.
- The CEO always knows where to send you to get the job done.
- If they try to pawn you off without seeing you, it means you have not delivered a powerful enough message and they're not interested. The solution? Fix it. Keep trying until you get an appointment.
- If you start lower than the top, there is danger. No matter how powerful people say they are or appear to be, they usually have to ask someone else for final approval – EXCEPT THE CEO. CEOs usually just ask their secretary or administrative assistant if they liked you. Get the picture?

*The benefits are obvious ...*

- The leader is always the decider.
- The CEO may not be directly involved in purchasing what you're selling, but his or her introduction after a brief interest-generating meeting can be the difference between sale and no sale.
- The power of being introduced by the CEO *down* to the decision maker is as real as you would hope it is.

**Beware of the handoff.** If the boss tries to hand you off too early (before the proposed 5-minute meeting), **don't accept it**. Say, "I appreciate your wanting to delegate, but the reason I wanted to meet with you personally is that this will impact your business significantly. I'd like 5 minutes to show you the highlights and get your reaction before I talk with anyone else in your firm. I know your time is valuable. If I take more than 5 minutes, you can throw me out."

### 4. Make your 5-minute meeting the best you ever had.

- Have a proposal in writing.
- Have notes on everything you want to cover.
- Have a list of anticipated questions and answers.
- Have samples or something to demonstrate.
- Have credibility builders – your best letter, something in print.
- Be early.
- Look as sharp as you've ever looked.
- Be knowledgeable – have answers in terms of how it works for the buyer.
- Be memorable – The thing that sets you apart, the thing that gets remembered is the thing that leads to the sale.
- Deliver – You have one chance. Don't blow it by not following through.

**It's the most challenging, rewarding fun you can have in sales!**

# The secret of top-down selling is the 4.5 R's …

- ## Be resourceful.
- ## Be ready (prepared).
- ## Be relentless.
- ## Be remembered.

*There is a 4.5 R -- Risk it.*
*It's the only way to make it happen. Go for it.*

The gift shop at the Guggenheim has a T-shirt that says *Start at the Top*. How much more of a wake-up call do you need? Call them and order a few today!

*I urge you to write yours. It builds your*
*character at the same time it lays it bare.*

# Your personal mission statement.

A personal mission statement is your affirmation, philosophy, and purpose
rolled into one. It's an opportunity to bring your goals into focus and
transfer your ideals into the real world.

It's a chance for you to write your own legacy. It's your personal challenge
to yourself. Sounds pretty heavy, but actually it's fun if you do it right. Here
are the ground rules:

- Define yourself.
- Who or what are you dedicated to (family
  person, children, etc.).
- Define your service to others.
- Tell how you will strive to get better,
  do new things, grow.
- Commit yourself to community service.
- Tell how it's getting done.

*Words that will help* … will, dedication, persist, honest, ethical, positive,
enthusiastic, fun, health, learn new things, listen, help, provide, encourage,
others, continually, example.

Use your goals and visions to define your mission:
- The examples you seek to set.
- The ideals by which you live or seek to live.
- The affirmations that you can use every day to
  make you a better person.

*The process takes time.* Write a first draft. Let it sit for a few days. Re-read it
slowly and make changes that you feel better express your true feelings.
Describe the things you think you are and the things you seek to accomplish
or become.

Don't be afraid or embarrassed to flatter yourself. You're writing this for yourself, not others. Affirm everything you think you are or think you want to become. Do it with a sense of pride and a spirit of adventure.

# Post it where you can see it every day. Sign it in big, bold felt-tip pen.

# Live it. Live it every day.

I'm attaching mine to use as a template for yours. Feel free to paraphrase. I'm sharing mine because it has helped me achieve some tough goals in some tough times.

I urge you to write yours. It builds your character at the same time it lays it bare. It serves as a beacon of light in the fog of life. It is a path to take that you build on every day. It is your mission.

# Jeffrey Gitomer
*Personal Mission Statement*

### I am a father ...
I will be a positive person and positive example.
I will encourage my children, give them self-confidence,
and help them understand the ways of the world.

### I will be a good person ...
I will help others when I am able, without sacrificing my goals.
I will say yes when I can, no when I can't.
I will be the type of friend to others that they hope I'll be.
I will not be ashamed or embarrassed to ask for help when I need it.

### I will seek business leadership positions ...
I will continue to be a leader by example
in sales, marketing, training, writing, and business consulting.

### My expertise and technology will position me to serve ...
businesses and individuals with the highest-quality plans, reports,
training, advice, business expertise, and customer support.

### I will strive to build quality long-term relationships ...
with my customers and vendors, and to deal fairly and honestly
with all people and companies I encounter. I will continually
endeavor to increase the level of service to my customers.

### I will help my customers discover the best solutions ...
to their sales, marketing, and management needs by listening, providing
information, and performing services to the highest standards of excellence.

### I will serve my community ...
in ways that reflect my commitment to co-workers, customers, and friends;
and show my appreciation for the help and support they and
the community have given me.

**I will be the best person I can be for myself so I can be my best
when helping others. I will be enthusiastic in all that I do.
I will do my best to maintain my health.
I will try to learn something new every day.
I will have fun every day.
I will rededicate myself to my positive attitude every day.**

## *Jeffrey Gitomer*

# The Book of Humor --

## The Biggest Secret

## Laugh Last!

Humor ...

If you're serious about succeeding at a sales career, it's time you started looking on the lighter side.

Go ahead, make me laugh.

Humor melts ice.
It warms the coldest of hearts.
It makes sales.

They'll be laughing all the way to the bank ... your bank.

*If I can get the prospect or customer to laugh,*
*I can get him or her to buy...So can you.*

# A funny thing happened to me on the way to a sale!

When you're on sales calls and prospects tell you no, start thanking them. Tell them that by saying *no*, they're helping you get one step closer to *yes*. Tell them how much you appreciate it. Tell them it takes you five no's to get one yes and you still need three more no's. *Ask them if they know anyone else who might not be interested, so that you can get the three more no's before someone says yes.* Tell them you need people to tell you *no*, because it helps you get to the yes quicker. It'll blow them away. Humor. How much of it do you employ when selling? Enough to make a sale?

**Humor is one of the most important communication strengths needed to master in the selling process.** If you can get the prospect or customer to laugh, you can get him or her to buy.

**Nothing builds rapport faster than humor.** It's a bonding mechanism that transcends (and reveals) all prejudice and prejudgments. It brings the selling process to a real level. It brings out the truth. I have found that many truths are revealed through humor. If you listen carefully to a prospect's jokes, it will often reveal philosophy, prejudice, and intelligence (or lack of it).

How can you use this powerful tool to make more sales? Here are a few guidelines:

• **Use humor in the warm-up of the presentation to set a happy tone for the meeting.** The earlier you get a prospect to laugh, the better. Laughter is a form of approval.

• **Don't make jokes at someone else's expense.** If the prospect knows the person (you never know who knows who), or is related to the person at the brunt end of the joke, you're dead meat. If it is repeated, I guarantee it will be mistold or altered, and will surely come back to haunt you.

- **Use yourself as the example or victim of the joke.** It shows you're human and can take it. It's also a safe form of humor.

- **Some people won't get the joke.** Silence at the end of a joke is pretty horrifying. Make sure it's funny to someone else before you tell it where it counts. But no matter how tested the material, some people's elevator stops before the top floor, and they will never get it.

- **Don't use ethnic humor or make ethnic jokes unless you're the ethnic.** That's not a guideline, that's a rule. I was challenged by a friend who said that telling someone an ethnic joke is implied approval for others to tell one. I have mixed feelings about that. I go back to truth in humor, and I'd rather have the prospect reveal himself or herself. But I do respect my friend's opinion.

- **Listen before you tell a joke.** Try to determine the type and demeanor of the person or people you're addressing. The wrong humor will kill you as fast as the right humor will let you live (and sell) eternally.

- **Try using personal experience rather than story-type jokes.** Something funny happened in your office, with your kid, or when you were a kid, rather than "two guys were walking down the street …"

- **If you tell a joke that prospects or customers have heard before, it is actually a negative to make them hear it again.** That's one great reason for using personal humor – they are sure to be hearing it for the first time.

- **Timing. Timing. Timing.** Humor properly inserted will turn the prospect or crowd in your favor. But be forewarned – there is *never* a right time for a political or religious joke told to someone you don't know. Don't use humor where it's not appropriate.

- **Keep a joke file.** Write down funny things or events so that you can remember them in selling or speaking situations.

- **There are humor tendencies.** Men and women tend to make jokes about the other gender. Religious groups are apt to take each other on. People in bordering states tend to be on the wrong end of the joke. In North Carolina it seems to be about farmers in West Virginia, but when I lived in Indiana, it was those farmers from Kentucky. And of course if you're from New York – everyone else in the world is a farmer.

- **Risqué jokes can be risky.** They will get you in trouble if you say them to the wrong person. Know the limits of your audience before engaging your mouth.

- **Turn questions into opportunities with humor.** You give a 30-second phone pitch and ask for an appointment at the end. *The prospect asks,* "How much does this cost?" *You say,* "Oh, I don't charge to make a sales call."

• **Don't dread cold calls; laugh them off.** There is a fear and dislike many salespeople have when it comes to cold calling. A salesman told me a story that he had a big fear of being thrown out of a company when making a cold call. I suggested to him that his strategy should be to only cold call on one-story buildings.

Adapt real-world humor to a real-world selling situation. I was making a presentation in a room full of smokers. I hate smoke. So I recounted a story where I was driving with my friend, Becky Brown, and she was talking about how tough it was to quit smoking and how hard she was trying but just couldn't. I asked, "Have you ever tried the gum – you know, that nicotine gum?" She said, "I tried it, but I couldn't keep it lit."

I made the sale. If you can make 'em laugh, you can make 'em buy.

# The Book of WOW

**"I am the greatest!"**
-- Muhammed Ali

Are you just another (business) card-carrying salesperson?

Does your pitch come straight out of a (tin) can?

Are they going to forget you as soon as you walk out of the door?

Are they going to take your calls again? Return them?

If you're not outstanding in front of the prospect, you'll be out standing in the street.

WOW …

**2.1**

*The WOW factor totally separates you from everyone.*
*Using WOW turns your prospect into a customer.*

# The WOW factor.
# Use it to land the big sale.

WOW is your ability to be different. The WOW factor and your closing ratio have lots in common. **If you don't WOW 'em, it's likely you won't sell 'em.** I went to New York to sell a publisher on a book idea based on my successful column on selling skills, *Sales Moves*. I used the WOW factor.

***Background and preparation.*** I developed a total WOW preparation. I had sample prototype book cover designs and mock-ups; I had a 15-page proposal including several letters of reference; I named the book *The Sales Bible*; I had the name trademarked; I had a multimedia presentation prepared by the Whitley Group; I had a daring marketing concept incorporating a computer disk and a package of wallet-sized flashcards to make it different from all other books on the shelf; I wrote my pitch and answers to every objection I could think of; I selected clothing I thought was appropriate; I was ready.

I selected 10 target publishers and contacted four before I arrived in NY. I made one solid appointment with the publisher I really wanted (a major publishing firm with a guy I'm calling Mr. Book).

This is how the appointment was made. It took me seven calls to get Mr. Book's name and extension number! Call number eight – BINGO. He answers his own phone. (He later said, "The phone is usually more important than what I'm doing.") I tell Mr. Book everything he needs to know in about 1.5 minutes – he seems interested. I tell him I'll send him a proposal and I ask him for a 5-minute appointment. He says, "The old 5-minute appointment bit. Did you read that in the Harvey Mackay book?"

I said, "Listen, Harvey Mackay is from Minnesota, I'm from Jersey. He learned that ploy from me!" Mr. Book laughed and said OK to a 5-minute appointment. (I sent Mr. Book my package by next-day air.)

**I had two mentors help me with my presentation.** Ty Boyd, the voice of Charlotte for two decades and one of the nicest people I've ever met, who put me on the right path; and Bill Lewis, who was in Manhattan and had published 20 books. (Every day I showed up at his place for an hour of coaching and encouragement. He was instrumental to my success.)

*The first appointment.* I walk into Mr. Book's office in midtown Manhattan and he says, "OK, Gitomer, I read your proposal. You've got 5 minutes." I start in immediately with background, get to the meat of my presentation in less than 2 minutes, put my prototype in his hands, sneak in two personal questions (for rapport), and finish my pitch in less than 5 minutes. Then I begin to question, listen, and take notes. (The longer he talks, the more questions he asks, the stronger my chances are.) *Forty-five minutes later, I'm still in there.*

Mr. Book says, "I'm interested. Leave me your stuff (my only copies), and let me run it by my CEO." Great. I've got three other publishers to see in the next three days, and this guy wants to keep half my tools. "When will you be meeting?" I ask lightly. "Before the end of the week," he says, trying to gain a position of power. (Here goes my risk statement.) "I have a slight dilemma, and I need your help," I said. "I've got several appointments over the next few days. Do you think you might have a chance to discuss this with the CEO by tomorrow?"

"I should be able to," he said.

"Great. Why don't we set up an appointment for the end of the day tomorrow?" I said, nailing him to the floor. "4:30 OK?" I ask. He says, "Looks fine to me."

I'm so excited I could scream. I walk back to my hotel singing and dancing. (In Manhattan you can do anything you want. No one notices, looks, or cares.)

I get back to my room and there's a phone message from Mr. Book under my door. I call. He says, "Can you make it a little earlier? I want to have a few other people present." "Yeah, sure," I reply in a millisecond. (If you ever want a dictionary definition of a buying signal, that was it.)

***The second appointment.*** I arrive 10 minutes early the next day. Mr. Book leads me into a conference room so that I can hook up my computerized (Whitley-prepared) presentation. In walks the national sales manager. I have to convince him why my book will sell. I turn on my computerized multi-media dog-and-pony show that has him leaning so far forward he about falls out of the chair. Now it's time to drag out every tool in my box. I talk about additional distribution ideas I have. I tell him I would be glad to go with him on selected sales calls. He is now totally convinced he can sell it.

We then negotiate "*What if we accept you?*" terms. Advances, royalties, and publicity. Mr. Book asks, "If I offer you this deal [he lists the bullet points] would you take it?" (There's a switch – now he's closing me.) "Yes," I say. He says, "I'll call you by noon tomorrow and let you know," and walks out of the room. Eighteen more hours of agony.

The third appointment. By 1:00 P.M., no call. I call him. He gruffly says he hasn't met Mr. Big yet and will call later. Tactically I tell him I'll stop by at the end of the day to pick up some of my materials. He says OK. I'm a nervous wreck. At 3:30 he leaves a message for me. I decide not to call back. At 4:45 I show up at his office. He keeps me waiting until 5:20. He comes out to greet me and says the magic words: *Let's talk business*.

***WOW!*** I just made the biggest sale of my life!

***I also failed.*** It is important to note that in success there are always failures. In all I contacted 10 publishers and two agents. All were cold calls. Six publishers turned me down or said I needed an agent before they would talk to me. One agent said no; the other has yet to call me back. WOW.

## *I'm saving the rejection letters so I can frame them around my book.*

*The WOW factor can be used by anyone.*
*The problem is that most salespeople*
*won't sacrifice enough to create it.*

# Are you using the WOW factor?

*One of the most powerful aspects of sales – being different.*
What is WOW? ... WOW is sales!
WOW separates the strong from the weak.
WOW separates the sincere from the insincere.
WOW separates the sales pros from the cons.
WOW separates the *yes's* from the *no's*.
WOW is the full measure of your sales power and the way you use it.

Are you WOW? Is WOW a factor in your selling process?
How do you WOW the customer?

You can measure how much WOW is in your sales effort by looking at the following 10 aspects of what make up WOW:

**1. Be totally persistent** – To reach the prospect, to get the prospect your information, to get information about the prospect, to appoint the prospect.

**2. Be totally knowledgeable about the prospect** – Your knowledge of the prospect and his or her business is often critical to completing the sale. Use the famous "Mackay 66" questionnaire as a guideline for how much information is needed. Go to www.gitomer.com, register if you are a first-time user, and enter the words "MACKAY66" in the GitBox.

**3. Be totally prepared** – Have a perfect presentation that you've rehearsed. Have a written proposal for what you want to accomplish or sell. Develop support tools and support documentation. Identify all possible objections, and prescript, test, and rehearse responses for each of them.

**4. Be 10 minutes early** – It is best to arrive a little early. It is always a disaster to arrive late. Carry a light load (only what you need for the show).

**5. Be totally professional** – Great clothing, professional accessories; briefcase, business cards. Have everything crisp and clean.

**6. Get to the point quickly, then question, listen, and question** – Talk straight to the point. Get your meat out in 5 minutes or less. Write down your thoughts when the prospect is talking. Don't interrupt.

**7. Totally separate yourself from your competition and everyone else** – Have creative, new ideas; have the sale in finished form (design done, preliminary layout, sample); have a WOW computerized presentation (multimedia); have a comparison chart of key areas where you beat the competition. Do things (professionally) no one else would do.

**8. Be totally confident in what you say and the way you act** – Build rapport first and keep building it during the presentation. Use humor, use humor, use humor. Act and speak as though the deal were done. Use total manners – think back to your mother screaming at you about how to act civilized and do it. *Don't confuse confidence with cockiness. One works; the other fails.*

**9. Don't be afraid to use sales tactics** – but don't be obvious. Get tie-downs, approvals, and commitments along the way. Don't leave without knowing where you stand. Don't leave without a written-down next action, deadline, and/or meeting.

**10. Be WOW yourself** – You must be positive, enthusiastic, focused, polished, and convinced. You must be outstanding enough to be memorable.

Here are 15 characteristics/words that epitomize a WOW salesperson:

| WOW Factor | My score: 1=lowest, 5=highest |
|---|---|
| 1. Persistent (relentless) | 1 2 3 4 5 |
| 2. Prepared | 1 2 3 4 5 |
| 3. Best | 1 2 3 4 5 |
| 4. Creatively different | 1 2 3 4 5 |
| 5. Funny | 1 2 3 4 5 |
| 6. Truthful | 1 2 3 4 5 |
| 7. Real (genuine) | 1 2 3 4 5 |
| 8. Compelling | 1 2 3 4 5 |
| 9. Fast and to the point | 1 2 3 4 5 |
| 10. Skillful | 1 2 3 4 5 |
| 11. Knowledgeable | 1 2 3 4 5 |
| 12. Courageous | 1 2 3 4 5 |
| 13. Memorable | 1 2 3 4 5 |
| 14. Long term | 1 2 3 4 5 |
| 15. Able to get to *yes* | 1 2 3 4 5 |

Add up your score and rate yourself.

$$70-75 = WOW$$
$$60-69 = AOK$$
$$50-59 = SO?$$
$$15-49 = DUD$$

Getting to WOW is identifying weaknesses in the preceding 15 areas, making a plan to strengthen them one by one, developing the self-discipline to carry out the plan, and taking action to practice and implement the changes. You can do it if you want it bad enough.

Are you WOW? Ask yourself …

- Would you buy it if you were the buyer?
- Do you have what it takes to stick with it, stick to it, and do it until it's done?
- Will the prospect be moved to act as a result of your presentation?
- Will the prospect go home or around the office and talk about you in a positive way?
- Do you epitomize the 15 WOW characteristics?

There is a challenge and sacrifice needed to put WOW into your selling process. If you have the fortitude to put the package together, then you must put your WOW in front of the prospect. Here are the final steps to incorporate WOW into your presentation. Notice that all are intangible:

- Focus on your target.
- Have your dreams ever present in your mind.
- Put your passion in your presentation.
- Don't ever let them see you sweat.
- Let them feel your belief in yourself and your product.
- Never quit.

# In sales it all boils down to one word … *yes.*
# To get there more often, use WOW.

*When you leave an appointment or a
networking event, will anyone remember
that you were there?*

# Remember me? I'm a salesman ... like all the others.

My cat, Lito, has a business card. She is our *corporate mascot* and plays a
vital role in my office productivity. Whenever I need an important paper,
Lito is lying on it. I give her card out in seminars and training programs for
fun and a laugh. But everyone who gets her card keeps it, shows it to
someone else, talks about it, and talks about me.

Being memorable is creating a vivid image in the mind of the prospect that
distinguishes you from others. What you do, how you do it. What you say,
how you say it.

How memorable are you? Do your prospects talk about you when you're
gone? Or are they talking about (and ordering from) your competitor?

*Here are some recommendations and examples of what has been
memorable ... and brought about business:*

**Spend money on your business cards.** They are the image you project
about the quality of your business. Take a look at your business card. Will
customers and prospects remember you from it? If someone gave it to you,
would you make a comment about it?

My friend, Richard Herd, prints his on the back of a deck of playing cards.
He has received thousands of comments about his card. He has people
talking about his card after a sales call. He also has lots of customers.
Coincidence?

My friend, Greg Gregory, is vice president of Builders Supply, a 53-year-old
business in Lancaster, SC. They supply lumber and building materials to
home builders throughout the region. Last week he had business cards
printed for his truck drivers. He considers them a valuable part of his team

and wants his drivers to be memorable to his customers. Gregory doesn't consider them drivers – he thinks of them as ambassadors of his company. His ambassadors are on the front lines with daily interface with his customers. They are ready to serve in a memorable way. WOW.

**Get with the times.** Want your business cards to be current with the rest of the business world? Better pull yours out of your wallet and double check that you've got the basics covered. And man, the information listed here is the bare minimum needed for conducting business today.

Does your business card (and every one of your employees' business cards) have the following information?

- ★ Name
- ★ Title
- ★ Company name
- ★ Company address
- ★ E-mail address
- ★ Company's Web site address
- ★ Phone (with area code)
- ★ Fax (with area code)
- ★ Cell phone (if applicable)
- ★ Company logo

You'd better make them memorable … and make them quick.

*A note about e-mail.* If you're a company of any size at all, meaning more than just you being a Lone Ranger at your desk in your den, get a real e-mail address. None of this Hotmail or AOL crap. Those accounts should be for personal use, not for professional communication. If you want your company to look like it's going to be around for more than 3 months, get yourself a domain name for your Web Site and for your employees' addresses. It's a minimal and worthwhile investment in your business.

**Respond with a personal surprise.** After I wrote an article on getting your foot in the door, Sheila Neisler of A Basket of Carolina, wanted to tell me that a gift basket was a good tool, so she hand-delivered one with personalized items: a book of quotes on winning and cat food (for Lito), among other things. She was talked about in this office for weeks. We have developed a business relationship that will last … because she dared to be memorable.

*Here are some elements that you can incorporate into a memorable marketing campaign:*

- ☛ Hand delivery.
- ☛ Fast delivery.
- ☛ Early service.
- ☛ Late (after hours) service.
- ☛ Delivering more than you promised.
- ☛ Personalized thank-you.
- ☛ Fax a joke.
- ☛ Quotation example (famous quote – book of quotes).
- ☛ A remarkable business card.
- ☛ Gift basket of things that are meaningful – banner from college, golf balls, personalized anything.
- ☛ Fax an article about the person's interest.
- ☛ A birthday call.
- ☛ "I was thinking about you" call.
- ☛ Personal attention – before, during, and AFTER the sale.
- ☛ Delivering a gift of thanks – gift basket, plant, flowers.
- ☛ Delivering a personalized gift of thanks – a book about the person's interests, a golf lesson.

# Do something that says, *"I took the time to get to know you AND I'm acknowledging my appreciation for your business."*

To be memorable, you need *personal* information from your prospect or customer. The famous "Mackay 66" takes personal information to a new level. To start, you must develop a form to gather the following data:

- Number of kids (in school? which one?).
- College attended.
- Favorite sports teams.
- Favorite restaurant, food.
- Type of car.
- Type of pet.
- Hobbies.
- Favorite magazine.
- Last book read.
- Prime goal.
- Last vacation – where.
- Trade publications read.
- Trade association involvement.
- Civic/community organizations.
- Hometown.
- Other places lived or worked.
- Present place of residence.

Getting personal information will facilitate follow-up if you use it properly. If you have the information, how will you use it to be memorable? Ask yourself one question: *Will they talk about you afterward to others?* If they will, you're on the right path.

The value and power of using the information you have must be strategized! Planning a memorable follow-up program for the client will get the results you want. Here are the planning elements to consider:

- ➤ The game plan (and budget).
- ➤ The objectives.
- ➤ The urgency (selling cycle time).
- ➤ The tools to be used.
- ➤ The verbiage of all writing … with impact.
- ➤ The verbiage of the pitch (phone, in person) … with impact.
- ➤ The objections – scripted responses.
- ➤ The implementation (and training).
- ➤ The measurement – documenting results.

*Being memorable and being remembered means doing creative, personal things. Things like …*

- ☆ If you have tickets, don't give them to customers. Go with them.
- ☆ Take them to their favorite restaurant.
- ☆ Donate to *their* charity in their *name*.
- ☆ Make them your Customer of the Month. Send them an award plaque.
- ☆ Share a family experience – Discovery Place, a Knights game, a picnic.
- ☆ Have a *customer* award program – Best, Most Fun to Talk To, Most Professional.
- ☆ Send a handwritten note with a personal message.

I was at a networking event last week. A Charlotte Fast 50 corporate president ran over to me saying, "Hey, Gitomer, show this guy your cat's card." "Have one," I said, "and have one of mine in case the cat isn't in. I usually handle her calls." … I'm printing another batch of Lito's cards.

**Author's note:** In February of 1999, my friend and companion of 14 years passed away in her sleep. I wish I could tell you how close we were even though we spoke different languages. To maintain her place in business history, we have named our publishing company Lito Press. Her first book was published in December 2002 and the company made a profit its very first week of business. Evidently, Lito's nine lives were not completely used up when she died.

# The Book of Questions

# Why ask "Why?"

Question:
• How do you build rapport?
• How do you determine prospect needs?
• How do you establish buyer confidence?

Answer: Question.

The technique of asking and answering questions is the heart of a sales presentation.

Without questions, you'll have no answers.

Without answers, you'll have no sales.

Without sales, you'll have no money.

Any questions?

2.2

*The question is the most important skill*
*a salesperson should master ...*
*The importance of asking one properly*
*lies somewhere between sale and no sale.*

# To sell or not to sell, that is the (Power) Question.

Two of the most important aspects of selling are asking questions and listening. **The proper questions will make the prospect tell you everything you need to sell him or her.**

Combine powerful questions with effective listening skills and you will have the power and self-discipline to uncover facts/needs, then formulate a response that moves the buyer to a decision.

Man, that sounds so simple. So why doesn't everyone buy when you try to sell them? Because ...

1. You're not doing an effective job of asking questions.

2. You're not doing an effective job of listening to the prospect.

3. You have a preconceived notion about the prospect – prejudging the type of person, anticipating answers, and interrupting dialogue.

4. You think you already know all the answers, so why bother asking questions or listening with full attention?

5. You have not uncovered the true needs of the prospect. How can you satisfy needs if you don't know what they are?

The most effective sales call is 25% questioning/talking and 75% listening. How does that compare with what you do? *"Oh, that doesn't apply to me,"* you say. *"My product is different. I need to talk more."* Bull-blank. That's just an excuse. What you're really saying is, *"I don't know how to ask a question effectively."*

How do you ask a question? In a word – open-ended. Avoid *yes* or *no* questions unless you're sure yes is a slam dunk – as in a tie-down question.

*Developing and asking Power Questions is the fulcrum point of your ability to understand the prospect's needs. Here are 12.5 challenges to the types and styles of questions you ask …*

**1. Is the question clear and concise?** Does the prospect understand the question, its meaning, content, and implication?

**2. Does the question require productive thinking before the prospect can formulate a response?** Have you put the prospect on the path toward your product or service as a result of the question?

**3. Does the question force the prospect to evaluate new information or concepts?** Are you building prospect credibility by asking superior questions that don't make people feel inferior, but do challenge them in a new way?

**4. Does the question make you seem more knowledgeable than your competitors by probing in new areas?** Are you separating yourself from the competition by asking questions the competition never thought to ask?

**5. Does the question lead the prospect (and you) to draw from past experience?** Are you asking prospects questions that make them share things they are proud of? *These are not only sales questions; they are rapport-building questions.*

**6. Does the question generate a response that the prospect has never thought of before?** New twists make you seem different, better, at the top of your game.

**7. Does the question provide a tie-down answer that moves the presentation process closer to a close?** Using question lead-in or ending words, like *don't you, isn't it, shouldn't you, doesn't it,* provides you with the opportunity for the prospect to say *yes* to a particular part of your presentation and move on to the next area.

**8. Does the question relate directly to the prospect's (business) situation?** The more direct the question, the more likely you are to get a direct response.

**9. Does the question relate directly to the prospect's objectives?**
Are you probing in areas that the prospect can relate to? Areas that make
the prospect commit to real answers?

**10. Does the question draw information from the prospect that
helps you make the sale easier?** Questions about how your product or
service will be used, what are his or her expectations.

**11. Does the question create an atmosphere that is positive and
conducive to make a sale?** Is the question provocative or provoking?
Don't make prospects mad when you ask a question – make them think.

**12. Are you asking a question back when a prospect asks you
one?** Prospect: *Can I get delivery in two weeks?* Salesperson: *Is that when
you need it delivered?*

**12.5 The ultimate question -- Are you asking a closing question?**
A question to which the answer confirms the sale.

*Do you have 10 or 12 different closing questions written down
to rehearse and use as the occasion arises? I'll bet you don't.*

Want to master the science of formulating and asking Power Questions?
Write two or three questions that respond to each of the 12.5 challenges
above, and incorporate them into your selling process. If you do, I'll make
you two promises:

1. It will be very challenging.

2. The reward for doing it will make you
   a better, more financially rewarded salesperson
   … forever.

# Questions are to sales as breath is to life.
# If you fail to ask them, you will die.
# If you ask them incorrectly,
# your death won't be immediate,
# but it's inevitable.
# If you ask them correctly, the answer is …
# a sale.

*Setting up the question is as important as asking it.*

# Setting up the question ... and lowering the boom.

In Ray Leone's insightful book *Success Secrets of the Sales Funnel*, he discusses questions as part of his sales philosophy. Leone says *the question* is the most important skill a salesperson should master, and I agree. He presents a three-level strategy in setting up and asking the question that could change the way you ask questions from now on.

*First stage* ... Make a factual statement that can't be refuted.
*Second stage* ... Make a personal observation that reflects your experience and creates credibility.
*Third stage* ... Ask an open-ended question that incorporates the first two stages.

OK, sounds pretty easy. Let's try it.
Here are three (concise) examples to illustrate this technique:

## Let's say I'm selling sales training.

*First stage*: "You know, Mr. Jones, sales staffs rarely meet the sales goals and quotas set for them by their boss or manager." *Second stage*: "My experience has shown me that when there is a lack of training there is often poor staff attitude and an absence of goal-setting and goal-achievement skills. Interestingly the staff tends to blame their inability to sell on other things and other people rather than take the responsibility themselves." (Now, *and only now*, is it time for you to drop the question.) *Third stage*: "How are you ensuring that your sales reps meet their goals and maintain a positive attitude?"
*Pretty cool, huh? Let's try another one.*

## Now I'm selling copiers.

*First stage*:"You know, Mr. Jones, document processing is an integral part of the operation of any business." *Second stage*:"My experience has shown me that many businesses fail to put enough emphasis on the quality and cost control of their documents. They fail to realize that every time a copy is sent to a customer, it reflects the image and quality of their business."

(Now it is time for you to drop the question.) *Third stage*:"How are you ensuring that the quality of your copies reflects the quality of your business?" *As an owner of a business, that question would make me think.*

## One more. Let's say I'm an accountant (as far-fetched as that seems).

*First stage*: "You know, Mr. Jones, most businesses don't plan long enough in advance for their best tax advantage." *Second stage*:"My experience has shown me that entrepreneurs lack the financial expertise to do their own planning, then blame it on a lack of time. That's what led us to put together this tax planner. It takes about an hour a month, is simple to use and can save you thousands of dollars every year." (OK, now it's question time.) *Third stage*:"How are you planning for your taxes for this year? With your permission, I'd like to review your return from last year and customize your planner for the type of financial situations you face day to day. I'm sure you're looking to save every tax penny you can and want an accountant who will fight the IRS to keep every dollar allowed you under the law, don't you?"

How the heck can you say *no* to that? You can't.

**This questioning technique is powerful.** It builds credibility and identifies needs at the same time. It works for any business or service. Don't take the examples too literally. Learn the concept and adapt it to your business. The object is to compel the prospect to think and respond to you in a different way. So different that it sets you apart from (above) the competition.

If you're going to use this technique successfully, write out the three stages and give it about five practice sessions to work out the kinks, refine your verbiage, and get familiar with the process.

After about 25 attempts, you'll own the technique and begin to see the real rewards.

*Sales solutions are easy once you identify the prospect's*
*problems, concerns, and needs ...*
*with questions.*

# Can you close a sale
# in five questions?

Questions breed sales. Using Power Questions to find facts is critical to creating an atmosphere in which a sale can be made. Ray Leone (*Success Secrets of the Sales Funnel*), who is probably as good a questioner as exists in selling, has issued this challenge: *Can you close a sale in five questions?* Here's a mixture of his technique and mine.

Sales solutions are easy once you identify the prospect's problems. This is only accomplished by well-crafted questions. Questions that extract information, needs, and concerns. *The sale is most easily made once you identify the prospect's real needs and harmonize with his concerns.*

This questioning technique can be used to qualify, identify true needs, and close the sale in five question steps. For this example, let's say I'm selling printing.

(Have a notepad out and use it as the prospect responds.)

*Question #1*: "Mr. Prospect, **how do you select** a printer?" (Variation: "How do you choose a printer?")

Prospect says, "Quality, delivery, and price."

*Question #2*: "**How do you define** quality?" or "**What does** quality **mean to you?**" (Ask the same "How do you define ...?" question for all three responses of the "How do you choose ...?" question.)

The prospect will give you thoughtful answers. Many prospects have never been asked questions like these and will be forced to think in new patterns. You may even want to ask a follow-up question or create a tie-down question here before going to Question #3. For example, the prospect says he defines *quality* as crisp, clear printing. You ask, "Oh, you mean printing that reflects the image of the quality of your company?"

*How can a prospect possibly say no to that question?*

*Question #3*: **"What makes that important to you?"** or **"Is that most important to you?"** or **"Why is that important to you?"**

This question draws out the true need of the prospect. Finding out what is important to them about printing and why printing is important are the keys to closing the sale. There may be secondary or follow-up questions to gain a clear definition of what is important and why.

*Question #4*: "If I could deliver the quality you demand so that the image in your printing reflects the image of your business to your customers, and I could do it in the time frame you require, at a reasonable [not the cheapest] price, **would I be** [variation: is there any reason I would not be] **a candidate for your business?"**

Of course you would! This is a feedback question that combines the data found in the first three questions. It's the classic "If I ... would you" question that makes the prospect commit. It actually quasi-closes the prospect. If there is a true objection (*We have to get bids ... Someone else decides ... I'm satisfied with my present vendor*), it is likely to surface here.

*Question #5*: **"Great! When could we begin?"** or **"Great! When is your next printing project?"**

The object of the fifth question is to pin the prospect down to a beginning date or time or quantity to start doing business. In many cases you can sell a sample order or trial. Where big-ticket products are involved (copiers, computers), a puppy dog approach will work best (leave your product for the customer to use for a few days), or take the prospect to visit a satisfied customer and see your product in operation and get a live testimonial.

This is not hard sell; it's heart sell. **Good questions get to the heart of the problem/need very quickly without the buyers feeling like they are being pushed.** Use the questioning process early and often. If you're doing a lot of talking and the prospects are not, you're boring the prospects and losing the sale. They don't care what you've got unless it serves their needs. The only way to identify those needs is to ask 'em.

Looking for a few additional Power Question lead-ins? Try these …

- What do you look for …?
- What have you found …?
- How do you propose …?
- What has been your experience …?
- How have you successfully used …?
- How do you determine …?
- Why is that a deciding factor …?
- What makes you choose …?
- What do you like about …?
- What is one thing you would improve about …?
- What would you change about …?
  (Do not say, "What don't you like about …?")
- Are there other factors …?
- What does your competitor do about …?
- How do your customers react to …?

To use questions successfully, they must be thought out and written down in advance. Develop a list of 15 to 25 questions that uncover needs, problems, pains, concerns, and objections. Develop 15 to 25 more that create prospect commitment as a result of the information you have uncovered.

# Practice.
## After about 30 days
## of asking the right questions,
## you'll begin to see the real rewards.

This is not hard sell;
it's heart sell.
Good questions
get to the heart
of the problem/need
very quickly
without the buyer
feeling like he or she is
being pushed.

# The Book of Power

## 2.3

## Income Statement

A Power Statement is electric with selling energy.

Are you energizing prospects with words of power ... or are your batteries dead?

Are you putting them to sleep or knocking them out?

Do you make a memorable impact on your prospects?

You better.

You can be sure you do when you use Power Statements.

Your brain is your power tool. Plug it in.

Turn your current into currency with your creative power.

*Power Statements make your product
or service outstanding, credible,
understandable, and buyable.*

# You are now under my Power (Statement).

What is a *Power Statement?* A statement that makes your product or
service outstanding, understandable, credible (incredible), and buyable. A
(nontraditional) statement that describes what you do and how you do it in
terms of the customers and their perceived use or need for what you're selling.

Where does the statement get its power?
## *Your creativity.*

You're trying to make a sale or the impact that leads to one. **The objective
is to persuade and motivate the prospect or customer to act.** *That's
what a Power Statement is designed to do.* If you do it right, it also
distances you from and sets you above your competition.

How do you create a Power Statement for your business? *Easy* – just think
of what you do in terms of how your customer will benefit. Not a boring
description, but a vivid, alliterative, benefit-filled picture – an energetic
group of words that has the prospect wanting more.

*Here's the mind-set needed for generating Power Statements:*
Don't sell drill bits. Sell the perfectly smooth holes they create.
Don't sell printing. Sell the brochures that will reflect your prospect's
image and impact her sales.
Don't sell cars. Sell the prestige and status you'll have, or the smooth ride.
Don't sell insurance. Sell safe, financially secure families protected from
tragedy.
Don't sell eyeglasses. Sell better vision and a stylish look.

## *Get it?*

Power Statements have several purposes and can serve many needs in completing and solidifying the sale. A Power Statement is ...

➤ A statement that makes a prospect think about what you do in terms of how he or she can use what you offer.

➤ A statement that builds your credibility with a prospect.

➤ A nontraditional statement that describes what you do and how you do it in terms of benefits to your prospect.

➤ A statement about what you do in terms of what your prospect needs.

➤ A statement that draws a clear line of distinction between you and your competitor.

➤ A statement that makes the prospect want to hear more.

➤ A statement that gives the customer a reason to buy.

➤ A statement that breaks down resistance.

➤ A statement that gives the customer more confidence to buy.

➤ A statement that makes a favorable impact on the prospect.

➤ A statement that links what you do and how it relates to the prospect.

➤ A statement that is memorable.

Power Statements creatively say what you do in terms of a prospect's needs. How do you respond when someone asks you what you do? I'll bet it's a boring one-sentence description that has the other person looking for someone else to talk to. Here are some examples of using Power Statements instead of the previous answer you gave to the question, *What do you do?* ...

• *Temporary Help*: We provide quality emergency and temporary employees for businesses like yours so that when one of your own employees is sick, absent, or on vacation there is no loss of productivity or reduction of service to your customers.

• *Men's Clothing*: Our experience has shown us that salespeople dress for their customers. We create the look you need to make that important presentation. *Variation*: Bruce Julian at Miltons Clothing Cupboard in Charlotte has a great power line: "When our customers have an important meeting or speech to make, they go their closet and select clothing they bought at Miltons." WOW.

## Power Statements are memorable opening lines. I went to one of those business opportunity (franchise) shows. Companies trying to sell businesses for $10,000 to $150,000. There were more than 100 businesses represented. Half were immediately recognizable by their national stature.

I took my tape recorder because I was sure I would hear dozens of gems. Wrong, franchise breath. They were disappointing (pathetic). After the first 20 or so duds, I was hoping to find just one. I did. As I walked by a booth loaded with Mickey Mouse products and clothing, a woman met me in the aisle and said, **"Mickey Mouse makes more money in a year than every company in this room … combined!"** Wow, what a line. I thanked her for making my day. She gave me a puzzled "You're welcome?"

### Power Statements generate interest and get appointments.
- *Generic-interest Power Statement:* Your key to profits is productivity. Last year we grew sales by more than 300% by providing items that arrived on time and aided our customer's productivity. In 30 days we can improve yours.
- *Generic appointment Power Statement:* I'm not sure if I can help you, Mr. Johnson. Let me explore some details with you for a few minutes (or over lunch). If I think I can help you, I'll tell you, and if I think I can't, I'll tell you that, too. Fair enough?

### Have you created your Power Statements yet?
Create your Power Statements now. Get out a sheet of paper in your sales meeting. Brainstorm them with your sales team. Bring in your most powerful salesperson – your president. Write your Power Statements for all situations. Why not take a fresh, powerful look at your selling expressions?

It's a great way to sell against the competition …

## *Overpower them!*

# The Book
## of
# Introductions

# Shake!

Introductions ...

Do they listen
to your pitch
with a friendly ear,
or pitch you out
on your rear?

Are you a sales
professional or a
professional visitor?

You've got a few precious
minutes to make a
powerful, professional
first impression.

If you can't open,
you can't close.

Knock, knock ...

**3.1**

*Your commercial is an opportunity to
provide information that creates interest and
response from people you network with.*

# The 30-second personal commercial ... How to write it.

When you go to a business meeting or are networking, you are on the lookout for contacts and prospects. Your commercial is your opportunity to provide information to create interest and response from prospects. It is the prelude and the gateway to a sale.

How effective is your commercial? *Do you even have one?*

Let's say you're out with a customer networking at her trade association meeting and she introduces you to a prospect. The prospect says, "What do you do?" If you're in the temporary staffing industry and you say, "I'm in the temporary staffing industry," you should be shot.

Your reply should be, "We provide quality emergency and temporary employees for businesses like yours so that when one of your own employees is sick, absent, or on vacation, there is no loss of productivity or reduction of service to your customers." *You deliver a line like that and the prospect can't help but be impressed.*

Now you have the prospect's attention. You ask your Power Question(s) to find out how qualified the prospect is. "How many employees do you have?" you ask. "Do you give them 1 or 2 weeks of vacation?" "How do you ensure that the level of service to your customers isn't reduced during these vacation times?" Make the prospect think.

Want to prepare or revise your commercial? Here's how:
Your objective is to have 15 to 30 seconds of information that ...

➤ States who you are
➤ States who your company is
➤ Creatively tells what you do

➤ Asks one or a series of Power Questions
➤ Makes a Power Statement that shows how you can help others
➤ Ends with why the prospect should *act now*

**After you creatively say what you do,
you ask a Power Question or series of questions
that makes the prospect think and respond in a way
that gives you needed information.**

This information allows you to formulate an *impact response* to show how you can help, and lets you know how qualified the prospect may be. The questions must be open-ended. (A question that gets the prospect thinking and talking. Not just saying *yes* or *no*.)

**There is no reason to tell a prospect how you can help
until you have uncovered what kind of help he or she needs!**

The Power Question is the most critical part of the process because it qualifies the prospect and sets up your impact (power) response. When formulating the Power Questions for your commercial, ask yourself these five questions:
1. What information do I want to get as a result of asking this question?
2. Can I qualify my prospect as a result of the question?
3. Does it take more than one question to find out the information I need?
4. Do my questions make the prospect think?
5. Can I ask a question that separates me from my competitor?

Here are some lead-ins to Power Questions that will expose areas of need:
• What do you look for ...?
• What have you found ...?
• How do you propose ...?
• What has been your experience ...?
• How have you successfully used ...?
• How do you determine ...?
• Why is that a deciding factor ...?
• What makes you choose ...?
• What do you like about ...?
• What is one thing you would improve about ...?
• What would you change about ...?
  (Do not say, "What don't you like about ...?")
• Are there other factors ...?
• What does your competitor do about ...?

- How do your customers react to …?
- How are you currently …?
- What are you doing to keep …?
- How often do you contact …?
- What are you doing to ensure …?

You should have a list of 25 Power Questions that make the prospect think and give you the information you need to strike.

Next comes your Power Statement. Re-read the section, **"You are now under my Power (Statement)"** in *The Book of Power.* This defines Power Statements completely.

Last, develop a call to action … a closing line, statement, or question that ensures another contact.

*Here is an example of a personal commercial:*
- **Name** … Hi, (hey) my name is Richard Herd.
- **Company name** … My company is (I'm the president of) Continental Advertising.
- **Creatively say what you do** … We impact your image, create sales, and ensure repeat business by providing innovative advertising specialties that keep your name in front of your customers and prospects.
- **Insert your Power Question** … How are you currently using ad specialties? (Variations: What are you doing to keep your name in front of your customers every day? How often do you contact your present customers? What are you doing to ensure that your name is in front of your customers more than your competitors'?)
- **Insert your Power Statement (How you help)** … (May be modified based on answers to Power Questions.) I think we can help you. We have creative brainstorming sessions with our clients where we bring together a small team of our people and yours. We place various items on the table that relate to your business and the customers you serve. This process creates dialogue that always leads to innovative products that complement your marketing plan and impact your customer's image of you. Not only is it productive, it's fun.
- **Why the prospect should act now** … Would you like to schedule a brainstorming session, or have lunch first and preview a few items to get a better feel for what I mean?

Use this example to help you write your own commercial. After you write it, rehearse it. Then go try it out and adjust it for the real world. Then really practice it (more than 25 times in real situations) until you own it.

## *Your Personal Commercial Worksheet*

- **Name** _____

- **Company name** _____

- **What you do** (briefly) _____

  _____

- *Power Question* _____

  _____

  _____

*(Ask more follow-up questions until you get the information you need.)*

- *Power Statement* _____

  _____

  _____

- **How you help** _____

  _____

  _____

- **Why prospect should act now** _____

  _____

  _____

**Instructions:** Fill out the form, read it from top to bottom, add a few personal pronouns, time it, practice it, and voila!

You now have
written the best
commercial
in the world,
but if you don't
deliver it properly,
no one will be
inclined to act.
Next page …

*Don't deliver too soon. Wait until you have enough
information from the prospect before you strike.*

# The 30-second personal commercial ... How to deliver it.

Can you deliver? You just wrote your personal commercial and now it's time to deliver it. Think of your personal business commercial as a pitcher in a baseball game. You want to make a pitch that's a strike, but all batters are not alike. They require different types of pitches – fast ball, curve, slider, and the ever-popular screwball. (Isn't it amazing how many screwballs we pitch?)

In order to pitch to the batter most effectively, you need to know what type of hitter he is. You need to know his hitting strengths and weaknesses. Every baseball team has a "book" on every other player in the league. They know how to pitch him and where the fielders should play in the event he hits the ball. It is no different in sales. You can't pitch the prospect effectively if you don't know what his needs are. You must know how to play each prospect. It's easy to get a strike in sales. All you have to do is ask your prospects questions. They will be delighted to tell you all about themselves.

Your objective is to deliver 15 to 30 seconds of information that states who you are, what you do, how you can help others, and why your prospect should act now. In the middle of your commercial (between *what you do* and *how you help others*), you are going to ask a series of open-ended Power Questions that will gather enough information for you to formulate a response that will lead to prospect interest and action.

## 10 Personal Commercial Delivery Rules ...
## (I'm tempted to say 10 Commandments, but I won't)

**1. Be brief.** Your remarks (other than questions) should be no more than 30 to 60 seconds.

**2. Be to the point.** Say something that creatively tells prospects exactly what you do in terms of their needs.

**3. Be remembered.** Say, give, or do something that will stay in the prospect's mind (in a positive, creative way).

**4. Be prepared.** Have your information at your command – rehearsed, practiced, and polished.

**5. Have Power Questions and Power Statements ready.** Prepare a list of questions and statements in advance and rehearse them.

**6. Get the information you need by probing first.** Ask power and follow-up questions that generate information, establish interest, show need, and allow you to give your information in a meaningful way. Ask your best questions and have your most concise message ready to deliver when the timing is right. Before you explain your problem-solving capabilities, know enough about the other person so that your information has impact.

**7. Show how you solve problems.** The prospect is bored hearing about what you do, unless you tell him in a way that helps or serves him. The prospect doesn't care what you do, unless what you do impacts him.

**8. Pin the prospect down to the next action.** Don't let a good prospect go without some agreement about what's next.

**9. Have fun.** Don't press or be pressured – it will show.

**10. Time's up.** When you have delivered your message, made your contact and secured the next meeting or action – **move on.**

**IMPORTANT: Don't say ANY words that aren't an integral part of your commercial.** Be as concise as possible. Be creative. If it drags, no one will listen or be inclined to act. Make your message in terms of the customer (*you, your*), not in terms of you (*me, I* ). Be original. Boring messages are forgotten immediately. Say, do, or hand out something that will be remembered. Ask open-ended, thought-provoking questions.

Your commercial can be used in various forms at a networking event, business or trade association meeting, trade show, PTA meeting, or church.

Be prepared. When you meet a prospect or a prospect comes up to you, are you ready? Test yourself:

- What do you want his or her first impression to be? How will you create that?
- How quickly can you qualify him or her?
- What kind of questions can you ask that will qualify your prospect and generate interest in what you do?
- Do you have a list of your Power Questions? Are they rehearsed?
- Do you have a list of your Power Statements? Are they rehearsed?

Let's say you're in the copier business. You're at a networking event or business meeting, you're well dressed, you're got your business cards, and you spot a prospect ...

**Give your name and company.** *Hey, I'm Jim Riggins, with Technocom.*

**Shake firmly.** (No one wants to shake hands with a dead fish.)

**Creatively say what you do.** We help businesses build their image through quality document duplication. You know every time you make a copy and send it to someone, it's a reflection and expression of the quality of your business. Your customer, prospect, or supplier subconsciously forms an opinion about your company when she sees the quality of your copy. We supply Toshiba copiers to some of Charlotte's finest businesses.

**Now ask an open-ended Power Question or series of questions.** *What type of copier do you have?* (Variations and additions: *What does your company do? How often does your present copier need repair? How many copies do you make per month? How many copies have you logged on your present machine? What type of policy do you have regarding the quality of copies you allow to be sent to a customer?*)

**Let the other person talk until you get a firm idea about how he or she can use your product or service. Don't talk too soon. Wait until you are sure you have the information you need to strike.**

**Make a Power Statement and show how you help.** *Some of our major accounts, like ... [said to gain some confidence] are people we've been dealing with for more than 7 years. Our experience has shown us that the copy quality we can maintain impacts the image our customer is trying to portray to his customer. You're concerned about your image, aren't you?*

**Solidify an action plan and get together.** *I'd love to have an opportunity to show you instead of telling you. If you give me your card,*

*I'll arrange a free 2-day test and demonstration; this way you get a chance to see if it works for you in your environment. When would be a good time to get together?*

The delivery of your commercial is successfully achieved when you are able to match your services exactly to specifically identified prospect needs. This can only be achieved with excellent preplanning and preparation.

*The statements you make and questions you ask must blend with the information you gather in order to score.*

*If you're going to play the game, it's a lot more fun when you hit a home run.*

## This is the personal commercial I give in my "sales lead" list business. You may get an idea or two from it.

- **Name** … Hi [sometimes I say, "Hey"], my name is Jeffrey Gitomer.
- **Company name** … My company is Business Marketing Services.
- **What I do** … Every week we publish lists of new businesses, new homeowners, and building permits that businesses like yours use as new sales leads.

☆ *Insert Power Question* … How valuable are new leads to your sales program? How do you generate those new leads?

- **How I help** … Our subscribers tell us that the leads provide them a valuable supplement to their regular lead-generation and referral program and also help new salespeople get off to a good start.

☆ *Insert Power Statement* … Have you ever seen the names of new businesses and permits published each week in the Business Journal? Are they useful? We sell them that information.

- **Why prospect should act now** … If you would like a free sample list to see if our leads can generate new sales for you, please give me your business card and I'll mail you one.

## Other Power Questions to open areas of need:
- How do you get your sales leads?
- Are new sales leads important to you?
- How many new leads do you generate per week?

*Actual time to deliver my commercial is 20 to 30 seconds.*

*When you get a referral, treat it like gold.*
*One third-party endorsement is worth a hundred*
*presentations, if you know what you're doing.*

# Got a referral?
# Here's the perfect approach.

You got it. The most coveted prize in selling besides a sale. A referral. How do you approach this person? How do you maximize the selling power of this referral? Here are eight rules to ensure your success:

*Rule #1:* **Go slow.** Timing is everything. Don't appear to be too anxious to get the sale (money). Proper setup (giving some value first) will breed a long-term relationship (more money) instead of just a sale.

*Rule #2:* **Arrange a three-way meeting.** Setting the stage for the first meeting/communication can be make it or break it. All three people (you, the referral, and the person who referred them) together sets a perfect stage. Here are the preferred methods of a first meeting with a referral and customer in order of preference (and effectiveness):

- Arranging a meal together (breakfast and lunch are more business; dinner is more open-ended and casual).
- Arranging to meet at a networking event.
- Arranging to meet at a social event (theater, ball game).
- Getting a personal (in-person) introduction.

If those methods are not possible or practical, try these:

- Getting a phone call to the referral from your customer telling of your impending call.
- Getting a letter of introduction.

NOTE WELL: These methods provide the best chance for success. A third party to sing your praise in front of the referral is a HUGE lever to the sale. One third-party endorsement is more powerful than 100 presentations.

***Rule #3:*** **You don't have to sell at the first meeting if your customer is with you.** In fact, the less selling you do, the more credible you will appear. You only have to establish rapport, some confidence, and *(Rule #4)* **arrange a second, private meeting** where you can get down to business.

***Rule #5:*** **Don't send too much information in the mail.** The mail, like the phone, is not where a sale is made. It's just a sales tool. Send just enough to inform and create interest.

***Rule #6:*** **Write a personal note to the referral within 24 hours.** Brief but positive. Don't slobber all over the note with thanks, and thanks again. Just tell him or her it was nice to get acquainted and you're looking forward to the next meeting.

***Rule #7:*** **Write your customer a note of thanks.** Include a gift if the sale will be of some significance (a *quality* ad specialty – something with your logo printed on it, or two tickets to a ball game). Your thanks and gift will encourage the customer to get you another referral.

***Rule #8:*** **Overdeliver!** Failure to follow up and deliver as promised makes you and your customer look bad to the prospect. Failure to deliver also eliminates any chance of another referral. This rule is the most important of them all; it is a breeding ground for your reputation.

# What kind of delivery reputation have you got?

One final real-world note. The least preferred or least productive way to use a referral, but the way it seems to happen most often, is a stone cold call (or letter) to a name, address, and number given to you by a customer or friend. It is where the referral is lost. PLEASE: Be creative. Make it a meaningful and personal connection. Get some information about the referral and his company before the first contact is made. Don't fall into the trap of calling or writing and saying, *"I was given your name by ..."* That sounds horrible.

Say instead, *"Hi (hey), my name is Jeffrey, my company is BuyGitomer, and you don't know me from a sack of potatoes. I've been doing business with [name of customer] for some time now, and she thought I might be able to help you in the same way I've helped her. I just wanted to introduce myself and get your address to send you some information I think you'll find of interest."*

Now say something CREATIVE to establish personal rapport from the information you were given by your customer. Try to get the referral to laugh. Then say, *"I'll call you back in a few days, and maybe we can talk over lunch. Thanks for your time."*

Don't be too windy. You're not going to make the sale on the phone. Say just enough to create interest and arrange an in-person meeting.

The referral is the easiest prospect in the world to sell. Ask any professional who hates selling (accountants, architects, lawyers) – they'll tell you that 100% of their new business comes from referrals. That's because they're not capable of making sales calls and rely on the fall-in-your-lap method of selling.

Take a lesson from
these professionals --
the referral is
the easiest-to-sell,
most powerful sales lead
on the planet.
The real secret is
how do you get them?
Simple two-word answer
… **earn them**.

# THE SALES BIBLE

### Part 3
### Please Allow Me to Introduce Myself

# The Book of Cold Calling

**3.2**

## You don't know me from a sack of potatoes.

Cold calls ...

Most everyone hates 'em.
Most everybody makes 'em.

Why not make
the most of 'em?

Have fun at 'em.
Make a game out of 'em.
Play to win.

Every *no* gets you
closer to *yes*.

# I have a sign on my company's front door that says … "Solicitors Welcome"

*What do salespeople think
of No Soliciting signs?*

# "No Soliciting,"
# the funniest sign in sales.

It seems every office building I go into has a sign on the door that says, *No Soliciting*. It has to be the funniest sign in sales. What a useless sign to post in front of a salesman. I'd like to have a dollar for every "No Soliciting" sign I've ignored. What is the purpose of this sign and whom does it deter?

It's interesting to me that many of the businesses that sport the sign have cold calling salespeople themselves. It's somewhat hypocritical to see No Soliciting on the door of a copier business, insurance broker, or temporary help agency.

What do salespeople think of *No Soliciting* signs? I polled the Early Risers Lead Club, the largest pure sales lead association in the Charlotte area, made up of entrepreneurs and salespeople. I asked how they felt and what they did when they encountered the dreaded sign.

"I go into the buildings so fast I don't see the signs," says Cindi Ballard, president of El El Interior Plantscapes. "I've been cold calling since 1976 and I've never had a problem."

"Once I was told '*No soliciting*' by a company," says Earl Coggins of Pony Express. "I said, 'I'm just trying to save you some money.' They said, 'Come right in.'"

"Most buildings are built with that sign on the door," says Richard Herd of Continental Advertising. "I feel like it's meant for other kinds of salesmen, not me. I ignore it and have never had a problem."

"I cold call on the telephone. That way I can't see if there's a *No Soliciting* sign on the door," says Bob Dillard of Bob Dillard Sales.

"Everyone's got one; it doesn't affect me," says Ward Norris, president of Crown Resources. "If they tell me 'No soliciting,' I say, 'I was so focused on meeting you and learning your name, I must have missed the sign.'"

"I take my glasses off just before entering so I can't see the sign," says Matt Keeble of Carolina Container Corporation.

"I got tossed out once," says Tom Barnett of PC Sales, "but one out of thousands isn't bad odds."

Out of 32 people polled in the Early Risers Lead Club, only 2 said they would respect the sign; 2 said they have fear but enter anyway; 28 (87.5%) said they ignore it. It is also interesting to note that the same salespeople think it's OK to ban the door-to-door peddlers selling candy, perfume, and pictures. You know, solicitors.

It's seems that salespeople from legitimate businesses believe that the sign is not aimed at them. I agree.

I was having a discussion with a company president and his sales manager. They have adopted a new policy NOT to screen cold sales calls. They feel that too many opportunities are missed by not listening to what a salesperson has to offer or say. What a great way to think. Of course, as sales warriors, we've known that all along.

## A word of caution ...
If you see a *No Soliciting* sign that is customized or handcrafted, they probably mean it, especially if the word *absolutely* is on it.

*To find out who decides,*
*make a passive statement*
*and ask an indirect question ...*
*"I've got some important information*
*about new computers. Who should I leave it for?"*

# Get to the decision maker on a cold call.

Getting past the *No Soliciting* sign is easy. It's getting to the decision maker that requires skill and finesse. If you use the line, "I'd like to speak with the boss," it will never get you to the boss without a major hassle. Don't ask to speak to anyone. The key to getting to a decision maker is to make an **indirect and nonassertive** request for "information only" from the secretary or administrative person. He or she will gladly give you all the facts you need to make the perfect follow-up.

**You can use the following technique if you're cold calling**
**in person or making a cold telemarketing call.**

Let's say you're selling computers ... "I need your help. My name is Jeffrey, and I've got some important information about computers. Who should I leave it for (or send it to, if calling)?" If you get the name, you MUST ask the following double-confirming questions: "Is she the person who decides on this type of thing? Is there anyone else who works with her on this type of decision?"

If the front-desk person says, "Just leave the information with me," ask him or her politely, "Are you the person who decides on computers?" They will usually back off quickly. If they don't, you must still be as nice as pie in requesting the all-important decider's name. Be gentle but persistent until you get the name. You may have to try three or four approaches.

**Don't quit until you get the name**
**and ask the double-confirming questions.**

How do you handle a *No Soliciting* sign and get to the decision maker?

I cold called every office in every (*No Soliciting*) office building in uptown Charlotte. I got off at the top floor and worked my way down each tower. I got tossed out of two offices. One actually called the sales police. *But they can only throw you out into the hallway!* You, of course, promise not to do it again, get on the elevator, get off at the next floor, and keep on cold calling. *No Soliciting* is actually more of a game than a rule.

The sign is meant for door-to-door-type sales crews who canvass an area trying to sell handbags, perfume, calculators, and wall hangings. If you have a legitimate, established business, making a cold call will not be offensive to most businesses IF YOU DO IT RIGHT. The best method is actually an *indirect solicitation.* You're only dropping off literature and asking a few questions.

If you're out making an appointed sales call, it's a great use of time to make a few *next-door neighbor* cold calls after that appointment. I always do. If there's a *No Soliciting* sign, I don't even think about it. The entire cold call process takes less than 5 minutes.

You don't have to solicit to make a cold call. Here are the guidelines to follow to ensure maximum *No Soliciting* success:

1. Ignore the sign.
2. Have literature and business cards.
3. Ask for help.
4. Offer to leave literature only.
5. Get the name of the decider.
6. Find out the title of the decider.
7. Write him or her a personalized note on your business card, attach it to your information, and ask for your package to be delivered ASAP.
8. Ask for (and get) the decision maker's card.
9. Find out when is the best time to call the decision maker.
10. Get the name of the person who helped you, and write it down on the back of the decider's card.
11. Thank the person genuinely for their help.
12. Leave.

*Try this pitch next time …*
"Hi, my name is [first name only] and I was wondering if you could help me. [Everyone wants to help.] I want to leave some information about [my product/service]. Who decides on that type of thing?"

"Oh, that would be Mr. Johnson," she gleefully volunteers.

Great, now I know the decision maker, but I'm going to double qualify while I'm on a roll. "What would his position be?" I query innocently. You'll get that answer, too. "Is there anyone else he works with on this type of decision?" I'm asking to find out if I've reached the biggest person. If I get questioned, I simply say, "We usually mail two packages of information if there are two people involved in the decision." That usually shuts the gatekeeper up.

Now I make a bold move. "I'm leaving this information and a note for him. I wonder if I could get his card." You'll get the card 90% of the time; 5% you'll get some facsimile of the card; and 5% of the time the boss himself will appear. If you're a female salesperson and the boss is male, the boss will appear twice as often. That's not a sexist remark; that's a fact.

"When would be the best time to call him?" I ask, trying to get the last bit of info before I wear out my uninvited welcome.

"Thank you so much for helping me. I really appreciate it," I say. "What was your name?" "Thank you, Susan." People love to hear their name associated with praise and thanks. If you do both, she'll remember you the next time you call and need to speak to Mr. Johnson.

Look at all the information you got! You may not have made a money sale the first time, but they bought your pitch and you're loaded for bear on the next call. Check out your prizes for being nice and nonpushy ...

1. The decision maker's name and card.
2. Whether he or she acts alone.
3. The decision maker has your information.
4. He or she has your card and personal note.
5. You made friends with the secretary.
6. You know the best time to call back.

My follow-up call will be made 24 hours later, and Susan will help me every way she can. Now all I need is an appointment, a contract, and a check.

*Good or bad, your opening line
will immediately establish an impression.
It sets the tone for the sale.*

# Opening is as important
# as closing.

On a sales call your professionalism is the first thing a customer or prospect sees. Then comes the impact of that all-important first line. **Your delivery, sincerity, and creativity set the tone for the rest of the conversation.** They also determine how the prospect listens. If you get attention and respect, you are likely to keep it throughout. If not, you're likely to leave empty-handed.

> *If you're on the phone, the opening line is even more important.
> It's all you've got. You can't say, "Look at my nice suit."
> You are at the mercy of (or the mastery of) your words.*

It is critical to understand that if a prospect doesn't know you, the only thing on his mind is *What do you want?* The faster you get to the point, the better.

Are there standard stock lines you can use? Sure there are. Should you use them? Sure you should, *but* … only if you are the master of them. It's not just what you say, it's how you say it.

Opening is as important as closing. If you can't get past the gatekeeper, you can never get to try for the prize. If you can't impress the prospect, you won't get the contract. And if you aren't perceived as professional, sincere, and competent, it will soon reflect in your weekly paycheck.

## Opening lines on a face-to-face cold call:
### 1. Can you help me?
This is by far the most effective way to begin a conversation. People love to help and don't feel *on guard* against a salesperson. Remember, the object is to get the prospect to listen. *Can you help me?* almost commands the other person to pay attention. Other lines that are effective are …

**2. I'd like to leave (or mail) you a brochure about (type of product or service). Who should I leave it for?**
This is known as indirect qualification and puts the gatekeeper at ease.
All you're asking for is a name, and all you're doing is leaving something, then you leave. She wants you out of there.

**3. I'd like to leave some information for the person who decides about (type of product or service). Who would that be?**
This is a bit more pushy, but it actually seems to work better.

In either #2 or #3, if you leave information, writing a personal note to the decider on the back of your business card goes a long way toward getting through on the follow-up call.

## Cold call (on the phone)
There are 7.5 rules to follow. *Always follow them.*

> 1. Smile when you talk.
> 2. Give your name and company.
> 3. GET TO THE POINT FAST (State your purpose within the first two sentences.)
> 4. Make it short and sweet.
> 5. Try to be somewhat humorous.
> 6. Offer or ask for help.
> 7. State that you have important information.
> 7.5 *Ask for the sale.* The "sale" may only be to get an appointment. But whatever your objective was when you picked up the phone ... persist until you get it.

For many years I have said, "Hi, my name is Jeffrey, my company is Business Marketing Services, and you don't know me from a sack of potatoes," then made my request. I could tell by the reaction (laugh or no laugh) who I was dealing with.

Avoid salesy-sounding lines like *Great weather, isn't it?* or the dreaded *How are you today?* or any lengthy description about you or your company before you get to the point.

## Phone follow-up

Use the same rules for cold phone calling and select from the following:

1. I've been thinking about what you do.
2. I've got the answer to your question.
3. I've got some important information that
   will impact your business.

**A majority of salespeople make the fatal mistake of asking, "Did you get the information I sent you?"** If the prospect says *no*, what do you say now, genius? You can fumble about how you sent it 3 days ago and how you can't understand how that could have happened, but that's lame, sounds defensive, and you have ruined any chances of making a positive call.

*Try saying this instead:*
"I'm calling about the information I sent.
*It wasn't completely self-explanatory,*
and I'd like an opportunity to discuss it
with you personally for about 5 to 10 minutes."

*If you want to gain immediate benefit from reading this today,* **make a list of the opening lines you use in your business,** *revise them, analyze them closely, and compare them with those of your co-workers. Try out your revised lines tomorrow. The results will surprise (and benefit) you.*

*If you use humor and get a blank stare,*
*you're dead --*
*but a cold call is a crapshoot anyway ...*
*why not have fun?*

# The cold call is fun ...
# if you think it is.

Cold calling is one reason many people shy away from a career in sales. Sales professionals who make a six-figure income will tell you that cold call training provided the basis for their sales success. Doubt it? Ask 'em.

Here is an 8-point game plan to begin succeeding at cold calling:

**1. Be exceptionally well prepared.**
• Know your best targets (preplan).
• Have a purpose (the big picture).
• Know your objective (get an appointment, get a name).
• Have a memorized script (lines, power lines, Power Questions).
• Have perfect materials and tools (ad specialties are good on cold calls).

**2. Don't apologize for anything, don't make excuses.** When you get there, get to your business. Don't say, "I'm sorry to interrupt." Just deliver your line.

**3. How you deliver your first line determines your success.** The impact of the first sentence will determine success or failure.

**4. Don't pay any attention to reluctance or fear issues.** Cold call reluctance is another way of saying, *"I don't know how"* or *"I can't plan"* or *"I don't like it when people reject me."* Develop a pitch, read positive books, stop watching the news, and believe you can succeed.

**5. Not everyone you call is a sale. Be prepared for rejection.**
People aren't rejecting you, they're only rejecting the offer you're making them. There, that feels better, doesn't it?

**6. Learn from those who tell you no.** Find out what caused them to say no or not be interested.

**7. Practice, practice, practice.** Unless you own your pitch, you'll sound contrived. Nothing's worse than a salesman sounding like a salesman.

**8. Have fun!** You're being paid to get the sales education of a lifetime. It ain't brain cancer; it's a sales call. Have a good time. Make someone smile.

Note: If you say, *"I hate cold calls!"* realize it is a self-induced mental state that is easily overcome by a series of cold call successes, sales, and commissions.

Here is a personalized formula to help you get better at cold calling:

- Identify your weaknesses and fears about cold calls. List them in detail.
- Create an action plan for weaknesses so that you can overcome and eliminate them one by one.
- Work on **one** every 30 days.
- Challenge yourself to succeed every day.
- Quit complaining … no one buys from a complainer.

Three of the most important parts of the cold call are *opening lines, Power Questions,* and *Power Statements.* They allow you to gather the information needed to qualify, determine the prospect's real needs, and sell.

Here are some examples of opening lines:
*Weak, door-closing openers:*
1. Could I have a few minutes of your time?
2. I was wondering if maybe you would be interested in ...
3. Is the boss in?
4. I have an idea that can save you money.
*Strong, effective openers:*
1. I need your help.
2. I know you actually run the place, but could I speak to the person who thinks they do?
3. Is the king in?
4. I need a loan for $50,000. I wonder if you could help me.
5. I was just next door with _____, and she thought I might be able to help you the same way I helped her company.
6. I was just next door with _____, and she recommended I stop by to see _____. Is she in?
7. My name is Jeffrey and you don't know me from a sack of potatoes ...
8. (In summer on a scorching day) I just fried an egg on my car and was wondering if you have any salt and pepper?

9. Can you point me in the right direction? (A receptionist with a sense of humor will quip, "Sure, which way did you come in?")

10. My boss said if I don't make a sale, I'm fired, so if you're not in a buying mood, perhaps you have a job opening.

### About being funny ...

- If you use humor and get a blank stare, you're dead – but a cold call is a crapshoot anyway ... why not have fun?
- The response (laugh or no laugh) will tell you exactly where you are.
- Laughing is agreement – tacit approval.

# *Why not go for it?*

**Power Questions ...**

- A question to make the prospect think.
- A question to let the prospect know you understand his or her business.
- A question that makes a prospect answer in such a way that he or she reveals information that leads to qualification, appointment, or sale.
- An open-ended question. Don't say, *"Do you ...?"* say, *"What do you ...?"* or *"How do you ...?"* or *"When do you ...?"*

**Power Statements ...**

- A statement that makes a prospect think.
- A statement that builds your credibility with a prospect.
- A nontraditional (nonboring) statement that describes what you do and how you do it.
- A statement about what you do in terms of what your prospect needs.
- A statement that is memorable.

Two more parts are *attitude* and *focus*. Positive attitude will impact the prospect, and proper focus permits you to use your skills to create action.

**Is there a most important part of the cold call? Yes ...**

# *Ask for the sale.*

*Prospects are just as motivated to avoid
losing something they already have
as they are to buy something new.*

# Elements of a cold call that can make it hot.

Cold calling is one of the most difficult parts of selling. An old sales cliché
says that the hardest door for a salesman to open is the car door.

To be successful at the science of cold calling, you must first define the
elements, functions, and formulas that comprise the call. Then, like all other
sciences, experiment (practice) until you have a method that works.
The basic elements that comprise a cold call are:

1. Deliver your opener.
2. Ask Power (thought-provoking)
   Questions to create meaningful dialogue.
3. Make Power (benefit) Statements to establish
   credibility.
4. Qualify the prospect as to need, desire,
   decision-making capability, and money
   (the ability to pay).
5. Gather information.
6. Get what you came for –
   make the next step in your sales cycle.
7. Have the right attitude and focus.

Here are several cold calling elements, guidelines, and techniques that have
proven to be effective:

• **Opening lines are important.** Deliver a smooth, sincere line. Say you're
a single woman and a guy comes up to you in some social circumstance and
says, "Don't I know you?" or "You're just the prettiest little thing I ever did
see." The first thing you think is, "This guy's a jerk. Get me out of here." It's
the same in cold calling. The opening line determines if you get to dance.

• **Opening impressions are important.** The way you look and come across in the first 30 seconds often (not always) determines your outcome.

• **After you deliver the opener, make the prospect think.** Your questions (*Power Questions*) and statements (*Power Statements*) are critical to gaining prospect confidence. Ask questions that show knowledge, imply prospect areas of weakness, and gather vital information. Make statements that are creatively descriptive, imply benefits, and build your credibility.

• **Get to the point fast.** The prospect is busy and will be insulted if you beat around the bush.

• **If you are asked for a price, give it immediately.** Try to do it in the most creative way you can, but give it.

• **Determine what your prospects need by ...**

> • Understanding the problems of their operation
>
> • Appealing to their sense of greed
>
> • Evoking their fears
>
> • Appealing to their vanity
>
> • Determining what their *customer* needs
>
> • Finding (searching for) the hot button –
> ***then pushing it.***

• **They will resist you.** So what? It takes seven exposures, seven tries to get the prospect to become a customer. If you quit after just one or two, the sale will go to the next guy/woman who shows up.

• **They will buy to solve a business problem or satisfy a need.** Statements and questions need to be pointed in that direction. Stress benefits (what's in it for them), not features (how it works). Emphasize what they will gain – profit, pride, reputation. Prove that they will avoid pain, loss, criticism. *Failure to express benefits in terms of customer needs will preclude the sale.*

• **Focus on *negative prevention*.** Get them to share what dissatisfies them. Motivate them to show discontent with their current situation. Tell them how they'll safeguard profits, eliminate worry, overcome fear, and avoid the terror of *customer complaints*. Prospects are just as motivated to avoid losing something they already have as they are to buy something new.

• **Gain buyer confidence.** Use every weapon in your sales-tool arsenal. Bring in testimonials, references, and similar situations whenever possible.

• **Attitude, humor, and action (persistence) will whip fears and rejection. Fear of failure doesn't exist if you believe it doesn't.** You will be rejected – the prospect will reject your offer – big deal! Edison, Lincoln, Babe Ruth, Colonel Sanders – these guys failed miserably thousands of times. Where would they be without their attitude to succeed? (And where would we be without their successes?) *You only fail when you quit!*

• **Set your own goals for achievement.** How many calls per day, how many appointments per day. Selling is a numbers game, but it will only work if you are prepared. You must work your numbers consistently to get them to pay. Push yourself to win. If you cold call enough people, you will make appointments (your objective), and you will make sales (your purpose).

• **Visualize it happening. Seeing is believing.** Believing is the first step to achieving. It's easier to do what you can see. Visualizing success helps eliminate fear of the unknown. Re-create those visual pictures in your conversation with the prospect.

• **Every time you go through a door, get what you came for.** Know what your objective is for this cold call. Close the prospect on the next step in your sales cycle. The biggest fear isn't making the call, it's asking for the sale. Focus on asking and push for it until you get it. Here are a few asks that work:

> • Which will be better for you …?
> • Who should I …?
> • If I … Would you …?
> • When can I …?

You are now armed with enough cold calling information to choke a horse. Don't let it stick in *your* throat.

### The best technique I can give you about the cold call?

# *It's a big game …*
# *have fun*
# *and*
# *play to win!*

# The Book of Presentations

## On with the show, this is it!

Presentations ...

Overture, hit the lights.
Now's your chance.
Get it right.

Can you tell the prospect
what he wants to hear?
Is he even listening?
Does he take you seriously?

Can you motivate him to act?
Can you give him enough
confidence to buy?
Or are you a one-act play?

Want your prospects
to scream ...
Bravo, encore?

2 minutes to curtain ...

4.1

*If you can establish common ground
with your prospects, they will like you,
trust you, and buy from you.*

# Want to make the sale easier?
# Establish prospect rapport first.

OK, everyone in sales sing, "Getting to know you, getting to know all about you, getting to like you, getting to hope you like me; getting to know you, putting it my way, but nicely." You are precisely singing the song that will make the sale easier to achieve.

**If you find common subjects or interests with a prospect,
you can establish a business friendship;
and people are more likely to buy
from a friend than a salesman.**

What do you do to establish rapport? Are you sharp enough to find something besides business after you open the conversation? Here are some techniques you can try on the phone, at the prospect's place of business, at your place of business, or at a networking event.

*On the phone* … It's likely that you're calling to make an appointment, so focus on four things …

> 1. Get to the point in 15 seconds.
>
> 2. Be happy and humorous.
>
> 3. Get to know something personal about the prospect.
>
> 4. Nail down the appointment.

You first begin to establish rapport by getting to the point! State the purpose of your call immediately. It's not necessary (and it's often a put-off) to ask the insincere "How are you today?" Just state your name, your company name, and how you can help the prospect. Once you've done that, there is a sense of relief on both sides. The prospect is relieved because he now knows why you've called, and you're relieved because the prospect hasn't hung up on you. Now you can go about the task of establishing some rapport and setting the appointment.

Is the prospect formal or friendly? **Try to use humor at least twice during the conversation (but don't force it). People love to laugh.** A quick, clean 10-second joke can do more for buyer rapport than 10 minutes worth of sales talk.

**You can gain insight by listening.** Prospect mood, hometown, and personality will all be revealed in just a few minutes on the phone. I listen closely for speech accent. It gives me a clue about where my prospect hails from – a great subject if you're well traveled or come from the same place.

**Listen for and be sensitive to the mood of the prospect.** If he or she is noticeably short or gruff, just say, "I can tell you're busy [or, 'not having the best of days']. Why don't we pick a time more convenient for me to call?"

**If you know the prospect, you can sell the appointment with a personal touch.** For example, if you're talking to a basketball fan, you might say, "I know I can help you reach your computer training needs. With a 10-minute appointment I can show you how we can help you in the first 5 minutes and have the other 5 to discuss who the Hornets should draft."

Remember, **people love to talk about themselves**. Getting people to talk about themselves will give you a chance to find common ground, establish rapport, and increase your chance to make a sale.

**Establish prospect rapport before you begin your pitch.**

The best way to win the sale is to first win the prospect. If you find common subjects or interests with a prospect, you can establish a business friendship.

## *People are more likely to buy from a friend than a salesman.*

What do you do to establish rapport? Are you observant enough to find something besides business to open the conversation? Here are some techniques:

**On an appointment in the prospect's office** ... This is the easiest place
to establish rapport. Look for clues as soon as you walk into the prospect's
place of business. Pictures, plaques, or awards on the wall; magazines
subscribed to that don't match the business. When you get in the
prospect's office, look for pictures of children or events, bookcase items,
books, diplomas, awards, desk items, or anything that reveals personal likes
and/or leisure pursuits. Ask about an award or trophy. Ask about a diploma
or picture. Your prospect will be glad to talk about what he or she has
accomplished or likes to do.

Try to engage prospects in intelligent conversation with open-ended
questions about their interests. It's obviously better if you're well versed in
the subject, but the point is to get prospects to talk about what makes
them happy. Use humor. Humor builds rapport because it constitutes
agreement (when the prospect laughs). Getting the prospect to laugh will
set the stage for a positive presentation.

*When the prospect comes to your place of business* ...When your
prospective customer comes to your place of business, it is more difficult
to establish common ground because you don't have the advantage of the
telling items that would be present in his or her surroundings. So, be
observant. Look at clothing, car, rings, imprinted items, their business card,
or anything that gives you a clue as to the type of person they are.

**Be friendly.** Ask open-ended questions just below the surface. (Surface
questions or talk about the weather, or did you find the place OK, should
be avoided at all costs.) Try to find out what they did last weekend, or
what they're doing this weekend. Ask about a movie or television show.
**Avoid politics, their personal problems, and don't lament your
personal problems.**

**People love to talk about themselves.** Ask the right question and it's
tough to shut them up. Your objective is to find a subject, idea, or situation
that you BOTH know about or are interested in.

**Be real.** It's as easy to spot an insincere salesperson as a skunk in your
living room. Both smell awful.

**One word of caution** ... Be aware of time. The time you are permitted to spend building rapport has a lot to do with where you live geographically. In the Northeast you may have as little as 30 seconds. In these situations I have tried to be direct immediately. Gain interest first. Then go for some rapport.

In the South, Midwest, Southwest, and West, you can spend 5 to 10 minutes establishing rapport. Don't lose sight of your mission, but ... I can assure you the mission is most likely to be accomplished if you make a friend before making a presentation. The key is getting prospects to talk about themselves. This will give you a chance to find common ground, establish rapport, and increase your chance to make a sale.

# *No rapport, no sale!*

*If the prospect says NO, it's most likely that
you failed to establish buyer confidence.*

# 15.5 get-real questions about establishing buyer confidence.

The prospect said NO! Rats.

Did you lose the sale or just fail to make it? You're sure that prospect should have bought. As you head back to the car, licking your wounds, you try to justify or figure out why the prospect turned you down.

Once you've answered the fundamental questions of self-doubt – Was I enthusiastic, friendly, and professional-looking? – you may have to probe a bit deeper for the true answers. Even though the truth hurts, the realization of what you failed to do is a big step in making the sale next time.

Let me save you some anguish. YOU FAILED TO ESTABLISH BUYER CONFIDENCE, Sparky.

You say, "Hey, Jeffrey, you're dead wrong – that guy really liked me." Maybe. But likability is only a part of the sales equation.

Take the Jeffrey Gitomer Establish Confidence Test and rate your ability. If you're willing to be objective about yourself and your abilities, ask yourself the following 14.5 revealing questions and rate yourself from 1 to 10 on each question. (1 = lowest to 10 = highest)

**1. Was I on time?** Did I show up 5 minutes early (good) or 5 minutes late (real bad)?

**2. Was I prepared?** Did I walk into my appointment with everything I needed to make the sale?

**3. Was I organized?** Did I have everything at my fingertips or was I fumbling?

**4. Could I answer all product questions?** Do I really have command of my product, or am I constantly "having to get back to you on that one"?

## 5. Did I make excuses or blame others about anything?

The sample wasn't shipped on time, the company didn't send the right information, etc.

## 6. Was I apologizing? Sorry I'm late, unprepared, don't know the answer, didn't bring the correct information, quoted the wrong price (ad nauseum).

## 7. Did the prospect probe personal issues about my company?

"If I buy," says Mr. Johnson, "how do I know you'll be here to service me in 6 months?"

## 8. Did the prospect ask doubting questions about my product?

What happens if it breaks down after the warranty, or, who else buys this product?

## 9. Did the prospect ask doubting questions about me? How long have I been with the company, or, how much experience do I have?

## 10. Did I name drop other happy, loyal customers effectively? Did I fail to use the name of a happy customer to answer a pointed question?

## 11. Did I feel as though I were on the defensive? Was I constantly answering questions dealing in subject matter other than my product/service? Could I prove my points?

## 12. Could I overcome all objections in a confident manner? Did I find myself unable to respond confidently about price, quality, and other issues blocking the sale when asked by the prospect? Did I try to fake it?

## 13. Did I down the competition? Did I berate my competitor (possibly the prospect's supplier)? Did I make disparaging remarks about the competition to try to make me/my product look better?

## 14. Was my prospect uninvolved in the sales presentation?

Did the prospect just sit there, or worse, do other things while I was talking?

## 14.5 Was I too anxious to make the sale? Was I too pushy? Was it obvious to the prospect that there was a commission involved?

Tough questions – but I ask them because confidence is elusive, tough to establish, and easily lost at the beginning of any relationship. These questions are designed for you to evaluate your sales performance and reveal your ability (or inability) to create prospect confidence from someone who just said no. The answers will lead you to the next sale better prepared to make it through with *confidence* rather than *manipulation*.

One of the primary lessons of sales is: If they like you, believe you, trust you, and have confidence in you, then they MAY buy from you. If any of those four elements is missing, the answer changes from sale to no sale.

When the prospect says "NO," it's most likely a vote of "no confidence."

**These questions are designed for you to evaluate your sales performance and reveal your ability (or inability) to create buyer confidence from a customer who said *no* or would not buy today.**

# In order for this exercise to work, you've got to be real with yourself.

Next we'll look at methods, techniques, and sales tools that will help answer these questions and show the link between gaining buyer confidence and the word *yes*.

*Buyer confidence must be established*
*by using sales tools, examples, and stories*
*the prospect can relate to.*

# 12.5 ways to make the prospect confident enough to buy.

Prospects won't buy if they lack confidence in you or your product. How do you establish buyer confidence? **Use sales tools, examples, and stories in a way that prospects can relate the use of your product to their business environment.** When is the appropriate time to begin establishing this? As soon as you can.

Besides the basic four – be enthusiastic, be on time, be friendly, look professional – these are the 12.5 most effective techniques I've learned …

**1. Be completely prepared.** A fumbling, excuse-making, apologizing salesperson builds zero confidence.

**2. Involve prospects early in the presentation.** Get them to help you or hold your samples. Something that makes them feel like they're on your team.

**3. Have something in writing.** An article about your company or product from a national news source will reek of credibility.

**4. Tell a story of how you helped another customer.** This creates a similar situation that the prospect can relate to.

**5. Use a referral source if possible.** "Mr. Prospect, you should call [name of company and contact name] to find out how we helped them."

**6. Drop names of larger customers or the buyer's competitors.** If you are doing business with a large firm, state it in a way that shows strength and competence rather than sounding like you're bragging.

(NOTE: Be extremely careful not to drop competition's names until you're sure it's appropriate. Sometimes it will work against you to be doing business with the prospect's competition.)

**7. Have a printed list of satisfied customers.** Include large and small accounts. Make perfect copies on good-quality paper.

**8. Have a notebook of testimonial letters.** Try to get letters that cover various aspects of your business: quality, delivery, competence, service, and extra effort. Be sure some of your letters answer the buyer's objections.

**9. Don't bombard the prospect.** Work your examples in as a natural part of the presentation. Let confidence build to a natural close.

**10. Emphasize service after the sale.** The buyer needs to be certain you won't sell and run. Talk delivery, training, and service.

**11. Emphasize long-term relationships.** The customer wants to feel that you will be there to help with problems, new technology, growth, and service. Give your home number.

**12. Sell to help, not for commissions.** Prospects can smell a greedy salesperson. It's a bad odor.

**12.5 The most important link to the process. Ask the right questions.** Go to *The Book of Questions* and read it 10 times.

Try to use your confidence-building tools as you would use trump in a card game. Play it when you need to. If the prospect asks you who else uses your product, drop your big-name customers, or give a list of satisfied customers. If the prospect asks about service, offer your testimonial letters to confirm your capability. **Don't play your cards too soon.**

If your business is relatively new, credibility will be a leading factor in getting the sale. You must sell your personal experience, desire to do a great job, and only ask for a small test order.

### Not once have I mentioned price as a credibility factor ...
# because it's not.

Being the least expensive won't get you anywhere if the prospect has no confidence to buy; and many times a low price actually scares the buyer.

There are circumstances that require different confidence-building techniques. They will be addressed in the next chapter. Eh, confidentially Doc, **read it!**

# Being the least expensive won't get you anywhere if the prospect has no confidence to buy. Many times low price actually scares the buyer.

*Buyer confidence must be
established and reconfirmed
in all phases of the selling process.*

# Where and when to establish buyer confidence.

The prospects won't buy if they lack confidence in you or your product. **Buyer confidence must be established and reconfirmed in all phases of the selling process.** Obviously the faster you establish confidence in the selling process, the easier it will be to get to the next phase of the sale.

Listed below are the prime selling opportunities to establish buyer confidence. Each situation calls for different types of confidence-building techniques.

***In a networking situation*** … If you only have time for one statement, make it one that will discuss the use of your product/service by a good company. "We were very fortunate to be awarded the toner cartridge contract from Duke Power. They selected us from among seven other bids." This begins the process of making the prospect feel confident in you.

***On the phone*** … Use only one item to establish confidence. *Just sell the appointment.* For example, "I believe we can help you get the computer training and achieve the productivity you need to cut operating costs. We just completed a similar project for Acme Manufacturing that used the same curriculum. Let me fax you a copy of a letter we received from them after the training was completed. I'd like to set up a brief appointment at your office to be certain this curriculum fits your needs exactly." *Your objective is to establish enough confidence to get an appointment – not make a sale.*

***On a cold call*** … Be brief. You must generate interest in about 30 seconds or less, or forget it. **Make a strong statement about how you can help the prospect.** Don't focus on how much money you can save them. That approach seems to be wearing thin. Talk about what you do for companies like hers, or how your product has worked for others.

If you're not in a *one-call close* business (over 90% are not), you only need to establish enough confidence to make the next appointment.

# Save your best stuff for your presentation.

***During a presentation*** … Your presentation – either at the prospect's place of business or in your office – is your big chance. **You walk in with your bag full of tricks, and use them one by one, like you're building a brick foundation.** Each time the prospect casts a shadow of doubt, you have something to counter that will make you shine …

- Letters from satisfied customers, articles, examples, comparison charts, and lists of satisfied customers that make the prospect secure enough to buy.
- Write things down. Let the prospect see professional respect for his time and the importance of the meeting.
- Your demeanor. Confidence begets confidence.

***On a follow-up call*** … Relax. Don't sound contrived or forced. If you force it, the prospect will begin to lose the confidence you worked so hard to gain. Have a specific purpose for calling; use similar situations (good things you've done for others), and specific benefits for the prospect as examples of why he should buy now. Have comfortable lead-in lines …

- I was thinking about you …
- I was thinking about your business …
- Someone paid you a compliment yesterday …
- Your name came up in conversation yesterday with …
- Something important came up you need to consider …

**How do you know if you have established confidence? Your phone calls are returned. You get the business, or the promise for it.**

It's actually easier to determine you *don't* have the confidence of the prospect. He starts handing you a bunch of pat-on-the-head responses like: "We'll get back to you in a few weeks." … "Our budget is spent." … "I'm not ready to buy yet." … "The board needs to meet and decide." … Or the ever popular, "Call me back in 6 months." **When you start hearing stalls, you have not established enough confidence for the buyer to proceed.**

*The key to being a professional*
*salesperson is not to sound like one!*

# Sales words and phrases to avoid at all costs. Honestly.

## *Create a new way to ask for the sale.*

My friend, Mitchell Kearney (pronounced Carney), is the best commercial photographer in this region. When shooting a subject, he never says, "Smile." That's got to be a major obstacle if you're a photographer. He says it makes him more creative to ask his subject for a smile without ever saying the word. I've looked at hundreds of his photos … most are smiling, so it seems his philosophy works. **Mitchell avoids the trite, unimaginative, insincere word that separates the professional from the amateur.**

How do you ask your customers to smile and buy today? Are you using words that offend the prospect? Are you using words that create confidence or ruin it? Are you projecting "I'm only here for the order"?

To get the sale, you must use superior word crafting to avoid sounding like an insincere salesperson. If you sound like one, you probably are.

### Words and phrases to avoid. Forever.

*Frankly* – a word that sounds insincere. All sales courses recommend dropping this word from your vocabulary.

*Quite frankly* – a double dose of the dreaded *frankly*. It makes me very suspicious of the person who says it.

*Honestly* – a word that is almost always followed with a lie.

*And I mean that* – No, you don't. This is probably as insincere a phrase as has been turned in the English language.

*Are you prepared to order today?* – Give me a break. This is an offensive, stupid, turnoff phrase. There are 100 better ways to ask prospects what their feelings are, or when they want to order.

*How are you doing today?* – When you hear this on the phone, you immediately think, *What are you selling, jerk?*

*Can I help you with something?* ... The universal anthem of all retail sales clerks. You'd think after 100 years of retail, they might have something more creative and customer service-oriented to say.

## Philosophies to avoid. Forever.

*Downing the competition* – Don't ever. It's not just a no-win situation; it's an absolute losing situation. My mother always told me that if you have nothing nice to say about someone, say nothing. If you down the competition to a prospect, you may be speaking to their relative or spouse, and it makes you look bad.

*Preaching ethics* – Don't ever say how ethical you are. Let your ethics shine through. The jails are full of televangelists and businesspeople who preached ethics. If you feel you have to prove yourself, use an example of how you performed or responded. Tell the prospect you want a long-term relationship, not just a one-shot order; but don't ever use the word *ethics*. When I hear it in a selling situation, I avoid that person at all costs.

The challenge is for you to rededicate yourself to helping and satisfying the needs of your customer or prospect. Your creative words and actions (the way you say it and the way you do it) are often the difference between getting a *yes* or *no*. They are the difference between getting the order and letting your main competitor get the order. It's enough to piss you off when your rival gets the business, isn't it? **Well, do something about it.**

How do you do it? You have to work at it. Get co-workers and other salespeople together and work at being different. Talented people in a room will create answers and positive results. Write it down. Practice. And have faith the results are certain to make you smile.

My experience has shown me that if you
have to say what you are,
you probably aren't.

Think about that
for a moment.
"I'm honest,"
"I'm ethical,"
even "I'm the boss,"
or "I'm in charge,"
usually indicates
just the opposite.

Doesn't it?

*Prospect involvement
lets them have a sense of ownership
that leads to a purchase.*

# Physically involving the prospect = more sales.

When I sold franchises in 1972, I drove a big new Cadillac. I would pick up the prospects at their home, and as I walked toward my car, I would say, "Gee, I have a headache, do you mind driving?" By the time Mr. and Mrs. Prospect got to my office, they wanted a car just like mine. They would buy the franchise I was selling to get a Cadillac with the profits they were sure to make. *I involved the prospect in the sale from the first 5 seconds.*

***How involved is your prospect when you make a presentation?***
*Tactile (touch, feel) involvement leads to the feeling of ownership. If you want to find out how receptive a prospect is to your product or service, get them involved early and often in the selling process.*

Usually it's easier to involve a prospect in a product sale than in a service sale. But if you use your creativity, you'd be amazed at how involved you can get someone. Below are some ideas to consider.

## Involvement in the presentation setup …
• Ask for help with an easel, slide projector, video machine.
• Ask for something – paper, special marker, board eraser.
• Ask him to plug things in or help you move something.
• Take the offered cup of coffee or soda.
• You can even call ahead to request that equipment be ready and in the room for your presentation (markers, projector).
• Getting the prospect involved in the set-up gives you additional opportunities for small talk and humor.

## Involvement during a product demonstration …
Having your prospects physically involved is the single most important aspect of the selling process. Let them run the demo, push the button, work the copier, drive the car, hold something, help you put something

together, make the call, fax the document. Get the picture?

Even though you know how to do it, you're not going to impress the prospect with a whiz-bang demonstration, you're going to bore him.

*Try to let the prospect lead the entire demonstration if possible.*
*The more the prospect does herself (successfully), the more ownership*
*she will take as she gets closer to a decision.*

Look and listen for buying signals: big smiles, words of praise, questions, exclamations.

## Involvement while explaining a service ...
Get the prospect to follow along. Read aloud. Play a part in the demonstration. Take a test. Do anything interactive that is fun and creates interest. A 20-minute pitch (monologue) is not nearly as effective as a 10-minute interaction (dialogue).

## Involvement techniques and questions ...
Ask open-ended and probing questions to determine how interested the prospect is:
• How do you see yourself using ...?
• If you could use this in your ..., when would you ...?
• How do you see this working in your environment?
• Do you see how easy it is to operate?
• What are the features you like best?
• Let the prospect sell himself – How do you think this will benefit you/your company?
• Ask the prospect if she can qualify or afford the product.

NOTE: When you have finished the demonstration, take things away from the prospect, turn things off, and remove all literature. This eliminates all distractions and keeps you in control of the selling process. If the prospect asks to play with something again or see something again – it's a buying signal. Close on it.

## Try to create some involvement that puts a pen in the prospect's hand ...

## This way he's ready when you give him an order form to sign.

*In a group sale,*
*it takes a consensus to rule in your favor ...*
*but it only takes one person to rule against you.*

# Group sales ... dramatically different from one-on-one.

Group sales separate the professional from the amateur. You must be skilled at sales, more skilled at people reading, and even more skilled at group dynamics. In a group you can sell 5 out of 6 and not make the sale. *Worse, you can sell 99 out of 100 and not make the sale.*

The problem in group sales is that you must please everyone. One night in a group presentation, a woman asked me what was my favorite color. I told her plaid. The group loved it.

My friend, Bill Lehew, is the master of group sales. He has sold thousands of people, all in groups of 10 to 500. Lehew says if you can sell a group of 100, selling one-on-one becomes duck soup.

After spending a few hours discussing and documenting the dynamics of the group selling process with Bill, *here are some guidelines that have proven to be successful in actual selling situations ...*

**Remember, a group is two or more. So even if you're presenting to two or three decision makers, these principles still apply.**

• **Look good, but look plain vanilla.** Dressing too far left or right of center can distract the audience. You want them to concentrate on what you're saying, not what you're wearing.

• Get there early and **introduce yourself to everyone**. Get to know some of them personally. Find and remember those who seem most enthusiastic.

• **Remember everyone's name.** This is considered by many as the sleeper of trump cards. People love to hear their names. Being recognized by name is a sense of pride among peers. It can definitely sway the opinion of the group in your favor. You may have to take one of those memory courses to do it, but Lehew claims it is one of his most valuable tools.

• **Get some information about the group in advance** – their history, goals, and achievements. Being able to talk to the group as an insider rather than an outsider has dynamic advantage.

• **Find the power person** – the one who (other than you) seems to have the attention of the group. Play to the leader.

• **Find the problem person** and address them head-on and early. Have solid answers to their questions and concerns. The "one rotten apple spoils the whole basket" rule applies here.

• **Uncover all objections by asking the group questions early.** Write down the group's concerns on a board or flip chart. Be sure to cover every one of them and check them off as you do.

• **Anticipate objections and cover them in the presentation.** You already know what they're going to ask. Why not have scripted answers?

• **Get interaction early.** Audience participation leads to a feeling of ownership … and a sale.

• **Get someone in favor to talk early.** Remember the names of those in favor when you walked into the room? Now's your time to play the card, and play to the group. One of them can sell the others better than 10 of you.

• **Address the numbers for those who are analytical.** If you have bean counters or logical types, they will be relentless to get the facts. Don't disappoint them. Give solid, hard-core, believable facts and move on to the emotional issues.

• **Win the group emotionally after you have made the numbers very clear.** This is the heart of the selling process. You must present solid emotional reasons of involvement, protection, benefit, and security to win the sale.

• **Give good handouts that are clear, concise, on high-quality paper, and that lead to a close.** Your company, your integrity, and your ability to make the sale often ride on the quality and understandability of your handout or sales literature. It must be first quality all the way.

"Humor plays an important role in group dynamics. Not funny stories, just being humorous can win a crowd – and create a favorable negotiating climate," Lehew says with a classic Southern drawl. "If they laugh with you, it makes them feel comfortable and in the mood to buy."

"It's totally different than one-on-one," says Lehew. "You can't afford to alienate anyone. In my years of experience, I have only found one way to consistently win the group – it's integrity. I know it may sound too simple and even a little old fashioned, but it is the basis of my success in group sales and the basis of my success in life."

I agree.

*The future of the sales presentation
is a laptop computer and
a portable overhead projector.*

# The 21st-century computerized sales pitch.

I have seen the future of the sales presentation.

International expert on computer presentations Bill Whitley and his creative genius associate, Arny Pickholtz, sat me down in my living room, plugged in their Macintosh laptop and portable overhead projector – totaling 7 pounds – and proceeded to show me a computerized sales presentation that I'm still reeling (and buying) from.

It was just an ordinary 3.5-inch floppy disk and an 80 MB Macintosh laptop, but it contained animation – a cartoon character named Norm who was smart, funny, and prepared to sell. They added 3-D computerized graphics that moved and talked. They incorporated an actual videotape clip that was somehow imported into the presentation, and Norm closed me at the end.

**I was sitting on the edge of my chair the entire time
(less than 12 minutes). I was stunned.
And I was sold.**

*These guys aren't **on** the cutting edge of sales technology –
they **are** the cutting edge.*

The technical, tactical, and persuasive advantages of a computer-assisted sales presentation are powerful and compelling ...

• **It is a weapon** ... It's a sales tool, an educational tool, and a training tool all at the same time.

• **It makes you look professional** ... And builds instant buyer credibility.

- **It sets you apart from your competition** ... An incredible competitive advantage.

- **You are seen as a leader** ... A computer presentation is the leading edge of technology.

- **It keeps you on course and eliminates omissions** ... A complete presentation that never fails to make its impact, even after 1,000 repetitions of the same pitch.

- **It's fascinating to the prospect** ... It will have the prospect leaning forward in the buying position from the first 5 seconds.

- **It answers the prospect's questions before they're asked** ... The right presentation takes the prospect's questions into consideration while it is being created and anticipates them as part of the pitch.

- **You can put in a qualifying test that the prospect takes** ... The answers to which can lead you to a sale.

- **It can be programmed to overcome objections specific to your product or service** ... When you hear an objection, you can alter the presentation to overcome the specific objection and close or go back to the pitch.

- **It can be used to ask a closing question** ... Or a series of closing questions – and the prospect interactively answers with ordering information or information that confirms the sale.

- **It's so good, it's scary.**

Yeah, you say, but how is it in a group? Better. I went to a dinner for 300 Branch Bank & Trust employees for the unveiling of three new banking products. The bank's regional president, David Crowder, used a giant screen to make the interactive, animated, song-and-dance presentation. The crowd loved it. At points in the presentation they were actually cheering wildly (remember these were bankers – people who don't get excited until you miss a payment). But most important – they were sold.

When it was over, I just sat there staring into space contemplating the possibilities.

*Think about it.* You walk into a sales appointment, plug in your computer, pop in a CD and the prospect (mesmerized) watches a state-of-the-art presentation. The computer gets him interactively involved, answers all his questions, overcomes all his objections, leads him to a close, and gets him to type in his name, address, and quantity ordered – all without the salesperson saying a word.

How much does it cost? According to Whitley, presentations start as low as $1,000, and all you need to get it going at the fundamental level is a laptop computer of any kind. "Small companies are not price precluded from this market," he says. "I think it's a wise move to start at any level possible and sophisticate your presentation as profits permit." Obviously, elaborate presentations can get quite expensive, but consider the possible results as you consider the investment.

And if you're thinking,
*I'll wait until the price goes down* –
I'll bet your competition's not.

And for those of you who say, "If it's so great, Gitomer, how come you didn't buy one?" **I did.**

*Epilogue:* A decade after the first *Sales Bible* came out, The Whitley Group no longer exists, and for the RIGHT reasons. I chose to keep this article in the book because Bill Whitley and his company were AHEAD of their time. Ten years ago, he was the ONLY one who was doing this, and it enabled him to turn around and sell his company for tens of millions of dollars. What are you doing that is ONLY? Ten years ago, they showed me a computerized sales presentation that blew my doors off. The point I am trying to make is the importance of being Internet savvy. You should be teaching a 14-year-old how to use and navigate on the Internet, not vice versa. Computers are cheap, Internet connection is cheaper, and both are 21st-century tools that are the gateway to your fame, fortune, financial freedom, fulfillment, and fun.

## THE SALES BIBLE

**Part 5**
**Objections, Closing, and**
**Follow-up ... Getting to *YES***

# The Book of Objections

## 5.1

# I object!

The sale starts when the customer says ***no***.

If you can turn ***no*** into ***yes***, you make the sale. Simple.

A sale is always made. Either you sell the prospect on ***yes***, or he sells you on ***no***.

You will hear the word ***no*** more than 116,000 times in your life.

Your challenge as a salesperson is ... change 500 of those ***no's*** to ***yes***. It will change your life ... and your bank account.

Don't take ***no*** for an answer.

Overrule objections.

Here's how ...

*Identifying the true objection.*
*Every time.*

# Will the real objection please stand up!

The customer says, "I object!" Or does he? Is it the true objection, a stall, or a lie? Euphemistically called *objection* or *concern*, it's actually the real reason a prospect won't buy now. What the prospect or customer is really saying is, "You haven't sold me yet." The prospect is actually requesting more information or more reassurance.

**There are very few actual objections. Most are just stalls.** This is further complicated by the fact that buyers will often hide the true objection. Why? They don't want to hurt your feelings, they are embarrassed, or they are afraid to tell the truth. A white lie is so much easier, more convenient, and less bloody than actually having to tell the truth, so they just say something to get rid of you.

These are the Top 10 Stalls/White Lies:

1. I want to think about it.
2. We've spent our budget.
3. I have to talk it over with my partner (wife, cat, mistress, broker, lawyer, accountant, shrink).
4. I need to sleep on it.
5. I never purchase on impulse – I always give it time to sink in.
6. I'm not ready to buy yet.
7. Get back to me in 90 days. We'll be ready by then.
8. Quality is not important to me.
9. Business is slow right now.
10. Our ad agency handles that.

*"We have a satisfactory source," "We need two other bids," "The home office buys everything,"* and *"Your price is too high,"* are also classic objections, but I didn't want to ruin the *Top 10* thing.

So, what is a true objection? **Most true objections are never stated –** 90% of the time when the prospect says, "I want to think it over," or gives you a stalling line, he or she is really saying something else …

## Here are the real objections …

- Doesn't have the money.
- Has the money, but is too damn cheap to spend it.
- Can't get the credit needed.
- Can't decide on his or her own.
- Doesn't have authority to spend over budget, or without someone else's financial approval.
- Thinks (or knows) he can get a better deal elsewhere.
- Has something else in mind, but won't tell you.
- Has a friend, connection, or satisfactory relationship in the business.
- Does not want to change vendors.
- Wants to shop around.
- Too busy with other more important things at this time.
- Doesn't need (or thinks he doesn't need) your product now.
- Thinks (or knows) your price is too high.
- Doesn't like or have confidence in your product.
- Doesn't like, trust, or have confidence in your company.
- Doesn't like, trust, or have confidence in you.

## Finding the *real* objection is the first order of business.
It's up there (in the list) someplace. Then (and only then) is successfully overcoming it and making a sale possible.

You can overcome an objection perfectly, but if it isn't the *real* objection, you'll be shaking your head wondering why the sale hasn't been made. When you get an objection, you must qualify that it is *true* and the *only one*. Qualifying the objection and overcoming it are of equal importance.

The problem is most salespeople are not able to get to the true objection *and* are not prepared to overcome objections when they occur. Why?

- They lack the technical (product) knowledge.
- They lack the sales tools.
- They lack the sales knowledge.
- They lack the self-confidence.
- They have not prepared in advance
  (often for the same objection they've heard
  10 times before).
- Their presentation is lacking.

*Or any combination of the above.*

*"The price is too high"* is the classic sales objection. To overcome it, you must find out what the prospect actually means or how high is too high. Half the time you hear it, you're dead. **The other side of that coin says that 50% of the time you hear a price objection, you have a shot at a sale**, and the prospect can be sold with the right words or phrases.

# Qualifying the objection and overcoming the objection are of equal importance.

*Overcoming the true objection.*

# Real-world objections ...
# Real-world solutions!

Objections. I love objections. Overcoming them is the true test of a salesperson. **The customer isn't exactly saying no; he's just saying not now.** *An objection may actually indicate buyer interest.*

The best way to overcome an objection? The Boy Scout motto – *Be Prepared!* But, since most salespeople are *not prepared*, this chapter contains the second best method. (The best method is detailed in the next chapter. No jumping ahead. This is a different way, and you may not always be able to use the best way.)

## *Why do objections occur?*

1. Because there are doubts or unanswered questions in the mind of the prospect (sometimes created by the salesperson).
2. Because the prospect wants to buy or is interested in buying, but needs clarification, wants a better deal, or must have third-party approval.
3. Because the prospect does not want to buy.

I guarantee you *will* get objections if ...

- You have not completely qualified the buyer, (Is he the real decider? Can he really afford it? What is the need and interest level?)
- You have not established need.
- You have not established rapport.
- You have not established credibility.
- You have not established trust.
- You have not found the prospect's hot button.
- Your presentation was weak.

- You have not anticipated objections in your
  presentation and overcome them before the
  prospect can raise them.

*Here are seven steps to identify the true objection and then overcome it:*

**1. Listen carefully to the objection being raised** ... Determine if it is an objection or just a stall. A prospect will often repeat an objection if it's real. Let the prospect talk it out completely.

**No matter what, agree with the prospects at first. This allows you to tactfully disagree without it starting an argument.**

If you believe it to be a stall, you must get them to fess up to the real objection or you cannot proceed. If you believe it's a stall, or want clarification, try these lead-in phrases to get to the truth:

- Don't you really mean ...?
- You're telling me _____,
  but I think you might mean something else.
- Usually when customers tell me that,
  experience has shown me that they really have
  a price objection. Is that true for you?

**2. Qualify it as the only true objection** ... Question it. Ask the prospect if it is the only reason he or she won't purchase from your company. Ask if there is any other reason he or she won't purchase besides the one given.

**3. Confirm it again** ... Rephrase your question to ask the same thing twice: "In other words, if it wasn't for _____, you'd buy my service. Is that true, Mr. Jones?"

**4. Qualify the objection to set up the close** ... Ask a question in a way that incorporates the solution: "So, if I were able to prove the reliability ..." or "If I were able to get you extended terms ..." or "If I were able to show you the system in a working environment, *would that be enough for you to make a decision?*" Or a variation, "*... would that make me a candidate for your business?*"

**5. Answer the objection in a way that completely resolves the issue** ... and in a way that the customer ties down to a *yes* answer. Use every tool in your box at this point. If you've got trump cards, play them now (a testimonial letter, a comparison chart, a customer you can call on the spot, a special time-related or price-related deal).

*Forget price* – show cost, demonstrate value, list comparisons, and prove benefits. If you cannot answer the prospect in a way that's different or sets you apart from others, you'll never close this (or any) sale.

Product knowledge, creativity, sales tools, your belief in yourself, your product and your company, and your ability to communicate, come together in this step. You must combine technique with assurance, sincerity, and conviction to get the prospect to agree with you and mean it.

## 6. Ask a closing question, or communicate in an assumptive manner ... Ask a question, the answer to which confirms the sale.

- "If I could ... would you" is the classic model for the close.
- "I'm pretty sure we can do this. I have to check one fact with my office. If it's a go on my part, I'm assuming we have a deal," *or* "I could meet with all the decision makers to finalize it."
- Use similar situations when you close. People like to know about others in the same situation.
- Ask, "Why is this/that important to you?" Then use, *"If I could ... would you?"*

## 7. Confirm the answer and the sale (in writing when possible) ...

Get the prospect to convert to a customer with a confirming question like:

- When do you want it delivered?
- When is the best starting day to begin?
- Is there a better day to deliver than others?
- Where do you want it delivered?

### Observation About Objections

There are mountains written about closing and overcoming objections. My philosophy is to learn as many of these techniques as you can from every book, tape, and seminar available.

## Then make sales in a way that you never have to use them -- by establishing relationships and friendships.

Sometimes you are precluded from the relationship or friendship, and the techniques are all that's left. That's why you need to know them all.

More tricks? There are thousands. One good one is to get approvals and confirmations from the prospect during the sale. This sets the yes tone for the close.

Read every book; listen to every tape. They all contain closes or ways to overcome objections. And most have usable ideas. Your job is to apply those techniques to your style and personality. No two salespeople are alike. Thank God.

**But the best trick is no trick -- it's friendship.**
**It's a warm, open, human relationship.**

These are the *Cliff's Notes* version of
*overcoming objections* to carry in your wallet.
You'll need a big wallet.

1. Listen to the objection and decide
   if it's true.

2. Qualify it as the only one.

3. Confirm it again, in a different way.

4. Qualify the objection to set up
   the close.

5. Answer the objection so that it
   completely resolves the issue,
   and confirm the resolve.

6. Ask a closing question, or
   communicate to the prospect in
   an assumptive (I have the sale in
   hand) manner.

7. Confirm the answer and the sale
   in writing.

# An objection
# may actually indicate
# buyer interest.

*If you can anticipate objections,*
*you can prevent them from occurring.*

# Objection Prevention.
## *A new way to enjoy safe sales.*

"Your price is too high." Rats. Don't you hate when you hear that? It's the number ONE objection in the world of sales. Why do salespeople continue to listen to it? Beats me.

There are no new objections. You've heard them all before. Can you imagine the prospect saying, "Your price is too high," and you responding, "Really, I've never heard that before." (Actually that response may be better than the one you're using.) Whatever business you're in, there are between 5 and 20 reasons why the customer won't buy now.

Some objections are stalls – delay tactics or hesitation by the prospect to tell the salesperson *no*. Both objection and stall are defined by salespeople in a single word: *frustration*.

Well, here's the way to cure what ails your sales: Prevent objections by discussing them in your presentation *before* the prospect has a chance to voice them. Prevention is the best medicine to cure objections.

Here's how the process works:

• **Identify all possible objections.** Meet with sales reps and customers. Brainstorm objections. Ask them for the top 10 objections they get. They'll flow like water.

• **Write them down.** Make a detailed list of every objection you have identified. Often the same objection is given in a variety of ways.

• **Script objection responses with closing questions for each.** In order to *prevent*, you must *prepare*. It may take some time to complete this task. Do it with your team and perhaps a few customers in the room. Create several scenarios for each objection.

• **Develop sales tools that enhance and support every response.**
Items like testimonial letters, testimonial videos, comparison charts, and
support documentation could enhance the objection-to-close process.
Companies must develop whatever is needed to make the salesperson
feel confident, supported, and able to make the sale easier.

• **Rehearse the scripts in role-play.** After the responses are written,
schedule several role-play sessions to get familiar with each scripted
situation, and try to make it sound natural.

• **Tweak the scripts.** After you role-play, there will be revisions to the
scripts. Make them immediately.

• **Try them out on customers.** Go to a problem customer or two. Tell
them what you're doing – they'll be flattered that you had the courage, and
they'll most often give you truthful responses.

• **Make final revisions based on real-world situations.** The real
world always changes a script or approach. Be sure to document revisions
every time you make them.

• **Keep the documents in a master notebook.** Give all salespeople
a copy. There is an added bonus to this system – when you hire a new
salesperson, he or she has a training manual that will provide immediate
insight and income.

• **Meet regularly as a group to discuss revisions.** There is always
someone inventing the *new* best way possible.

It's so simple, it works. The key is to know the objections that are likely to
occur, and script the answers or responses into your regular presentation so
that when you come to the end of your pitch, there's nothing to object to.

Here are 7.5 tools and phrases of objection prevention you might consider
adding to your scripts and incorporating into your presentation as part of
this process:

**1. Similar situations** – Stories about customers who had the same
or similar problem or objection who bought in spite of the objection.

**2. Testimonial letters** – Some of them can be closers, for example,
*"I thought the price was too high, but after a year of lower maintenance
cost, I realized the overall cost was actually 20% lower than last year.
Thanks for talking me into it."*

**3. A story or article about your product or your company** –
To build support, credibility, and confidence.

**4. A comparison chart** – Compare the competition apples to apples and use it when the prospect says he wants to check around.

**5. Say, "Our experience has shown ..."** – One of the most powerful verbal lead-ins to preventing an objection.

**6. Say, "We have listened to our customers. They had a concern about ... Here's what we did ..."** – To get the prospect to see his potential objection disappear, and how you listen and respond.

**7. Say, "We used to believe ..., but we have changed and now we ..."** – As a method of preventing a myth from recurring (reputation for poor service, high price, etc.)

**7.5 Prepare yourself.** – You know the objection is coming. You've heard it before. Be ready with questions, answers, and sales tools when it arrives.

If you can overcome an objection in your presentation before the prospect raises it, you are more likely to make a sale.

# *The real world ...*

If you can anticipate objections,
you can prevent them from occurring.
Sounds simple. It just requires preparation and practice.
It takes time, creativity, and focus to make it happen.
Please try it.
Your reward for superior effort
will be superior sales ...
which leads to a superior wallet.

# Overcoming objections series ...

*The sale starts when the customer objects.* Most often customers won't tell you the real objection first; they just stall. A master salesperson can get through the stall to the real objection. The next pages are dedicated to the objection. The ones you hear all the time, like ...

> I want to think it over.
>
> I want to check with two more suppliers.
>
> Your price is too high.
>
> I have to talk it over with my partner (boss, wife).
>
> I'm satisfied with my present supplier.
>
> We've spent our entire budget for the year.
>
> Get back to me in about 6 months.

Sometimes these are true objections. Most of the time they are stalls, or worse, untruths.

## The key to overcoming objections lies in ...

- Your knowledge of selling skills.
- Your knowledge of your product.
- Your knowledge of your prospect.
- The relationship you have built with your prospect.
- Your creativity.
- Your attitude.
- Your sincere desire to help your prospect.
- Your persistence.

None of these things has anything to do with price.
Some of these things may relate to cost.
*All of these things have to do with value.*

*Each chapter in the objection series will focus on a single issue so that you can get as much practical, usable information as possible. The objective is to give you a technique you can use when you make your next sales call.*

> ***Rule #1*** *... Before you can overcome*
> *an objection and make a sale,*
> *you have to get down to the **true** objection.*

## What do you say when the prospect says ...

# *"I want to think about it."*

The prospect says, "I want to think about it"? Don't you hate to hear that?

Let's say you're trying to sell Jones Construction a new copier. Jones is interested, but gives you the old line about thinking it over.

**"Thinking it over" is a stall,
not a true objection.**

*You can only make the sale if you find out what the
true objection(s) is and creatively overcome it.*

*This will get Mr. Jones off the fence and onto the order pad ...*
**Salesperson:** Great! Thinking it over means you're interested. Correct, Mr. Jones?
**Jones:** Yes, I am.
**Salesperson:** You're not just saying, "I want to think about it" to get rid of me. Are you? (said in a humorous vein)
**Jones:** Oh, no, no, no. (laughter)
**Salesperson:** (seriously) You know, Mr. Jones, this is an important decision. A copier is not just a duplicating device. Every time you send a copy out to a customer, it reflects your company's image. I'm sure you agree with me. Is there anyone else in your company you will be thinking it over with? (Meaning: Is he deciding alone, or are others involved?)
**Jones:** No, just me.
**Salesperson:** I know you are an expert at building; your reputation speaks for itself, but I'm an expert in copiers. In my experience in the copier industry over the past 6 years, I've found that most people who think things over develop important questions that they may not have answers for ... since the image of your business is on every copy you make. Why don't we think it over together so that as you develop questions about the copier, I'll be right here to answer them? Fair enough? Now, what was the main thing you wanted to think about? [*At this point you will begin to get the real objection(s).*]

NOTE: If Mr. Jones had said he was going to think it over with others, you must think it over with all parties in the same room, or you're dead.

*50% of the time when the prospect says,
"I want to think it over,"
it really means he or she ...*

- **Doesn't have the money.**
- **Can't decide on his own.**
- **Wants to shop around.**
- **Doesn't need your product now.**
- **Has a friend in the business.**
- **Knows he can buy it cheaper elsewhere.**
- **Doesn't trust or have confidence in you.**
- **Doesn't trust or have confidence in your company.**
- **Doesn't like your product.**
- **Doesn't like you.**

*The other 50% of the time he will buy.
The prospect can be sold
if you use the right words or phrases.*

**What do you say when the prospect says …**

# *"We spent our entire budget, honest!"*

"We spent our entire budget" is one of the best put-offs a prospect can give you. But take heart – **it's only a real objection about half the time**.

- Sometimes you can find another budget category.
- Sometimes you can get a bigger boss to make a variation or exception.
- Sometimes the prospect will just use the line to get rid of you.
- Sometimes it's the truth – but I'd love to have a dollar for every lie.

To overcome this objection, you must first find out if the prospect is telling the truth. There are several hidden meaning possibilities: "We spent our whole budget" may actually mean "I can't afford it," *or* "I can buy it elsewhere cheaper (or better)," *or* "I don't want to buy from you (or your company)," *or* "I already have a satisfactory vendor," *or* "I don't want what you've got."

## Here are a few ideas to get the prospect off dead center …

- *Mr. Prospect, let me tell you about our deferred payment plan. If you sign for 2 years now, we can delay payments for 6 months until your next budget, then simply accelerate payments.*
- *If my service solves your problem, is there any reason why you can't make the necessary changes to be included in your budget?*
- *Who would have the authority to exceed the budget? When can we set up a meeting with them?*

To find out if the prospect truly wants to buy but actually does not have the money in the budget, here's a great method to use:

**Salesperson:** If the budget wasn't used, would you buy my product?
**Prospect:** Oh, yes!
**Salesperson:** When is the next budget meeting?
**Prospect:** July.

*NOTE: You must now ask the following questions and write down the answers.*

"What type of proposal do I need to submit?" "Date due?" "Can you get me a sample of a previously submitted proposal?" "Are there others I should submit it to?" "Will you give me a letter of endorsement?" (A letter of endorsement by a manager attached to the budget proposal can be the deciding factor.) "Can I present my proposal in person at the meeting so that any questions can be answered?" (*Any hesitancy on the part of the prospect to answer these questions probably means the budget is not the true or only objection.*)

You might still be able to get a sale or partial sale this year. Begin to ask about the present situation: "Is there anyone else who might be able to rearrange this year's budget to find some money? ... Is there any money left in approved items that is unspent? ... Can we categorize this purchase in another heading that has money left to spend (office equipment, promotion, dues and subscriptions, publicity, advertising)?"

A bit more pushy approach is, "Are you sure you can get it approved?" Prospect says *yes.* You say, "Buy now. I'll bill you now, but it's due after the budget approval."

"No money in the budget" is among the most difficult objections because you don't know if it's the truth, and if it is, there's serious follow-up that must be done. If you submit a proposal for budget approval, it must be concise, without error, all terms and conditions spelled out, and on time.

## You must qualify the fact that the prospect wants your product.
Then you can get an endorsement for next year, and potentially some business this year.

**What do you say when the prospect says …**

# *"I want to check with two more suppliers."*

It's frustrating when you have just made a great pitch, you know you have the best product, you have explained every benefit, but the prospect says, "I have to check with two other suppliers." What the heck can you do or say to get the sale today?

The best salespeople are trained to respond to objections and make closes at the appropriate moment. They go to a presentation prepared with every tool that enables them to make the sale now. Below is a technique with a little-used but powerful sales tool that can win a sale and impress the prospect with your thoroughness.

*SCENARIO:* Mr. Jones needs a cellular phone for better and faster business communication, has appointed you, listened to your pitch, but says he wants to look around.

### *This is probably not his true objection.*

Your objective in this situation is to position Mr. Jones in a way that he will buy today or state his true objection. Try this on indecisive Mr. Jones …

**Salesperson:** You know, Mr. Jones, many of my customers wanted to do the exact same thing before they bought their cell phone from me. I'm sure you want to know you're getting the best phone and the best service for your dollar. Correct?

**Jones:** Yes, absolutely.

**Salesperson:** Can you tell me a few of the things you'll be checking (comparing)?

**Jones:** (Whatever Jonesy says first and second are the real objections – unless he's just trying to get rid of you)

**Salesperson:** After you have compared these items [name them] with other companies and found ours to be the best, I'm sure you'll buy from us. Correct, Mr. Jones?

**Jones:** Yes, I will.

### (OK, it's time to nail Mr. Jones.)

**Salesperson:** Great! Many of our customers want to shop and compare before they buy; but we both know this can take a lot of your valuable time. The reason you're buying the cell phone in the first place is to give you more time. Isn't it? So, to save you the time, we have shopped the competition for you. Here is a chart of our top 20 competitors, their products (show an 11 x 17 chart completely filled in), their services, and their prices for you to review. Take time to point out how you compare favorably in each area, especially those areas of concern voiced by Mr. Jones.

### Now, Mr. Jones, when do you want to sign up for your cell phone plan?

NOTE: Mr. Jones is now pleasantly surprised at how well you did your homework and in shock that he will have to decide now, or else begin to state his true objections. (See *"I want to think about it,"* earlier in this chapter for a list of the true objections you are likely to get.)

### A chart that compares your products, services, and prices with those of your competition can get your prospect to buy now instead of look around.

*A variation of this tactic ...*
**Offer to do the comparison on your time.** Have Mr. Jones tell you what he's going to compare. Tell him you'll file a written comparison, and whoever wins, wins.

Mr. Jones will say, "I don't want you to go to all that trouble." You respond, "Mr. Jones, your business means a lot to me. I don't mind doing this. It'll give me a chance to make sure we're on top of our game. Besides, we've never lost in a competitive comparison."

Now, with the most guts you can muster, say, "Did you want to go ahead and sign up now, or wait until the comparison is over?"

**What do you do when the prospect says …**

# *"I want to buy, but the price is too high."*

Mercedes-Benz is one of the most expensive cars in the world. Some people say, "The price is too high" … the company sells thousands of autos worldwide. Mercedes is one of the wealthiest companies in the world.

*"The price is too high"* has been a cry from buyers since the open market in Damascus, 2,000 years ago … but they still bought.

*"The price is too high"* is a classic objection. **To overcome it, you must find out what the prospect actually means.** Assuming he or she wants to buy now, and the person you're speaking to is the sole decider, there are actually five possible meanings behind this objection …

1. I can't afford it.
2. I can buy it elsewhere cheaper (or better).
3. I don't want to buy from you (or your company).
4. I don't see, perceive, understand the cost or value of your product or service.
5. I'm not convinced yet.

About half the time you get a price objection, you will not make the sale. That leaves a 50% opportunity window. Open it.

## Here are some probes you can try …

• *Prove affordability:* "What we will do for you costs less in comparison to what it will cost you if you don't hire us and proceed on your present course."

• *Challenge:* "What are you willing to pay?" "What price can you afford?"

• *Get a feel for the difference:* "How much 'too high' is it?"

• *Talk about value and tomorrow:* "Mr. Jones, you're thinking about pennies per day. We're talking about value over a lifetime."

The one that has worked best for me is: **"Would you buy it from me now (not today) if the price were lower?"** (Assume the prospect says *yes*.) "You mean other than price, there is no reason we can't do business?" (Note: I have double-qualified the prospect on the price objection to determine it is the real, true, and ONLY objection.) "If we can figure a way to make it affordable, will you take delivery [or *begin* or *order*] right away?"

If the prospect says *yes*, then you have to *creatively* figure out a way to change the terms, offer a discount, offer a future credit of items to enhance value, compare price to cost (over a term), or simply resell at the original price. **The key is to prepare these answers in advance.** You know the objection is coming. Why be surprised?

If prospects want your product or service bad enough, they'll figure out a way to afford it. Just because they say the price is too high, doesn't mean they won't buy. What is actually being said many times is **"I want to buy. Show me a way."**

# Just because a prospect says, "The price is too high," doesn't mean he won't buy today.

# What do you do when the prospect says …

# *"I'm satisfied with my present source."*

Great, just what you wanted to hear. But don't get discouraged with this one; it's actually pretty easy to get an opening and begin a relationship if you can get the prospect talking. Just because he's satisfied now doesn't mean he'll stay that way.

*Realize that what your prospect is saying is that their existing supplier is the best they've been able to find.*

You may have a better product, price, availability for delivery, service, training, or warranty. The prospect is only telling you he's satisfied from *his perspective*. He doesn't really know about you or your company yet.

*Knowing the reason why the relationship is satisfactory will help you understand how to proceed.*

Here are the top 12 reasons your prospect likes the vendor he's currently using …

1. Price or great deal (perceived value).
2. Quality of product/service.
3. Has a special business relationship.
4. Has a personal relationship.
5. Has used this supplier for years.
6. Doesn't know any better – only thinks he's getting a good deal or good service.
7. Vendor "helped me when I needed it."
8. Great (friendly, immediate) service.
9. In stock – immediate delivery.
10. Personalized service/does favors.
11. Told by others, "This is who we buy from."
12. Is lazy, has a vendor, doesn't want to change, isn't spending his own money (not the boss).

**Find out which one of these 12 reasons applies to your situation before you start to overcome this objection …
or you're wasting your time.**

• *Get information about the present vendor:* "What do you like most about the vendor you're using?" and "Is there anything you would like to see changed?"

• *Show a difference:* "We have recently introduced new technologies that go beyond your present equipment and would appreciate an opportunity to demonstrate them."

• *"Give us a try":* Suggest that the prospect use your service for a trial period of 30 to 90 days, or take a trial order, or give you a small percentage of the business to prove yourself.

• *Issue a challenge:* "I'm sure you will agree, Mr. Prospect, that as a businessman, you owe it to your business to continue to actively seek out the best value." A satisfied buyer may indicate a complacent supplier. Offer to do all the comparative work.

• *Give an experienced response:* "Mr. Jones, when I personally have a satisfactory vendor, I still need another vendor as a point of reference to make sure I'm getting the best price, selection of products and value."

• *Question their selection process (not their selection):* "What standards do you judge your vendors by?" Raising the question of standards will get the prospect thinking about future performance, not just the past.

*The four keys to success with this objection are ...*

**1. Find out how the relationship with his present source began.** Get a historical perspective. Find out how he began with his present supplier.

**2. Ask the two important open-ended questions:** "What are the things you like most about the vendor?" and "What would you change if you could?"

**3.** If you get a chance to give some information, you'd better make it sound great. **Be sure to stress that you have long-term relationships with your customers.** Tell the prospect you're interested in slowly cultivating one with him and you don't expect a total switch, but an evolution of judgment and proof by performance. Say you'd like the same opportunity you gave (present supplier) back when you issued him that first order.

**4. Go for the sample or trial order.** Something small to get your foot in the door, and prove your worth to the prospect.

If prospects have a good long-term relationship with their present supplier – and you really want the business – start building a relationship with them now. Get your *Mackay 66* filled out and start using it. There is no better way. Tell prospects you want to begin the same way they started with their present source. Go slow, start small, and win big.

# What do you do when the prospect says ...
# *"I need home office approval."*

More than half the time you hear the line "I need home office approval," it's a lie – a stall tactic that frustrates and deceives. The challenge this objection presents is to find out if it's the truth (or true objection).

**Ask the prospect pointed questions about the home office approval process:** "How long does it take? ... Does one person decide or is it a committee? ... If it's a committee, when does it meet? ... Can I submit a proposal? ... Do you have a sample proposal or suggested format? ... Can I contact the decision maker?"

**Challenge the prospect:** "No problem. I understand. Let's contact them right now while I'm here. That way I can answer any questions they might have." The objective in making the appeal to call now is to determine if the prospect is telling the truth that home office approval is really needed. If the prospect tries to make some excuse why he can't call now, chances are home office approval is NOT needed. If you detect hesitation or uneasiness on the part of the prospect, he is probably less than 100% truthful.

**Direct questions will expose a prospect.** If you don't believe the prospect is being truthful, go back to the pitch and find out the real objection.

**Whether the prospect is telling the truth or not, the key question to ask is** ... "Tell me, Mr. Prospect, if you didn't need home office approval, would you buy?"

If the prospect says *yes*, you have crossed the first bridge to making the sale with or without home office approval.

**Look for ways around the problem.** Sometimes the local manager has a discretionary budget. Sometimes there is a dollar limit, so if you divide your invoice into several smaller ones, it might fly. Be creative.

**Prevent the objection by qualifying first.** ... There are ways to avoid this objection. How well did you qualify the prospect prior to making the appointment? You should not ask the blunt question, "Are you the sole decision maker?" It sounds too "salesy" and is somewhat insulting to the prospect. Just rephrase it. Try this one: "Is there anyone else you work with on decisions (situations) like this?" The object is to find out if anyone else is involved in the decision BEFORE you make your presentation.

The unfortunate aspect of this objection is that it's a convenient put-off for the prospect who doesn't want to (or have the guts to) just say no. It can be a large, disappointing wheel-spinning exercise. Take heart, though. I've flown to many home offices and brought back paper.

If you really want the business, go for it. Don't let a home office get in the way of you and a big order. Go to the home office and bring back business.

Someone is.

**What do you do when the prospect says ...**

# *"I have to talk this over with my ..."*
# *Uh oh!*

*When you hear the words "I have to talk this over with ...," you realize
you've done something very wrong.*

You didn't qualify the prospect very well, did you? OK. What do you do now?

*When others need to approve the deal, besides qualifying the buyer
better, you must take four action steps ...*

      1. Get the prospect's personal approval.

      2. Get on the prospect's team.

      3. Arrange a meeting with all deciders.

      4. Make your entire presentation again.

If you think you can get around these steps, think again. It's obvious you're
looking for shortcuts or you would have properly qualified the buyer.
If you would have just asked, "Is there anyone else you work with on
decisions like these?" this whole mess wouldn't be taking place. Would it?

*Back to the reality of the four steps ...*

**1. Get the prospect's personal approval.** "Mr. Jones, if it was just
you and you didn't need to confer with anyone else, would you buy it?"
(The prospect will almost always say yes.) I ask, "Does this mean you'll
recommend our product to the others?"

Now I go through a checklist that seems a little redundant, but I want to
uncover any areas of doubt, so I ask ...

    ✔ Is the price OK?        ✔ Is the product OK?

    ✔ Is the service OK?     ✔ Is the company OK?

    ✔ Am I OK?             ✔ What doubts do you have?

    ✔ Do you like it well enough to own it?

*(Note: Revise these questions to suit what you sell. Revise them in a
more personalized way. The objective is to nail down absolute approval.)*
Get the prospect to endorse you and your product to the others, but don't
let him (or anyone) make your pitch for you.

**2. Get on the prospect's team.** Begin to talk in terms of "we," "us," and "the team." By getting on the prospect's team, you can get the prospect on your side of the sale.
• "What do WE have to do?"
• "When can WE get them together?"
• "When does the team meet next? It's important that I am present because I'm sure they'll have questions that they will want answers to."
• "What can I do to be a member of the team?"
• "Tell me a little bit about the others." (Write down every characteristic.) Try to get the personality traits of the other deciders.

**3. Arrange a meeting with all deciders.** Do it any way you have to. Leave several alternative *open times* from your date book. Use the alternatives as a reason to get back and solidify your meeting with the decision-making group.

**4. Make your entire presentation again.** You only have to do this if you want to make the sale. Otherwise just leave it to the prospect. He thinks he can handle it and will try his best to convince you of that.

**The best way for you to make this (or any) sale is to be in control of the situation.**
**If you make the mistake of letting your prospect become a salesperson on your behalf (goes to the partner instead of you), you will lose. Every time.**

*An alternative method …*

**Ask the prospect if he's sure the partner (wife, boss) will want to do the deal.** If the prospect says, "Yes, I'm sure," you say, "Great! Why not just approve the purchase now [sign the contract], and get their approval? If you call me tomorrow and tell me no, I'll tear up the contract. Fair enough?"

**You can avoid and prevent this objection with three words …**

# Qualify the buyer!

## What do you do when the prospect says ...

# *"Call me back in 6 months."*

Is it just a polite way of saying no? *Are you willing (do you have the guts) to bottom-line the prospect?*

Pat me on the head and tell me to go away. That's the real meaning of *"Call me in 6 months"* (or any nebulous "get back to me" after some period of time). The prospect is really saying no! To overcome this stall, you must find out what true obstacles are in the way.

Does the buyer really want your product? Is there someone else? Is your price too high? Can the prospect afford what you're selling?

Fact is, if the prospect says *"Call me in 6 months,"* you haven't found the true reason for the stall (and may not want to know). The real reasons for this objection are ...

1. You have not established enough rapport.
2. You have not established enough buyer confidence.
3. You have not established enough need.
4. You have not established enough value.
5. You have not established enough trust.
6. You have not established enough desire.
6.5 You have not established a sense of urgency to buy today.

You've done all that? The prospect is telling you the truth? Baloney. If you are looking for some *truth in rejection*, try looking a bit deeper. The real reason might be one of these:

- The prospect isn't the true decider.
- The prospect doesn't have the money.
- The prospect doesn't like your company.
- The prospect doesn't like your product.
- The prospect thinks your price is too high.
- The prospect has a friend or relationship established to buy or get your product or service in some other (more beneficial) way.
- The prospect doesn't like you.

## TRY QUESTIONS:

What will be different in 6 months?

Is there a particular reason you prefer that I get back to you in 6 months?

What is preventing you from taking action today?

**BIG QUESTION:** Are you willing (do you have the guts) to bottom-line the buyer? Do you have the courage to ask him, "Are you really saying NO?"

If you want to begin the process to overcoming this objection (stall) and find out where the sale is, do any one or combination of the following:

- Ask the prospect, "Do you see yourself buying in 6 months?"
- Find out who else is involved in the decision by asking, "How will the decision be made?"
- Ask the prospect, "Could you purchase now and pay in 6 months?"
- Show that by purchasing now the prospect will save/earn back some or all of the purchase price in 6 months.
- Show how a delay can cost more than purchasing now.
- Ask if he has looked at the cost of delay.
- Show how the advantage of purchasing now outweighs the hidden expense of waiting.
- Show the difference between spend (cash outlay) and cost (total value of the sale).

**BIG ANSWER:** Wherever the answer lies (and often the prospect does just that), one fact is clear: A 6-month, 6-week, or 6-day stall is not the fault of the prospect. You have not uncovered the true desire, need, or objection. It is not an issue of blame – it is an issue of responsibility – yours.

# The Book of Closing

5.2

# Pleeeease ... I'll be your best friend.

Closing ...

That was your first close.
And sometimes it worked.

The sale belongs to the
closer ...
It pays (big commissions)
to master the science of
the close.

All your work, all your
preparation, comes down
to one final question.

The close is a delicate
balance between your
words and actions and the
prospect's thoughts and
perceptions.

Here's how to ask for the
sale and get it!

*Any question asked by the prospect*
*must be considered a buying signal.*

# What are the 19.5 early warning signals that the prospect is ready to buy?

*Question:* When is the prospect ready to buy?

*Answer:* He'll tell you if you just pay attention.

*The links between the presentation and the close are buying signals.*

Recognizing signals to buy is the first step toward a close in the science of selling. Listen to the buyer. He or she will give you signals.

When you're giving your presentation, the buyer will gesture, question, play with your product, or in some way communicate that he is inclined to purchase. As a professional salesperson, your job is to recognize the buying signal and convert it into a sale.

*Here are 19.5 signals (questions) to look for:*

**1. Questions about availability or time.** *Are these in stock? How often do you receive new shipments?*

**2. Questions about delivery.** *How soon can someone be here? How much notice do I have to give you?*

**3. Specific questions about rates, price, or statements about affordability.** *How much does this model cost? What is the price of this fax machine? I don't know if I can afford that model.*

**4. Any questions or statements about money.** *How much money would I have to put down to get this?*

**5. Positive questions about your business.** *How long have you been with the company? How long has your company been in business?*

**6. Wanting something repeated.** *What was that you said before about financing?*

**7. Statements about problems with previous vendors.** *Our old vendor gave us poor service. How quickly do you respond to a service call?*

**8. Questions about features and options** (What will it or you do?). *Is the sorter standard or optional?*

**9. Questions about quality.** *How many copies per month is the machine rated for?*

**10. Questions about guarantee or warranty.** *How long is this under warranty?*

**11. Questions about qualifications** (yours or the company's). *Can all of your people answer questions on the phone?*

**12. Specific positive questions about the company.** *What other products do you carry?*

**13. Specific product/service questions.** *How does the manual feed operate? Do you select the person or do I?*

**14. Specific statements about ownership of your product or service.** *Would you provide paper each month automatically? Will you come by each month to pick up my accounting? Suppose I like her and want her to work for me full-time?*

**15. Questions to confirm unstated decisions or seeking support.** *Is this the best way for me to go?*

**16. Wanting to see a sample or demo again.** *Could I see the fabric samples again?*

**17. Asking about other satisfied customers.** *Who are some of your customers?*

**18. Asking for a reference.** *Could I contact someone you did temp work for using Lotus or WordPerfect? Do you have a list of references?*

**19. Buying noises.** *I didn't know that.... Oh really.... That's interesting.... That's in line with what we've been doing.*

**19.5 Your ability to convert the signal into a sale ...** *Every one of these buying signals (questions) can be turned into a closing question that will lead to a faster sale – if you do it right.*

**How do you answer these questions?** Good question! A buying signal. I'll tell you in the next chapter.

# Recognizing buying signals is critical to your success as a salesperson. You will go past the sale if you fail to recognize them. And many do.

*If you answer a prospect's question with*
*yes or no, you may be going past*
*the sale without making it.*

# When you answer a prospect's question, avoid two words -- *Yes* and *No*.

When a prospect asks me a "yes" or "no" question, *I never answer yes or no.* When a prospect asks me any question, I try to answer in the form of a question – or ask a question at the end of my answer. This establishes the two central objectives of selling:
1. I'm in control of the presentation.
2. I might be able to close the sale now.
When you answer a prospect's question, avoid two words: *yes* and *no.*

If you answer a prospect's question with "yes" or "no," you may be going past the sale without making it.

Think about it for a moment. **When a prospect asks you a question, it is often a buying signal.** How do *you* answer a prospect's questions? As a salesperson, your highest skills are called upon when a prospect asks a question or shows an interest in buying. Your first inclination is to answer the question in the affirmative, if you know it to be true. *For example:*

• "Do you have this model?" *Yes.*
• "Does it come in green?" *Yes.*
• "Can you deliver on Tuesday?" *Yes.*
• "Are these in stock?" *Yes.*

**All of the above *yes* answers are not only wrong, they are answers that prolong the sale unnecessarily.**

You are also inclined to answer the prospect in a straightforward manner.

## *For example:*
- "What is your delivery lead time?" *Usually 2 weeks.*
- "How much notice do I have to give you?" *24 hours.*
- "When will the new model be out?" *January 30th.*

## These answers are also wrong. Very wrong.

### *The rule is ...*
## Use the prospect's question to confirm the sale.

*In other words, after you get the prospect's signal, form a response question that implies the answer and confirms that the prospect wants to buy what you're selling.*

*It's not as complicated as I just made it sound.*
## Here are some examples of confirming questions:
- "Do you have this model?" *Is this the model you want?* If the prospect says *yes*, all I have to do now is find out when he wants delivery, and I'm finished.
- "Does it come in green?" *Would you like it in green?*
- "Can you deliver on Tuesday?" *Is Tuesday the day you need it delivered?*
- "Are these in stock?" *Do you need immediate delivery?*
- "What is your delivery lead time?" *How soon do you need delivery?*
- "How much notice do I have to give you?" *How much notice do you usually have?*
- "How soon can someone be here?" *How soon do you need someone here?*

## You can also answer directly and still pose a closing question immediately thereafter. *For example:*
- "When will the new model be out?" *January 30. But we have special incentives to take the copier now. Let's compare which will be the best way for you to go. Fair enough?*
- "Do you have references?" *Here is the list. If our references are satisfactory, when would we be able to get our first assignment?*

## Here's the magic process:
1. Recognizing a buying signal is the sales discipline.
2. Being able to construct a response question (much more difficult) requires creativity and practice.
3. Delivering the response soft and smooth is the mark of the master professional salesperson. And usually the one who makes the sale.

Is there a secret to perfect question formation and delivery? Yes! And the answer is the same as the immortal question a tourist asked of a New York City cab driver: "How do you get to Carnegie Hall?" *Practice.*

*There are thousands of ways
to ask for the sale.*

# How to ask a closing question.

Thousands of pages have been written on closing the sale. You can have the best presentation in the world, you can be an expert in your product or your field of endeavor, but if you don't know how to close the sale, dining out for you will probably mean a drive-thru window.

The experts (J. Douglas Edwards, Zig Ziglar, Tom Hopkins, Earl Nightingale, etc.) define closing as: *Asking a question, the answer to which confirms the sale.* After you ask this all-important question, it is critical that you follow the oldest rule of selling: *After you ask a closing question, SHUT UP! The next person who speaks, loses.*

*There are thousands of ways to ask for the sale ...*
But you can set the tone for closing by telling the prospect what you want (the purpose or objective of your meeting) when you walk in the door. *Then, ask for the sale as soon as you hear the first buying signal.* An important guideline in asking for the sale is to try to eliminate *no* as a possible response to your question. You may not get the coveted *yes* as a result of eliminating the word *no*, but you will get dialogue or objections that will eventually lead to a *yes*.

Formulate your closing question in a way that responds to the prospect's main need or desire.

For example ... "Mr. Jones, would you like these T-shirts in light or dark colors?" or "How many shirts do you want in the darker color you said you liked?" or "Would you like delivery before or after the first of next month?" or "When did you want these delivered?" or "Are you paying by check or credit card?"

These are examples of using time, choice or preference methods – simple techniques that eliminate *no* as a response.

**Let the buyer decide,
but don't give him or her *no* as one of the choices.**

Other closing questions offer a possible *no* response. Before you ask this type of closing question, be sure you have confirmed the prospect's interest and he has given you concrete buying signals.

*For example* ... You're trying to sell Mr. Jones a fax machine. Jones says he needs a machine by Tuesday, **but has not yet said he is buying from you.** You ask, "Would you like me to deliver your new fax machine Monday evening?" *That is a solid closing question.* You have given the prospect the option of saying no, but it is unlikely he'll use it. (Even if Jones says *no*, ask: "When *would be* the most convenient time to make delivery?")

**The key is to ask for the sale in a sincere, friendly manner. Don't push or use high pressure. If you just stop talking after you ask the closing question, the tension in the air mounts real fast.**

A minute seems like an hour when the room is silent.

Self-confidence is important. The buyer will buy if you believe he will. Most salespeople don't ask for the sale because they're afraid of rejection, uncomfortable about the money, or not sharp enough to recognize the buying signals of a customer. I'm glad none of those apply to you.

# The oldest rule of sales still holds true ...

When you ask a question,
the answer to which confirms the sale ...

# Shut up!

*In my experience I have found the biggest flaw in failing to secure the order is the salesperson's inability to know when and how to ask for it.*

*The sale belongs to the closer.*
People love to be closed.

*The sale is more likely to be made
if the prospect can take ownership before
she actually commits to the sale.*

# Two breeds of the Puppy Dog Close.
## Breed 1 ... Simply irresistible

How can you adapt its power to your sales process?

The easiest way to sell a puppy is to give it to the prospective owner (and the kids) overnight "to see how they like it." Just try to get that puppy away from the kids the next morning. Thus the name Puppy Dog Close. It is an incredibly powerful sales tool that is used (with variation) by sales professionals around the world.

*Think about it for a moment.*
- Test drive the car.
- 30-day free trial membership.
- Try this in your home for 7 days.
- First issue of the magazine is free.
- 2-day demo of our copier in your office.

**All these are forms of the Puppy Dog Close.**

**We're telling the prospect ...** this product is great but you may not know it until you touch it, try it, take it home, or use it. If I can get the prospect to touch and/or try my product, I'm more likely to get him to buy it.

**It's ownership before the sale. It breaks down resistance to the point of acceptance.**

You can enhance the use of this tool with the words *if you qualify*; this means you can determine if prospects can afford your product before they try it out ... then if they want to keep it, financing is prearranged.

Obviously not all businesses can use the Puppy Dog Close, but more and more corporate sales strategies call for trying to get the product into the hands of the buyer for a test or trial as part of the selling process.

Salespeople know statistically the sale is more likely to be made if the prospect can take ownership before he or she actually commits to the sale.

When you try on a new suit or dress, before you actually make the purchase, you see yourself owning it …The fit, the feel, the look, and the salesperson chortling how good it looks, are often more influential than the price. You can almost see yourself at the office or trade show in your new clothing … then you say, "OK, I'll take it."

If you doubt the power of this close, go to a pet store and ask if you can have a puppy overnight for evaluation. You might want to take your checkbook along, just in case.

How old is the Puppy Dog Close? God gave Moses the 10 Commandment Tablets: "Try them," he said. Pretty strong close. Still working. After 5,000 years he still has billions of customers.

◆ ◆ ◆ ◆ ◆ ◆

*If you chase the world, it runs from you.*
*If you run from the world, it chases you.*
*– Hari Dass*

## *Breed 2 … Let the dog chase you*

When I was 16, I decided to get a puppy. Early one morning the puppy got away. She ran for blocks through the neighborhood as I chased her fruitlessly. I was panicked. Surely the dog would get hit by a car. I ran home as fast as I could to awaken my dad to get in the car and find my dog. Dad reluctantly began to get out of bed. I spun to race to the car – and tripped over the dog.

*The sales moral of the story is:* Let the prospect chase you. Sometimes you're better off baiting or challenging the prospect. Often we are so eager to sell, we don't give the prospect enough room to buy.

*There are variations of this technique that are from the old school of selling but are still worth looking at …*

**The negative sale** ... (take it away if the buyer shows interest) has been touted through the years as the most powerful selling device. When motel franchises were first sold in the 1950s, a salesman would come into town, visit a local bank, and say there were "only" 10 shares in this new motel at $50,000 per share. He would ask the banker for leads – and get them.

He would make group presentations that started out, "I believe all the shares are spoken for, but I'll go through my presentation, take your application, and if I get a cancellation, I'll give you a call." I was with my friend's dad that day. He eagerly filled out the application. To his amazement, he was called – someone had canceled. We found out later everyone was called.

Good tactic? Well, it worked. Ethical? You decide.

**The "Can you qualify?" sale.** Rather than pushing the prospect to buy, you challenge him to be *qualified* (have the money, get the credit) to purchase. Often used in door-to-door sales, or big items requiring credit, like cars and mobile homes. You can laugh at it, but it still is the backbone of the sales efforts of many national companies.

*How soon do you close a sale?*
*As soon as you walk in the door!*

# Eat dessert first!

You're at one of those banquets where they put out the salad and dessert before anyone arrives. So, when I sit down, I immediately eat the dessert. People are anywhere from surprised to shocked. If they make a comment, I ask if they're going to eat theirs. If they say no, I ask them to pass it over.

If someone gives me a choice of apple pie and ice cream or lima beans, I'm not an idiot. Dessert is to eating as closing is to selling. It's the best part. Tradition says do it last – I say do it first.

I begin to close the sale within 10 seconds of entering a prospect's office. I state my objective of the meeting, and I tell him or her what I would like to do. I tell them my three strategies of business …

> ➤ I'm here to help.
> ➤ I seek to establish a long-term relationship.
> ➤ I'm going to have fun.

Stating your objective and philosophy at the outset puts the prospect at ease. It gets the meeting off to a great start. It establishes credibility and respect. And it clears the way for meaningful information exchange and rapport building.

Tell the prospect what you want when you walk in the door.
*Then, ask for the sale as soon as you hear the first buying signal.*

We were raised to think in patterns set by others. To be as successful as you want to be, it may take getting out of those traditional patterns. Most people don't get out of their comfort zone. Most people don't attain the level of success they set out to achieve. I wonder if there's any correlation between those two statements.

## Don't save room for dessert …
## Eat it first. It's a sweet way to close.

*Understand how your product is used*
*so that you can understand*
*how to sell it most effectively.*

# The most powerful close in the world is not a close.
## *The Understanding Close*

Product knowledge is useless until you know how your product is used on the job to satisfy and profit the customer. On the surface this seems simple, but I challenge you as to how far you have gone to understand how your customers actually use your product or service on a real-world, day-to-day basis. How do they use it in their work environment?

*Understand how your product is used so that you can understand*
*how to sell it most effectively.*

In most cases, the end user is not the purchaser. The person who buys the copier or computer is often not the person who runs it every day. The end user is the person who will lead you to important sales information.

It's easy to find out. Go visit your customers. Watch, ask, and listen.

➤ Go watch your product being used.

➤ Ask questions about their likes and dislikes.

➤ Ask what they like best.

➤ Ask what they like least.

➤ Ask what they would change and how they would change it.

➤ Ask about service they've received after the sale.

➤ Observe the operations made by everyone connected.

➤ Ask if they would buy it again.

➤ Ask if they would recommend it to a business associate.

➤ Write down or record everything they say!

*Seeing your product in action and questioning its use puts a new (and powerful) perspective on how you sell it.*

- It's customer insight at its highest level.
- It's product knowledge that no factory training can provide.
- It's the best (and least-used) opportunity to gain knowledge about a customer's real needs.
- It's a chance to see the benefits of your product in action.

## When your visit is over ...

- Document it.
- Thank your customers for their time.
- Report what changed as a result of it.
- Make recommendations.

## Try to measure the value of these five benefits ...

1. You've built incredible rapport.
2. You've taken giant relationship steps.
3. Competition will have a tougher time getting in the door.
4. You've gained indispensable knowledge that will lead you to more sales.
5. Your customer now sees you as a consultant rather than a salesman.

Now when you're on a sales call, you can discuss using the product in the customer's work environment, and have a hands-on basis for your expertise. You can ask questions that get the prospect talking about use after purchase. ("If you purchased, how would you use this differently than the one you have now? My experience has shown me ...")

## And if you do it right, it's not only a learning opportunity -- it's a selling opportunity.

# The Book of Persistence

**5.3**

## Blood, Sweat, & Commissions

Persistence ...

I could retitle this
The Book of Pest Control.
How to follow-up without
bugging the client.

Persistence
(with the right attitude)
is the key to success.

If you believe in your
product, if you believe in
yourself, then you march
to success.

Obstacles can't stop you.
Problems can't stop you.
Most important of all, other
people can't stop you.

Only you can stop you.

Persistence is your desire
to succeed combined with
your creative presence.

Your persistence must be
as relentless as the tides.

Roll on ...

*The method or system you use
to organize your follow-ups
can make or break the sale.*

# No follow-up system? No sale!

Since 98% of all sales are NOT made on the first call, follow-up is as important as any part of the selling process. **Follow-up starts early.** When you respond to an inquiry call, either by phone or by appointment, that first sales call you make is actually a follow-up.

*You must have an organized
method or system of following up if you want to make the sale.*

There are several types of follow-up systems. Pick one that works for you, your type of business, the size and complexity of the sale, and one that you will use faithfully.

*Here are the choices:*

**1. ACT Database** – This program (and others like it) are specifically designed for contact management, organization, and sales follow-up assistance. It's a bells and whistles organization system with e-mail merge and date-to-follow-up alarm reminders and a bunch of other fields to help track (and keep control of) the sale. This program lets you retrieve data a number of different ways such as by company name, contact name, phone number, city, state, or e-mail address. There are a number of programs like this to choose from (ACT is what we use at my office). Get one that is the most user friendly and has the options you need.

**2. Get a PDA** – This is an easy device to learn and use, and it is wireless. Aha! Wireless is the way to go in the 21st century. A PDA, regardless of brand, will keep all your important information like names, phone numbers, e-mail addresses, appointments, and notes right at your fingertips while you are away from your desk. And it is light enough and small enough to fit in your pocket or your purse.

**3. Use a Card Scanner** – Forget the old way of saving stacks of business cards. That just takes up room in your desk drawers. Invest in a card scanner. It is only about one hundred dollars, and well worth the money considering the time and space it will save you. The card scanner does all the data entry work for you. You just insert the card into the scanner, and it will copy the image and all the information and upload it electronically to your personal database. The scanner copies the exact color, picture and information on the card and stores it in your database for you, so there is no need to keep the hard copy of the card anymore. You have it on file, electronically, on your desktop!

**4. 3 x 5 or 5 x 8 card file (staple business cards to save time)** – a combination of the business card and notebook system; great if many follow-ups are needed before a prospect commits to a sale. Many people with desk jobs tend to use this system, and I don't know why.

**5. Daytimer** – good because you usually have it handy to write notes and meeting dates. It's bad because you're constantly rewriting, and nothing is in any kind of order. A daily planner/calendar is a must in conjunction with any system to keep your appointments and notes of the moment – but even this is going the way of the computer. (Get literate if you're not.)

**6. Yellow pad** – not a very good system. Pages get lost, constant recopying, and you panic when you misplace the pad.

**7. Scraps of paper** – guaranteed to make you look bad, lose sales, and eventually find a new career.

*Notes to better productivity ...*

- Have special 8.5 x 11 lead sheets around the office for inquiries instead of message pads. Have a checklist and plenty of lined note space on the sheet to determine what type of follow-ups need to be or have been made, and when. Even if you use another system, the lead sheets provide information necessary to get the sale off on the right foot.
- Update all information the same moment you receive it or do it.
- Photocopy everything once a week. Keep backup copies in case of loss.

*Tracking is critical in the follow-up process.*
*When you have all your information on computer,*
*your mind is free to create.*
*That's part of the secret of sales achievement.*

*By creating unusual sales tools and using the ordinary tools effectively, your sales will increase significantly.*

# Sales tools are a vital part of the follow-up process.

Your ability to create follow-up selling tools can significantly enhance your image with the prospect and make the sale more often.

*Sales tools are the most underemployed weapon in the selling process.*

Defined as an aid or prop in the selling process, sales tools can be a tremendous boost to productivity, especially if several follow-ups are needed to make the sale.

There are everyday tools like the phone, fax, letters, brochures, and literature, but the extraordinary salesperson creates out-of-the-ordinary tools to entice the prospect to buy now and to choose his or her product over the competition.

Review the tools listed below and see if they might be effective in your sales game plan …

• **Personal note (imprinted with your company name and logo, greeting card size)** … handwritten. Better and more effective than the common business letter. Gives the prospect the feeling that you care.

• **A package of letters from satisfied customers** … No salesperson is more persuasive than third-party endorsements.

• **A third-party mutual friend endorsement** … An incredibly powerful tool. Your friend is far more influential than you.

• **Support articles** … Like a copy of a favorable article recently printed that can give you an additional reason to mail and call. It doesn't have to be about your business. It's better if it's about his business or best if it's about his personal interests.

• **A videotape supporting your product/service** ... Prepared by you or your supplier; if a picture is worth 1,000 words, a video is worth 1,000,000.

• **Meet at a networking event (lead club, chamber function, etc.)** ... Business/social engagements are the heart of business life.

• **An invitation to your facility** ... Building the business relationship by showing yours with pride. A welcome sign for the visitor, and happy, enthusiastic greetings by all members of your team. Make the tour memorable. Serve great food, issue tickets, give a memento. *Ask yourself:* Will the prospect go back to his office and talk about this visit? If not, change it so he will.

• **Ad specialty** ... Small, useful (Post-it Note pad, coffee mug, T-shirt), or unusual item that will be used, seen, or talked about.

• **Lunch appointment** ... Spending a few extra dollars can often lead to the sale. It will also get the personal information that leads to a relationship.

• **After-work meeting** ... Meeting the prospect after hours can be more relaxed and informative. Get to know and like your prospect. People will buy from their friends first.

• **Tickets** ... Sporting events, cultural events, and seminar tickets are appreciated and can help build a relationship. (Go with the customer.)

• **Letters and faxes** ... Can be used effectively if short, informative, and humorous.

• **Telephone** ... The second most powerful weapon in selling (live visits being the first). Calls can set up meetings, give information, and close the deal; but calls can get redundant, and many times don't get returned. It's also hard to get a signed contract over the phone, and checks don't squeeze through the little holes very well. **Use the phone with respect, stay in control at all times, always have a purpose for calling, and NEVER get off the call without having set the next meeting or contact, as well as confirming it.**

Additional telephone information, and *how to follow-up without feeling like you're bugging the prospect* is in the next chapter.

## Sales tools build sales ... if you use 'em.

*I'd love to hear about tools that you use.*
*Fax your best or most unusual tool to 704/333-1011.*

*Missed Opportunities*

# Tickets!

They are the most coveted perk in business.
Sporting events, theater, and concerts can make
a prospect's or customer's mouth water
(and pen drip with ink).

## Don't just give them away!
## Go *with* the prospect or customer.

*It's a great opportunity to build the friendship and
strengthen your grip on his or her business.*

*If you are creative, helpful, and sincere
in your follow-ups, the prospect will not
perceive you as hounding him or her.*

# Most sales are made after the seventh *no.*

It takes 5 to 10 exposures (follow-ups) to a prospect to make the first sale.
The prospect may not actually say *no* seven times, but each time you
follow up and the prospect doesn't buy, he's saying, "Not now, buddy; do
something else for me; I'm still shopping around; I haven't met with my
partner; try again later; in short, you haven't sold me yet."

*As a professional salesperson, you'd better have what it takes
to persevere through the follow-up process and not quit.*

Be willing to put forth the effort it takes to get past the seventh *no*
and get the sale ... *or consider taking a job with a salary.*

*Here are some follow-up guidelines to ensure early closing success ...*
• Know your prospect's hot buttons (things you think will make the
prospect buy), and work with them in constructing your follow-up plan.
• Present new information relative to the sale.
• Be creative in your style and presentation manner.
• Be sincere about your desire to help the customer first, and put your
commission second.
• Be direct in your communication. Beating around the bush will only
frustrate the prospect (and probably cause him to buy elsewhere).
Answer all questions. Don't patronize the prospect.
• Be friendly. People like to buy from friends.
• Use humor ... Be funny. People love to laugh. Making your prospect
laugh is a great way to establish common ground and rapport.
• When in doubt, sell benefits.
• Don't be afraid to ask for the sale. Often.

If there were a formula for following up it would be ...
new information + creative + sincere + direct + friendly + humor = SALE
*... but there isn't an exact formula.*

Every follow-up is different, and elements from the above guidelines must be chosen as called for. Here are a few lead-in lines you might try so that you don't feel uneasy about how to start the conversation:

- I thought of a few things that might help you decide …
- Something new has occurred that I thought you would like to know about …
- There has been a change in status …
- I was thinking about you and called to tell you about …

Don't say: "I called to see if you got my letter [info or whatever]." It sounds dumb and it gives the prospect a way out. If he doesn't want to talk to you, he'll say, "No, I never got it." Where does that leave you? Nowhere.

Why not try: "I sent you some [name the stuff] the other day and I wanted to go over a couple of things with you personally, because they weren't self-explanatory …"

*It's likely you won't bug the prospect if …*

- He's a salesman himself.
- You have something new, creative, or funny to say.
- You're short and to the point.
- He's genuinely interested in your product or service.
- He returns your calls right away.
- He likes you.
- He seems to need what you're selling.

*It's likely you will bug the prospect if …*

- You call more than three times without a returned call.
- You ask dumb or pushy questions (probably because you didn't listen well in the first place).
- You are perceived as insincere.
- You exert pressure too soon or too often.
- You are rude to the prospect or anyone on his staff.

*Follow-up* is another word for persistence. Your ability to follow up will determine your success in sales. Ask any professional salesperson the secret for success. He or she will answer …

# persistence.

*Somewhere between diapers and getting*
*our business card printed, we forget how*
*tenacious we need to be to make that sale.*

# You've been selling
# since you were a kid!

*I would like to acknowledge Joe Bonura, of Bonura Training Systems,*
*whose excellent seminar provided the inspiration for this story.*

How many *no*'s are you willing to take before you give up the sale?
Remember when you were 7 years old, in line with your mother at the
supermarket, and asked, "Mom, can I have this candy bar?" *That was a*
*closing question if there ever was one.*

"No," she replies. You, the master salesman, ignore the first *no* and respond,
"Please, can I have the candy bar?" Mom is a bit put off by now; with her
mind preoccupied with the grocery tab, she says, "I said NO!" *No* number 2
is now safely out of the way, and you respond, "Aw, come on, PLEASE!"

Now the momma prospect is emphatic. "Absolutely NO," she thunders *no*
number 3. (Sometimes she will actually spell it out: N-O.) *No* number three
is now out of the way. Time to move in for the kill. Let's try to find out
what the objection is here. "Why can't I have a candy bar, Mom?" This is a
classic example of a direct question going straight at the real reason for the
first three *no*'s. How did you learn these sales skills so early in life?

"Because it'll spoil your dinner," she responds, true to form. Now is your big
chance. Overcome this objection (the fourth put-off), and it's in the bag
(the grocery bag, that is). "No it won't, Mom. I promise to eat it after
dinner," you reply in your most sincere tone.

She's on the ropes now, about to cave in, but being the true sales-reluctant
prospect, she isn't going to just cave in. "Well, I don't know," she weakly
states the fifth negative response. You see your opening and immediately
bellow, "PLEASE!" in that endearing kid mixture of song and whine. "OK,"

she says. "But don't you dare eat it until *after* dinner." (She has to get out of the loss gracefully, so she emphasizes the caveat "after dinner" to save face to the cashier, who is grinning.)

VICTORY! You made the sale, and it only took five *no*'s to get it. You were prepared to go at least 10. Possibly risk a hit or two on the butt, and in some cases actually throw a fit in public. Think about that for a second. When you were 7, you were willing to risk public embarrassment, corporal punishment, and verbal abuse to make the sale.

*Somewhere between diapers and getting your business card printed, you forgot how tenacious you need to be to make that sale.*

If you're looking for the best examples of how to overcome the obstacles and objections to sales, just sit back and reminisce. The candy bar, the first date, staying out after curfew, getting the keys to the car, getting a raise in allowance, getting off punishment to go to the dance or getting a date … all sales. All were full of *no*'s and objections. But did you hang in there against all odds? Were you willing to risk? Willing to take a beating? Did you eventually make the sale?

*I'll bet your closing ratio as a kid was better than 90%.*

**How much money would you be making if your closing ratio were that high today? Forget candy bars -- you'd have enough cash to buy the entire grocery store.**

On average it takes seven impressions, exposures, *no*'s, or objections to get the sale. What's the secret to getting to the seventh *no*?

# *Persistence.*

*Mail is a quick, inexpensive way
to get in front of your customer
or prospect more often.*

# Stamp out competition with a 37¢ sales call.

How often are you in front of your customers or prospects? *Answer:* Not as often as you should be. It takes 7 to 10 impressions to get a sale and begin to build a relationship. You can get there more quickly if you use the mail. If you can't be there in person, send a letter.

An effective communication by mail can solidify a deal. Do it once a week and the number of new orders, volume of repeat business, and percentage of customers remaining loyal will drastically increase.

Sometimes the writing is already done for you. Cut out or photocopy an article about something that pertains to your customer's business, or something you know he's interested in. Put a Post-it Note on the article saying, "Saw this and thought it might be of interest to you," and sign your first name. It will be remembered.

*Here are 13 valuable mail-ways to get in front of your customers and prospects ...*

1. Thank-you note for an order.
2. Thank-you note for a referral.
3. Thank-you note for continued (and valued) business.
4. Short note about a positive meeting or phone call.
5. Article from a magazine or newspaper about his business.
6. Something about his competition.
7. A joke, cartoon, or something funny.
8. Announcement of a new product.

9. Special sale or offer.

10. A newsletter (from your company).

11. A hot lead.

12. Notice of a meeting or seminar that might be of benefit to him.

13. A reminder of a pending order or reorder.

None of the above costs more than 75¢ including paper and postage. What a value! You get a sales call, more orders, build goodwill, build loyalty, build a long-term relationship, and make the customer or prospect feel great.

*Use personal handwritten notes whenever possible. We use them ourselves because we know our customer appreciates the time it took to send a handwritten note.*

*Have trouble putting it into words?*
*Go to The Book of Communications –*
*The sales letter will work, if you get it write.*

A 37¢ communication is an inexpensive
sales tool that can help you win and keep a customer ...
especially if a competitor is calling.

*Faxing is instant contact.*
*Sometimes it can be the difference*
*between your order or your competitor's.*

# The fax machine will breed sales if you harness its power.

A fax demands attention. When a fax is received, it is hand-delivered (and read) immediately. Faxing is still a technology where many salespeople have yet to discover its power and immediacy.

If speed of response is important to your selling process, the fax looms large as a vital tool. It can actually be your competitive edge if used properly.

Faxing provides instant information. I have often faxed documents in the middle of a (telephone) sales conversation.

*Here are 21.5 selling reasons to fax someone today ...*
1. To be first with important information.
2. To get back with a price, a quote, or a proposal for a prospect's immediate need.
3. To get information or a letter (or an invoice) to a prospect who claims he never got it in the mail.
4. To change a contract.
5. To get a solid selling message through when your call isn't returned.
6. To beg for a returned phone call, or tell a prospect his voice mail is out of order.
7. To punch a point; to emphasize.
8. To answer a question about something germane to the sale (same day as question was asked).
9. To warn of an impending price rise or change in product.
10. To introduce a new product or service.
11. To thank.
12. To inform.
13. To congratulate.
14. To remind of a date or deadline.

15. To confirm an appointment.
16. To pass around a great joke or cartoon (A word of caution – Many folks on the receiving end will see your humor, so keep it clean).
17. To entertain with a humorous fax cover sheet.
18. To send an urgent request to meet because of a pending change (price increase, increase in productivity, new technology).
19. To show a referral letter from a satisfied customer.
20. To show an article that appeared in a local or national publication that supports the need for your services.
21. To send something that shows you know about the prospect's business/industry.
21.5 *To demonstrate a sense of immediacy that indicates your desire to serve and respond quickly – a vital component in building a long-term business relationship.*

*Fax your way to the prospect's heart and wallet.*

Proper use of the fax is one thing. Improper abuse of the fax is another. Like all aspects of sales, timing is the essential ingredient.

A fax is to sales as trump is to bridge. You only play trump when it is to your maximum advantage to do so. Misplay your cards and you will lose the hand and probably the game. Overusing or abusing the fax destroys its ability to work in your favor.
• Avoid words like urgent, critical, and emergency.
• Don't use the fax in place of a cold call, or as a first contact.
• Don't fax your brochure or a sales pitch. It will be file-thirteened in a New York minute (38 seconds).

## Consider these facts about the fax:

• **The fax still gets immediate attention.** You have a page or two to get information to your prospect – use the space wisely. Say only what is necessary to achieve your next objective.

• **Creativity is essential.** If your fax is clever, different, and contains concise information, you will gain confidence and attention.

• **Always fax on the *fine* or *detail* setting.** It takes longer, but when your fax comes through crisp and clear to your prospect, it reflects the quality of your company … and vice versa.

• **The fax machine will breed sales** – if you harness its power.

E-mail immediacy? That will come in my next book – Stay tuned.

**All-time great ideas in selling ...**

# Fax a copy
# of your
# daily appointment book
# with open dates
# and times circled.

*(You can even show an appointment listed
with a competitor.)*

# *Cover it!*

Let your fax cover sheet reflect your creativity. Don't be afraid to use a little humor. Lawyers have fancy notices on their cover sheet that basically say, *"If you read this fax and it is not addressed to you, your eyes will fall out, and you'll burn in hell."*

To keep things in perspective, I created my own set of fax rules that appear on my fax cover sheet:

1. Deliver this document at once to the person named above.
2. Don't read the fax unless it's directed to you, nosy.
3. Our phone # is 704/333-1112 if you need to call.
4. Our fax # is 704/333-1011 if you need to fax.
5. Hurry up.

I get about five comments a week
about how someone enjoyed our fax cover sheet.
How many do you get?

*The big question is*
**Do you leave a message?**
*The big answer is*
**It depends!**

# Oh, *NO!* ... not voice mail -- AAHHHHH!!!

*Press 1* ... if you want to leave a message.

*Press 2* ... if you don't think your call will ever be returned.

*Press 3* ... if you've already left three messages, haven't had your call returned, and want to send a bolt of lightning directly through the phone and strike the butt of the person who won't return your call.

*Press 4* ... if you want to shoot the person who installed this voice mail.

Voice mail can be the scourge of the salesperson, but it doesn't have to be. Voice mail is a tool used to establish contact. It is not used to make a sale. Your objective is to leave a message that will elicit a return call.

*Your option is to ignore voice mail*
*and use your resourcefulness to get in*
*direct contact with your prospect.*

*Here are 5 guidelines that define the sales perspective of voice mail:*

    1. It's a game – play to win.

    2. It's here to stay – know how to get around it.

    3. Know when to leave a message
       (and when not to).

    4. Know how to leave a message that will get
       a response.

    5. Be resourceful. Be creative. Be memorable.

*The big question is* Do you leave a message? *The big answer is* It depends! Since there is no cut-and-dry answer, why not develop a method that works for you? **Don't listen to what everyone else says. There is always a way around it and there is always a way to get your call returned. Figure out a way to make voice mail work *for* you.**

## Do leave a message if ...

• You've spoken with the person before and gotten positive feedback.
• You're following up a good (interested) lead.
• You have valuable information the prospect really needs to know.
• You have a *prepared* message that has enough impact to get the prospect to respond.

## Don't leave a message if ...

• It's a cold call or exploratory call.
• It's likely you're selling something the prospect already has.
• It's likely you're up against an existing relationship.
• You're trying to raise funds for a charity.
• You're selling insurance, stocks, or financial planning services.

## Getting around voice mail and getting directly to the prospect ...

• Press "0" to get an operator or secretary.
  Ask if the prospect can be paged.
• Tell the operator you don't want voice mail and ask how you can reach your prospect live.
• Tell an administrative person you got lost in the voice mail options, you're not a college graduate, and can they please help you. If you *nicely* act exasperated, you can get someplace – especially at the CEO executive administrative level.
• Find the administrative person and get the prospect's schedule of normal arrival and departure.
• Get someone else to book a tentative appointment.
• Call before the gatekeeper arrives
  (7:45 to 8:30 A.M.).
• Call after the gatekeeper leaves
  (5:15 to 6:30 P.M.).
• Call the sales department – they'll tell you everything if they think you can help. Plus they're more fun to deal with than administrative types.
• In a larger company, call the publicity or public relations department – it's their job to give out information.
• Find a champion or comrade – someone within the company who likes you or believes in what you do.

**Use your fax machine as an alternate way to get through ...**
- Fax pages from your appointment book with open dates and times circled (show an appointment listed with a competitor).
- Fax a joke or cartoon.
- Fax a referral letter from a satisfied customer that relates to his business.
- Fax an urgent request to repair his or her voice mail. Tell the prospect to notify the company that sold the system to come fix it because you have left several messages and they're evidently not getting through, so the only thing you can figure is that it's broken. ("Surely, Mr. Jones, you're not ignoring my calls.")

*(See the section on harnessing the selling power of the fax ... for more ideas.)*

Voice mail is not all bad. It's great when you're in the middle of a sale and need to get important or timely information to a customer. Voice mail is helpful when you are trying to reach an existing customer. It's just frustrating at the beginning of a sales cycle.

Your challenge is to beat voice mail by using the one sales tool you always carry with you – your brain.

*Just a note on hypocrisy:*

Part of total quality is totally returning phone calls.
If I had a dollar for every executive preaching TQM
who doesn't have the courtesy to return a call,
I could buy my own voice mail system
and not return his call.

# It's a shame that returning phone calls can't be made mandatory.

*Leaving messages is a risk.
If you do, create a message
that will get response.*

# "Leave a message and I'll be glad to return your call" … Not!

*"Press 1 if you'd like to leave a message. I'll be glad to return your call as soon as I can."* Right. And Santa will bring you a pony if you're a good little boy.

*"Press 2 if you're selling something I don't want."* That's a lot closer to the truth.

Why won't they call you back? When you get someone's voice mail and decide to leave a message, what steps can you take to ensure that your call will be returned? Lots.

*If you leave a message, here is a collection of techniques that have gotten calls returned:*

• **First name and number only (in a very businesslike manner).** It seems that calls are returned in inverse proportion to the amount of information left.

• **Be funny.** Clean wit will get response.

• **Be indirect.** "I was going to mail you important information and I wanted to confirm your address."

• **Offer fun.** "I have two extra tickets to the Hornets game and I thought you might be interested. [Here's the sure shot:] Please call me if you can't go so that I'm able to give the tickets to someone else."

• **Remind the prospect where you met if it was a positive first meeting.**

• **Dangle the carrot.** Leave just enough information to entice.

• **Ask a provocative or thought-provoking question.**

*Note:* **There is never a reason to give your sales pitch on voice mail.** No one is there to say yes. Your objective is to make contact. Your objective is to provide enough information to create positive response.

## An all-time classic technique ...

was offered by Thomas J. Elijah III, of Elijah & Co. Real Estate, at a SalesMasters™ meeting. Thomas said, "Leave a partial message that includes your name and phone number, then pretend to get cut off in midsentence as you're getting to the important part of the message. Cut it off in midword. It works like a charm because the prospect can't stand not knowing the rest of the information or thinks his voice mail is broken."

*Here are a few examples of the Elijah Method:*
Leave your name and number, *then* deliver half a sentence to peak interest:

- Your name came up in an important conversation today with Hugh ...
- They were talking about you and said ...
- I have a deal that could deliver you a hundred thou ...
- I'm interested in your ...
- I have your ...
- I found your ...
- I have information about your ...
- Your competition said ...
- I'm calling about your inheritance ...
- Are you the [person's full name] who ...
- We wanted to be sure you got your share of ...
- I'm calling about the money you left at ...
- Hello. I'm calling for Ed Mc ...

I had to call Elijah recently to get some information. I tried his technique on him, cutting off my message in midsentence. I said, "I'm going to quote you in my column this week and I need ..." He called me back in under 3 minutes laughing hysterically. This technique could revolutionize message leaving. I've been using it ever since, and it works. *Be careful about how far you go on the humor with someone you don't know.*

If you're making several calls, make sure you document your messages so that you can be on top of it immediately if/when your call is returned. There's nothing worse (or more stupid) than getting a returned call and having no idea who it's from.

Voice messaging companies say that voice mail helps companies route messages faster, and the recording system offered by voice messaging reduces errors and allows complete messages to be left. True, but many of the people who have voice mail (especially the ones you're trying to reach) use it as a dodge.

If you're thinking about buying voice mail, don't just look at convenience. Before you make a commitment to a specific system, *consider the impact on your customers.*

*Will they be better served? Will you maintain friendly, human service in spite of the voice-mail system?*

**Don't confuse *voice mail* with *automatic attendant* systems. Automatic attendant, where the computer actually answers the phone, is the single worst business invention ever.**

Here is the most customer-friendly type of voice-mail system to use:

1. Human answers.
2. Human determines if the person you're calling is in by ringing their phone and monitoring the response.
3. If not in, human returns and says, "Mr. Jones is not in. Would you like me to help you personally, take your message personally, or would you like to leave a detailed message on his or her voice mail?"
4. You faint from the shock.

Press 1 if you hate voice mail. Press the hot button of the prospect if you want to get a call back and make the sale in spite of it. Press on.

# If you do leave a message on someone's voice mail, ask yourself, "Would I return this call?"

# If you hesitate to say *yes*, change your message.

**All-time great ideas in selling ...**

"Leave a partial message
that includes your name and
phone number and
pretend to get cut off in
midsentence as you're getting
to the important part of the message."

*-- Thomas J. Elijah, III*

*Take a risk.*
*Take a chance.*
*Use your creativity.*
*Don't be afraid to make a mistake,*
*don't be afraid to fail, don't worry about*
*rejection, and don't quit just because*
*some yahoo won't see you.*

# Can't get an appointment?
## Try harder. Try smarter.

*The guy won't appoint me.*
*I can't get an appointment.*
*He didn't show for his appointment.*
*He won't commit to an appointment.*
*She won't return my phone call.*
*He has rescheduled me three times in 2 weeks.*

Welcome to the reality of a salesperson. The above situations are not problems – they are symptoms. When these symptoms (excuses) occur, there are unstated but obvious objections. Pick the one that applies to you. If you think none of these apply to you, think again:

- You haven't established enough interest.
- You haven't given any value.
- You haven't created or uncovered need.
- You are unable to or have not established rapport.
- The prospect is already doing business with someone she is satisfied with.
- You have been talking (telling) instead of asking (selling).
- The prospect doesn't see you as important enough to carve out time to meet.

- The prospect feels "sale" rather
  than "relationship."
- The prospect has an unfavorable impression
  of you, your company, or your product.

Get creative, Jack (Jackie). You're not going to let little things like that prevent you from achieving your objective. Are you?

### *Here are some strategies and tactics that have worked:*

• **Get referred.** Find someone you know who knows who you want to appoint. Get this person to call Mr. Elusive for you if possible (to smooth the way, or find out the real reason he won't see you).

• **Use the fax.** Send a referral letter, a top 10 list, a cartoon, or your schedule for next week with the open times circled. Use the fax to open the door.

• **Send a plant, flowers, or a small gift.** You will be amazed how much ice you can melt with a small gift. Flowers can get through a brick wall no matter how thick it is. The right gift basket will bring a remarkable response.

• **Get close to the administrative person who knows your prospect best.** Find out what your prospect likes. His typical schedule – arrival and departure times. Gather information.

• **Arrange to meet the prospect at a networking event.** Trade association meeting, chamber of commerce event, ball game. Want to know where he'll be? Ask the prospect's administrative person or sales team.

• **Send a provocative letter without being provoking.** Ask questions or make statements in the letter that make the prospect think. Don't sell your product; just pique interest and sell an appointment.

• **Cold call at a time when you know (from the administrative person) he'll be there.** The best time is before the workday begins or after it is over.

• **Take a risk; take a chance.** Use your creativity. Don't be afraid to make a mistake, don't be afraid to fail, don't worry about rejection, and don't quit just because some yahoo won't see you. If you believe you can help the other person, never quit.

# All-time great ideas in selling ...

*Want a few closing lines to get the appointment? Here are three:*

1. If you must use the dreaded alternative-choice close, ask it this way: *Would you rather have breakfast or lunch?*

2. A better approach is to ask the prospect when are his open (best) times to meet, then suggest a meal.

3. The best approach is honesty. *My objective is to help, Bill, but I don't know if I can. We'll exchange information at lunch. If I feel I can help you, I'll tell you; and if I can't help, I'll tell you that too. FAIR ENOUGH?* It's hard to say *no* to that.

*BONUS: There are benefits that transcend getting the appointment. Using your creative power achieves four other purposes:*

1. It will enable you to achieve your short-term goal of appointing the prospect (and perhaps make the sale).

2. It will provide you with a proven method of approach that will work again for you and for others.

3. It will prove that your creativity is a tool you can begin to rely on.

4. It will make you feel great that you persisted and achieved your goal.

# The Book of Lamentations

> "You can't be a winner if you're a whiner ... wiener."
>
> *-- Jeffrey Gitomer*

6.1

*You don't have to sell it …*
*95% of the time the customer will buy it!*

# When bad sales happen to good people.

There's good and bad in all professions. Sales is no exception. Surveys show the only thing lower than a salesman in the minds of many Americans is a politician.

I got a call from a guy who said he went to a car dealer with cash wanting a new car. The salesman was so bad, he left without purchasing, still hasn't purchased, and has told 25 to 50 people how bad the experience was. Unfortunately this is far from an isolated experience. There are thousands of examples of poor salesmanship. But it isn't you. Is it?

Every business owner and sales pro reading this will swear, "It can't happen here." And they are dead wrong. Salespeople get cocky, think they know it all, think the customer is stupid or unwise to their tactics, treat everyone in the same manner, and end up losing the sale.

They fail to focus on the fundamental elements to position the customer or prospect for the buy. Relax – you don't always have to *sell* it. If you do it right, 95% of the time the customer will *buy* it!

Here are 10 common mistakes made by know-it-all salespeople (who actually know little or nothing at all):

**1. Prejudging the prospect** – Either by looks, dress, or speech, you have made up your mind what type of person this is … whether they have money or will buy.

**2. Poor prospect qualification** – failure to ask the right questions about what the prospect wants or needs before the selling process begins.

**3. Not listening** – concentrating on a *selling* angle instead of trying to understand how the prospect wants (needs) to *buy*.

**4. Condescension** – acting or talking above (talking down to) the prospect. Making the buyer feel unequal in the selling/buying process. Lack of respect.

**5. Pressure to buy today** – If you have to resort to those tactics, it's because you are afraid the customer might find a better deal elsewhere. Also indicates a "no relationship" attitude.

**6. Not addressing needs** – If you listen to prospects, they will tell you exactly what they want or need. Sell back something that addresses those needs, and the prospect will buy it. Don't sell in terms of you, sell in terms of the prospect.

**7. Telegraphing closes and hard selling** – "If I can get you this price, will you buy it today?" is a repulsive sales line reserved for salespeople in need of training, or salespeople who like losing sales. When you close, don't make it obvious.

**8. Making the buyer doubt your intentions** – If you change from friendly to pressure at the end of the presentation, or change terms or prices, the buyer loses confidence – and you lose the sale.

**9. Lack of sincerity** – *Sincerity is the key. If you can fake that, you've got it made*, is an old sales adage. It's half true. Sincerity is the key to building trust and establishing a relationship with a prospect who will become a customer if you are successful at conveying the feeling.

**10. Poor attitude** – "I'm doing you a favor by selling you. Don't ask me to go out of my way, because I won't."

Here is an easy self-test to determine if you are losing customers. *Can you answer yes to these?*
♥ Do I know my prospect's needs before I begin the selling process?
♥ Am I addressing the needs of the prospect during the sale?
♥ Do I look at the prospect when she is talking?
♥ Do I take notes and ask questions to strengthen my understanding?
♥ Would I buy from me if I were the customer?
♥ Am I sincere?
♥ Will this customer bring another back for the same treatment?

I hope you can answer no to these:
✗ Do I use (high) pressure tactics to get the customer to buy today?
✗ Do I have to resort to telling the customer about some sales contest or sob story to try to elicit the sale?
✗ Do I use antiquated sales tactics and think my prospect is too stupid to know?
✗ Do buyers doubt my intentions?
✗ Are contracts being canceled after the prospect goes home and thinks about it?

Whenever you're frustrated or mad at a salesperson, please don't be too hard on him or her. *Usually, in situations when poor salesmanship is at fault, the blame goes to the person who trained them.*

> *Failure is an event, not a person.*
> *-- Zig Ziglar*
> *People aren't afraid of failure,*
> *they just don't know how to succeed.*
> *-- Jeffrey Gitomer*

# 18.5 characteristics of sales career failures.

We are each responsible for our own success (or failure). Winning at a career in sales is no exception. To ensure a win, you must take a proactive approach. Prevention of failure is an important part of that process. If you find yourself saying, *"I'm not cut out for sales,"* … *"I'm not pushy enough,"* … *"I hate cold calling,"* … *"I can't take the rejection,"* … *"My boss is a jerk,"* … or *"My boss is a real jerk,"* you are heading down the wrong path.

Here are 18.5 recurring characteristics and traits of people who thought they could hit a home run in a sales career. But they struck out in their attempt – many of them with their bat on their shoulder – failing to swing at the ball as it passed them by for a called third strike.

*How many of these apply to you?*

**1. You don't believe in yourself.** If you don't think you can do it, who will?

**2. You don't believe in your product.** Failure to believe that your product or service is the best will show. Lack of conviction is evident to a buyer and manifests itself in low sales numbers.

**3. Failure to set and achieve goals. Failure to plan.** Failure to define and achieve specific long-term (what you want) and short-term (how you're going to get what you want) goals.

**4. You're lazy ("slack" in the South) or just not prepared to make the sale.** Your self-motivation and preparation are the lifeblood of your outreach. You must be eager and ready to sell, or you won't.

**5. Failure to understand how to accept rejection.** They're not rejecting you; they're just rejecting the offer you're making them.

**6. Failure to master the total knowledge of your product** (failure to know your product cold). Total product knowledge gives you the mental freedom to concentrate on selling.

**7. Failure to learn and execute the fundamentals of sales.** Read, listen to tapes, attend seminars, and practice what you've just learned. Everything you need to know about sales has already been written or spoken. Learn something new every day.

**8. Failure to understand the customer and meet his or her needs.** Failure to question and listen to the prospect and uncover true needs. Includes prejudging prospects.

**9. Failure to overcome objections.** This is a complex issue. You are not listening to the prospect; you are not thinking in terms of solution; you are not able to create an atmosphere of confidence and trust suitable enough to cause (effect) a sale. People aren't afraid of failure; they just don't know how to get to success.

**10. Can't cope with change.** Part of sales is change. Change in products, tactics, and markets. Roll with it to succeed. Fight it and fail.

**11. Can't follow rules.** Salespeople often think rules are made for others. Think they're not for you? Think again. Broken rules will only get you fired.

**12. Can't get along with others** (co-workers and customers). Sales is never a solo effort. You must team with your co-workers and partner with your customers.

**13. Too damn greedy.** Selling for commissions instead of helping customers.

**14. Failure to deliver what you promised.** Failure to do what you say you're going to do, either for your company or your customer, is a disaster from which you may never recover. If you do it often, the word gets out about you.

**15. Failure to establish long-term relationships.** Trying to make commissions leads to failure through insincerity, failure by lack of service, failure to be motivated by anything but money.

**16. Failure to understand that hard work makes luck.** Take a close look at the people you think are lucky. They (or someone in their family) put in years of hard work to create that luck. You can get just as lucky.

**17. Blaming others when the fault (or responsibility) is yours.** Accepting responsibility is the fulcrum point of succeeding at anything. Doing something about it is the criterion. Execution is the reward (not the money – money is just the by-product of perfect execution).

**18. Lack of persistence.** You are willing to take no for an answer and just accept it without a fight. You are unable to motivate the prospect to act, or are unwilling to persist through the 7 to 10 exposures it takes to make the sale.

**18.5 Failure to establish and maintain a positive attitude.** The first rule of life.

*The 18.5 characteristic that leads to sales failure:*
## B.T.N.A.
*Big Talk No Action*
*Too busy bragging about the sales you're going to make*
*and not busy enough making them.*

Failure is not about insecurity. It's about lack of execution. There's no such thing as a total failure. Zig Ziglar has the answer: "Failure is an event, not a person."

There are degrees of failing. Here are 4.5 of them. What degree are you?

      1. Failing to do your best.

      2. Failing to learn.

      3. Failing to accept responsibility.

      4. Failing to meet quotas or pre-set goals.

      4.5 Failing to have a positive attitude.

If you are weak in any one of the above 18.5 areas, it is urgent that you make a change as soon as possible. Sales weaknesses are like cancer – mostly self-inflicted due to bad habits and neglect, easy to uncover, hard to cure – but not impossible. It takes outside help and regular treatments to maintain excellent sales health.

# The Book of Competition

☆ Dancing with the competition?
Watch your step ................... 224

## 6.2

> ## "Of course you know, this means WAR."
> *-- Bugs Bunny/Groucho Marx*

Competition ...

Gentlemen,
start your sales pitch.

To the victor go the sales.
All's fair in love and sales.
I'm in the mood for sales.

Carl Lewis won the 100-meter dash three Olympics in a row. Who came in second? Who cares?

Are you going for the gold ... or will you come in second?

There's no prize for second place in sales.

When you're in a foot race with your competition, here's what to do ...

*Never say anything bad about
the competition -- ever.*

# Dancing with the competition?
# Watch your step.

How do you feel about your competitors? You say, "I have a great relationship with my competitors." Right, if you needed $50,000 or your business would fold, I guarantee your *friend* the competitor would send you a *bon voyage* note. Get real. Competitors may talk to you, they may be civil to you, and they may even appear to help you – but ask them if they wish you were dead or alive, and I'm betting on the funeral home.

*They help me, they send me business, they call me to discuss common problems, there's enough business for everyone* – all are statements your competitors are hoping you'll say while they systematically plan to destroy you. That's life in the jungle of business (and especially sales).

Friendly competition – there's a good one. "Now let's play fair. I got the last sale, so you can have this one." My butt. Friendly competition is kinda like friendly snakes. They'll turn and bite you in a heartbeat, and it's *real tricky* to tell the poisonous ones from the safe ones.

Competition is a lot like an unknown snake. Potentially poisonous, not someone you want to get real close to, it's best to know all you can about them, respect 'em, and always carry a snake bite kit with you – just in case.

*Facts about the competition and their feelings about you:*

- ❤ Some are OK.
- ❤ Some will co-operate.
- ❤ Some are ethical.
- ❤ Some like competition.
- ❤ Some will like you.
- ❤ Some will trade business with you.
- ❤ Some will help you.
- ❤ Most won't. Most don't like you.

*How to deal with competition ...*

- Know where they stand in the market.
- Know who their major customers are.
- Are they taking business from you, or are you taking business from them?
- Have they captured any of your employees?
- Get every piece of their information (sales literature, brochures).
- Get their prices.
- Shop them every quarter. Know how they sell and what they feature.
- Identify where they are weaker than you and play on it.
- Learn where they are stronger than you and fix it ... IMMEDIATELY.

*When you are up against competition on a sales call ...*

- Never say anything bad about them, even if the prospect does.
- Praise them as worthy competition.
- Show them respect.
- Show how you differ – how your benefits are better.
- Stress your strengths, not their weaknesses.
- Show a testimonial from a customer who switched to you.
- Maintain your ethics and professionalism at all times – even if it means biting your tongue until it bleeds.

My friend, Jim Collins, president of Leasing Legends, somehow obtained a sweatshirt imprinted with the name of his fiercest competitor. It hangs on the wall over his copy machine where everyone can see it. It has a sign next to it that says in big bold print "THE ENEMY."

Collins has a relationship with this competitor. They speak on the phone; they meet and talk at trade shows. But the reality of it is Collins wishes they were out of business, and vice versa.

And for those of you getting ready to write me one of those "There's plenty of room for everyone" letters. Suppose there wasn't. Suppose there was only room for two businesses to survive in a market, and there were three businesses out there. Still going to write me? I suggest you go back and mind the store as though it were true.

# Competition does not mean war ...

# It means learn, it means prepare, it means be your best.

# The Book of Customer Service

7.1

## "To serve is to rule."

*-- Lao Tzu*

Are you serving others the way you expect to be served?

Make your customer happy. Keep your customer happy. Forever.

If you don't have the time or the interest to do so, someone else will.

Sell them and serve them so that you can sell them again.
And again.

Where does customer service begin? In the next decade, it will BEGIN with a 100% satisfied customer. Start now.

Don't let your customers sing "I can't get no satisfaction."

Here's how to create memorable, legendary customer service ...

*Satisfactory customer service*
*is no longer acceptable.*

# The secret of great customer service ... Ty Boyd.

*Customer service* is one of the most maligned terms in our language. So often as customers we are disappointed in the service we receive (or the attitude attached to the service) that we go elsewhere. Amazing. The company made the sale, got the customer, and then, through an act of rudeness, indifference, poor follow-up, bad service, slow response, or the like, lost the customer it fought so hard (and spent so much) to get.

Seems ridiculous, but it happens thousands of times every day. It's happened to each of us many times. And, boy, do we talk about it. In fact, **statistics show a disgruntled customer tells 20 times more people than a satisfied one.**

How good is your customer service? Once you make the sale, are you as intense to keep the customer as you were to get the customer?

I attended a Ty Boyd seminar called The Spirit of Customer Service. I thought I was going to get a great lesson from a great speaker. I was wrong. I got an unbelievable series of lessons from a master presenter. I was rewarded with more than 100 rules, lessons, and examples about what to do and what NOT to do in the never-ending quest to serve (and preserve) the customer.

How do we lose customers? Ty offers the Seven Deadly Sins of Service:
1. Putting money or profits ahead of service.
2. Complacency brought about by success (getting fat).
3. Organizational layering without creating teamwork (people blaming others or whining "It's not my job").
4. Lack of proper employee training, recognition, or retention.
5. Not listening – Anticipating the answer before hearing the situation.
6. Isolationism – Not paying attention to the customer or the competition.
7. Lip service, or worse, lying.

We have probably been victims of every one of these sins at one time or another. Yet if I ask you if you commit any of these, you'll say *NO*. Guess what? Someone's lying or living in fantasy land waiting for tickets to the Ross Perot Inaugural Ball.

Customer service is a complex issue critical to the ongoing success of any business. *It's easy to go astray without guidelines and standards.*

*Some of Ty Boyd's wisdom about customer service includes ...*
- Satisfactory customer service is no longer acceptable.
- Customer service begins at 100%.
- The customer's perception is reality.
- A mistake is a chance to improve the company.
- Problems can create beneficial rearrangements.
- Make the customer feel important.
- Learn and learn how to ask questions.
- The most important art – the art of listening.

Ty spoke in detail about refining the skill of listening. It is a vital key in the customer service process. As salespeople, we are prone to talk way too much. Sometimes we lose sales and customers because we fail to hear their true needs and desires. Ty offered the following rules to maximize your listening skills and increase customer satisfaction:

1. Don't interrupt. ("But ... but ... but ...").
2. Ask questions, then be quiet. Concentrate on really listening.
3. Prejudice will distort what you hear. Listen without prejudging.
4. Don't jump to answer before you hear the ENTIRE situation.
5. Listen for purpose, details, and conclusions.
6. Active listening involves interpreting.
7. Listen to what is not said. What is implied is often more important than what is spoken.
8. Think between sentences.
9. Digest what is said (and not said) before engaging your mouth.
10. Demonstrate you are listening by taking action.

Sounds simple – it is! Just focus on it.
(Read the sections *"Want to close more sales? Listen more!"* and *"Learn to listen in two words ... Shut up!"* in *The Book of Communications*.)

*To tell a customer no at L.L. Bean,*
*you must get senior management approval.*

# Outstanding customer service is a powerful sales tool.

Customer service is the never-ending pursuit of excellence to keep customers so satisfied that they tell others of the way they were treated in your place of business.

Is that the way your customers feel? If they do, you're among 5% of American businesses. The other 95% fall short of that mark, according to Ty Boyd. For years, Ty has compiled information and spoken worldwide on Customer Service.

Every business has a different definition of customer service because of the diverse types of their products and services. The constants among them are the attributes of customer service.

Here are the 12 key attributes presented in Boyd's seminar. How many are present in your company? If you can't answer *yes* to all of the attributes below, you're losing customers to your competition. That's a comforting feeling, isn't it?

1. Dedication to customer satisfaction by *every* employee in the company.
2. Immediate response to the customer (now, not tomorrow).
3. Individuals taking responsibility for customers' needs (no buck passing).
4. Do what you say and follow up immediately.
5. Agreement with and empathy for the complaint or situation of the customer.
6. Flexibility to serve specific needs of individual customers (the ability to go beyond *policy*).
7. An empowerment of employees to decide.

8. Consistent on-time delivery.
9. Deliver what you promise before AND after the sale.
10. A *zero-defects* and *error-free* delivery program.
11. Outstanding people to serve customers and implement customer service.
12. Smile when talking on the phone.

### "Write down and live your customer service policy,"
says Ty Boyd (*passionately*).

*Here are some examples, presented by Ty, of American corporate leadership and innovation in customer service:*

**Auto Zone** – Named their service WOW Service and they live up to it. They have a GOTTChA program – *Get Out To The Customer's Car and Assist.* They use the WITTDTJR philosophy – *What It Takes To Do The Job Right.* Do you? Auto Zone has high-energy, knowledgeable employees dedicated to greeting and helping customers, with a special emphasis on helping women feel informed about the products they need – never selling more than is absolutely needed. Their stores are alive and customers can feel it.

**Nordstrom** – Their entire service policy to employees is: *"Use your good judgment in all situations."* Seminar attendees who had shopped there cited example after example of service way beyond the call of duty, including going to competitors to buy products they are out of or don't stock and delivering them to customers at no additional charge.

**L.L. Bean** – Before an employee can say *no* to a customer, he or she must have senior management approval. Think about that.

The philosophy is simple …
*Legendary service builds fortunes in repeat customers.*
*Poor service will drive your customers to your competition.*

Every time you encounter a customer, try this …
*Measure the value (and profit) of a customer over 10 years,*
*and you begin to look at them in a whole new way.*

Ty has written a list of *51 Ways to Get Closer to the Real Boss, Your Customer.* Here are a few samples:

• Have top management people make sales calls regularly.

- Install a customer *hot line*.
- Make it a policy to return all inquiry or complaint calls within 1 hour.
- Set a goal to resolve every complaint within 24 hours ... then shorten it to 12 hours.
- Have your top staff/management personally answer complaints.
- Create a slogan centered around "[Our Company] means SERVICE." Put it on your walls, on your letterhead, on your literature, on uniforms. Tattoo it on your forehead.

I recently gave a two-part seminar on understanding the customer to a company of 65 employees. In the first part we went over what it takes to have a memorable customer service team and used the examples above. A week later, when I walked into the second part of the seminar, the entire staff had "CFC means Service" on yellow Post-it Notes stuck to their foreheads. It was great.

Want the entire list of 51 Ways to Get Closer to the Real Boss, Your Customer? Log onto www.gitomer.com, register if you are a first-time user, and enter the words "Ty Boyd" in the GitBox.

*When a customer has a complaint,*
*you have an opportunity*
*to solidify your relationship.*

# Customer complaints breed sales ... if you handle them correctly.

The customer is always right. Except when he or she is wrong, which is most of the time. In sales, right and wrong don't matter. It's the perception of the customer that matters. Keeping the customer satisfied and happy is what matters. What's the best method of handling the dreaded CUSTOMER COMPLAINT? Try the *Personal Touch Method*.

Here is a formula I have developed and used over and over. To institute this method, you must first and foremost TAKE RESPONSIBILITY, even if the fault isn't yours or you won't be the one who handles it. The customer doesn't care. He's pissed. He just wants you to handle it. Now.

Here are *15 steps to taking responsibility when dealing with unhappy or dissatisfied customers*. Not only does this method work, but it provides for a self-analysis at the end to prevent the problem from recurring. All 15 steps must be used, or you risk losing your customers.

1. Tell them you **understand** how they feel.
2. **Empathize** with them. (Cite a similar situation. Tell them that it makes you mad too. Tell them a similar thing happened to you.)
3. **Listen** all the way out. Make sure customers have told you everything. Don't interrupt. **Ask questions** to understand the problem better and to **find out what it will take to satisfy them**.
4. **Agree** with them if at all possible. (Never argue or get angry.)
5. Take notes and **confirm** back that everything has been covered, and that they have said all they want/need to say.

6. Be an **ambassador** for your company. Tell the customer you will **personally** handle it.

7. **Don't blame others or look for a scapegoat.** Admit you (and/or the company) were wrong and **take responsibility** for correcting it.

8. **Don't pass the buck.** *"It's not my job,"* ... *"I thought he said,"* ... *"She's not here right now,"* ... and *"Someone else handles that"* are responses that are never applicable or acceptable to the customer.

9. **Respond immediately.** When something is wrong, people want (and expect) it to be fixed immediately. The customer wants it perfect.

10. Find some **common ground** other than the problem. (Try to establish some rapport.)

11. **Use humor** if possible. Making people laugh puts them at ease.

12. Figure out, communicate, and **agree upon a solution** or resolve. Give customers choices if possible. **Confirm it** (in writing if necessary). **Tell them what you plan to do ... and DO IT!**

13. **Make a follow-up call** after the situation is resolved.

14. **Get a letter** if you can. Resolving a problem in a favorable and positive way strengthens respect, builds character, and establishes a solid base for long-term relationships. Tell the customer you would appreciate a sentence or two about how the situation was resolved.

15. **Ask yourself: "What have I learned, and what can I do to prevent this situation from happening again? Do I need to make changes?"**

*It is important to be aware of some practical realities when trying to accomplish the task of satisfying the customer:*

- ♥ The customer knows exactly how they want it, or exactly what they want, but may be a lousy communicator and not tell you completely, or tell you in a way that is difficult to understand. **If the customer cannot state his complaint in a clear and concise manner, it's up to you to help him do so.**
- ♥ Remember, you're the customer elsewhere. Think about the level of service you expect when *you're* the customer.
- ♥ Every customer thinks he's the only one you've got. Treat him that way. Make the customer feel important.
- ♥ The customer is human and has problems just like we do.
- ♥ The customer expects service at the flip of a switch.
- ♥ It all boils down to you.
- ♥ The customer's perception is reality.
- ♥ How big a deal is it to try to give customers what they want?

## *Recovery is powerful ...*

When you satisfy an unhappy or dissatisfied customer, and you can get him to write you a letter telling you that he's happy and satisfied now, I'd say you have a solid shot at a long-term relationship.

### *If the problem is left unresolved, the customer will surely find your competition.*

# Customers talk ...

*to their associates, friends and neighbors.*
*Here is the number of people they will talk to based*
*on how well you handle their complaint.*

**3** ... if you do a good job

**10** ... if you do a great job

**25** ... if you do a bad job

**50** ... if you do a really bad job

**and you will be on the 6 P.M.**
**news if you do a horrible job.**

*How are yours talking about you?*

# The Book of Communications

## Say What?

Communications ...

Communication is the lifeblood of the selling process.

Communication is not just talking.

It's getting your mission accomplished by a combination of
talking,
writing,
listening,
and doing.

Complete communication with your prospects, your customers, and your associates must be your purpose.

Talk it up,
listen up,
do it up,
so you can write it up.

Communication = Sales!

8.1

*Make an appointment*
*1 minute following your sales meeting.*
*You'll be pumped.*
*Why not take it out on a prospect?*

# A weekly sales meeting
# is a place to create new sales.

Sales caffeine. The early morning sales meeting.

Sales staff meetings are a vital link between what your company expects the sales team to do and what actually gets sold in the trenches. It's a place where marketing is converted to sales. But how often is the opportunity provided by these meetings lost? Answer: Too often.

Sales meetings should be a forum for reporting, goal achievement assistance, encouragement, problem solving, training, sharing, and communication. The purpose of a sales meeting is to get the sales staff primed and pumped to sell. Notice I've left two things off the menu – whining and complaining.

Why do salespeople hate sales meetings?
See how many of these apply to your meeting:

1. Salespeople already know everything.
2. The meetings are usually boring.
3. The meeting has no agenda.
4. The meeting is run by someone who can't run a meeting.
5. Salespeople think they could be out selling (and earning).
6. The meetings are usually boring.
7. There is always a bunch of talk about forms, paperwork, and assorted nonsales drivel that takes twice as long as it should and will probably change again next week.

8. Meetings don't have enough real-world selling situation lessons.
9. Sales meetings mean the dreaded sales report is due (which contains as much fantasy as fact).
10. And did I mention, the meetings are usually boring?

If you want to rate your own weekly meeting, ask yourself this question: *If the meeting were not mandatory, who would show up?* Uh oh.

Last week I attended a well-designed Monday morning sales meeting.

- They had an agenda and stuck to it.
- Each member of the staff of seven was given an opportunity to present or lead one portion of the meeting.
- They had a sales lesson about how to introduce themselves, how to create buyer interest, and where to network.
- There was some, but very little administrative stuff.
- There was 15 minutes for product knowledge.
- At the end of the meeting, everyone got to tell about their best sale of the past week.

The 2-hour meeting kept the staff involved and in learning mode. It was one of the rare sales meetings I have attended that produced no gripes and great sales information.

How do you have a great sales meeting every time? Preplanning and preparation. Let lots of people have their chance to lead. Set an agenda that will work, be fun, be productive, include participation by everyone, and STICK TO IT.

## *Here are some criteria to consider:*

- **Very little administration.** Five minutes tops.
- **Don't do boring things** like go over new forms, company policy, personal disputes, and what went wrong. Figure out a better, faster way to communicate. Try this – have an instruction sheet for the new form and just pass it out. CLUE: Salespeople don't pay attention to administrivia anyway.

• **Don't present problems unless you have thought of some solutions to go with them.** This rule applies to everyone. It gets people solution oriented.

• **Do fun things that help salespeople feel good about themselves.** Awards; share success stories.

• **Do things that help salespeople learn more about their profession.** Have a mini-lesson on one topic per week. Have it prepared and presented by one of the sales team.

• **Do things that help salespeople earn more money.** Thrash out objections and obstacles that create roundtable discussion. Role-play solutions.

• **Bring in people from the real world.** Have one customer attend each week and tell why he or she buys from you. You'll be amazed, but this is a powerful dose of reality. The customer will dissect the BUYING process (way more powerful than you trying to learn the SELLING process).

• **Have meetings early in the morning.** Have great food and great coffee ready early.

• **Make people be on time.** Fine late ones/reward early ones. START ON TIME no matter what, and END ON TIME no matter what.

• **Stress the positive.** Support your people in public, especially among peers. If you have a negative about an individual, say it to him or her privately.

A sales meeting is a place to plan this week's sales. Some people use the forum to threaten and complain; some use it to encourage and learn – guess who wins?

## The Best Sales Meeting Idea ...

Make an appointment 1 minute following
the sales meeting with a hot prospect.

You should be pumped.
Why not take it out on a prospect?

*You should close that sale 110% of the time.*

*Get to the point in the first sentence.*

# The sales letter will work, if you get it write.

How important is a sales letter?

I have received hundreds of sales letters of all different types. Introduction, literature enclosed, just met you, after the presentation, follow-up, here's the information, thanks for the order – you get the idea. Most have a specific purpose. Most are not very good (uninspiring). OK. Most of them are PATHETIC.

The skill of drafting *sales words* on a letter is an integral part of the sales process, because it creates an impression of you and your company when the customer or prospect reads it.

Here's how it works. If you write a great letter, they think you're great. If you write a creative letter, they think you're creative. If you write a dumb letter …

Some salespeople have a hard time coming up with the appropriate words. Not because they can't write, but because they don't know the rules of writing.

*Here are some rules and guidelines to help turn your sales letters into sales:*

1. State your objective or the purpose (get to the point) of your letter in the first sentence. You can even use a headline above the body of text.

2. Use short paragraphs. (for emphasis)

3. Edit, ~~edit, edit~~. Take out every word not integral to the purpose or objective of the communication.

4. Keep the letter short. One page; three paragraphs. The shorter it is, the better chance you have of the letter being read and understood.

5. Don't make the prospect vomit when he reads your letter. Make the letter easy to digest. Avoid heavy syrup. Half the adjectives, half the prepositional phrases, and most adverbs can be eliminated. Look behind commas to see if the entire phrase is worthy of keeping. Most of the time it's not.

- Use bullets to break up the monotony.
- Make the letter easy to read graphically.
- Use bullets to make the letter seem (or be) short and sweet.
- Use bullets to emphasize the most important points.
- Indent the bullets.

6. Don't say, "Thank you for the opportunity"; instead, try, "We are proud to offer."

7. Don't bold your name – **bold what's important to the prospect.** Your name is among the least important words in the letter.

8. Don't make it sound like a rubber stamp.

9. Don't sell your product too much – just sell the next action step in the sales cycle and build some confidence and rapport. Don't use the letter as a sales pitch; just use it as a sales tool.

10. Do the extra – the unexpected. Enclose an article or something pertaining to the customer's business or just a good cartoon. Something that makes your prospect think you went beyond the norm to serve and communicate.

11. Personalize it. Talk about a ball game, child, event.

12. Solidify the next contact or event – date it and time it.

13. Hand write whatever you can.

14. Edit out (almost) all words that end in "ly."

15. Avoid superlatives ("est").

16. Avoid the word "unique."

17. Never say "again, thanks." It's not necessary to thank anyone again. Once is enough; twice is groveling.

18. Don't misspell a word. One man misspelled "potato" and he paid for it dearly, perhaps for a career. Luckily he didn't have a very important job.

19. Use an example (or similar situation) the customer/prospect can relate to.

20. **Bold stuff** to get people's attention – but only when absolutely necessary.

21. Ask for a response.

22. Use a nice, nonbeg, professional closing like: "Thank you for your time and consideration. I'll call you Tuesday."

23. **Sign your first name only.** There are some – but rare – occasions when this is inappropriate (a letter of agreement where both people must sign, or a formal quote that might end up in a corporate office for approval).

24.5 Very truly yours (and I mean that), Jeffrey Gitomer.

P.S. If you want to make your plea or point twice, use a P.S.

*Here's a tough rule.* Let your letter sit for a day, then re-read it. How does it sound to you? If the answer is thin or hokey, you may want to start over.

*Here is a tougher rule.* Ask someone *smart and impartial* to critique your letter. Learn to accept criticism, and use it as a learning tool.

*Here's the toughest rule.* Ask yourself how this letter would be different from your competition. Suppose the sale was based on the originality of your cover letter. Would you ever make another sale? Uh oh.

Knowing the rules AND practicing them will lead to effective letters. Effective letters lead to prospect rapport and confidence. Prospect rapport and confidence lead to sales.

*Listening is arguably the most important
aspect of the selling process,
yet it's usually the weakest part
of a sales professional's skills.*

# Want to close more sales?
# Listen more closely!

Have you ever had a course in listening skills?

*How to listen* lessons were never offered as part of any formal education.
It's amazing to me that the skills we need the most for personal success
were never taught in school.

Listening is arguably the most important aspect of the selling process, yet
it's usually the weakest part of a sales professional's skills.

We listen to TV, radio, and CDs, and we can recite chapter and verse the
next day, or sing the songs word for word. But if your spouse or child says
something to you, you say, "What?" or "I didn't hear you."

How often do you ask people to repeat what they said? How often do you
hear, "You weren't listening to a word I said." There are reasons for poor
listening, and thank goodness I'm writing them – otherwise you'd be forced
to listen. Here are the fundamental lessons:

**LISTEN LESSON #1.** *The two biggest impediments to listening are:*

    1. You often have an opinion (of you or what
       you're going to say) before you begin listening.

    2. You often have made up my mind before you
       begin listening, or before you hear the full story.

**LISTEN LESSON #2.** *The two important rules of effective listening must be observed in this order or you will not be an effective listener.*

    1. First, listen with the intent to understand.

    2. Second, listen with the intent to respond.

**LISTEN LESSON #3.** *Think about the way you listen right now:*

- Are you doing something else when someone is speaking?
- Do you have your mind on something else when someone is speaking?
- Do you fake listening so that you can get in your comments?
- Are you waiting for a pause to get in your response, because you already know the answer?

**LISTEN LESSON #4.** *At some point you stop listening. When does that occur?*

- After you have formulated your response.
- After you have been turned off by the speaker.
- When you decide to interrupt someone to say something.
- When the person speaking isn't saying anything you want to hear.

**LISTEN LESSON GUIDELINES.** *Here are 14.5 guidelines to observe that will maximize your listening skills, increase your productivity, reduce errors, gain customer happiness, and help you make more sales:*

    1. Don't interrupt. (But ... but ... but ...)

    2. Ask questions. Then be (veweey, veweey) quiet. Concentrate on the other person's answers, not your thoughts.

    3. Prejudice will distort what you hear. Listen without prejudging.

    4. Use eye contact and listening noises (um, gee, I see, oh) to show the other person you're listening.

    5. Don't jump to the answer before you hear the ENTIRE situation.

    6. Listen for purpose, details, and conclusions.

    7. Active listening involves interpreting. Interpret quietly or take notes.

8. Listen also to what is not said. Implied is often more important than spoken. HINT:Tone of speech will often reflect implied meaning.

9. Think between sentences and during quiet times.

10. Digest what is said (and not said) before engaging your mouth.

11. Ask questions to be sure you understood what was said or meant.

12. Ask questions to be sure the speaker said all he or she wanted to say.

13. Demonstrate you are listening by taking action.

14. If you're thinking during speaking, *think solution*. Don't embellish the problem.

14.5 Avoid all distractions.Turn off the cell and pager. Close the door. Clear your mind, and both sit or both stand in close proximity.

## LISTEN LESSON #4.5 *What causes people not to listen?*

• Sometimes people are afraid to hear what is about to be said, so they block it out. Don't be afraid to listen.

• Sometimes you take the other person for granted – spouse, parent, child.

• Sometimes you're mentally preoccupied with other things.

• Sometimes you're just rude.

• Sometimes the person grates on you, so you don't listen.

• Sometimes you have other things on your mind.

• Sometimes you know the person speaking and have prejudged them.

• Sometimes you don't respect the other person and block the listening process.

• Sometimes you think you already know what is about to be said.

• Sometimes you think you know it all …
  or is that all the time?

There are many secrets to becoming a good listener, but the one that encompasses them all is:

### *Just shut up!*

*A person who seems to have all the answers usually isn't listening.*

# Learn to listen in two words ... Shut up!

It's amazing how much you can learn by just keeping quiet. People think you're smarter if you're quiet. You learn more by listening than by speaking.

*Effective listening leads to sales – lots of them. Listening is arguably the most important aspect of the selling process, yet it's the weakest part of a sales professional's skills.*

## How well do you listen?

Answer each statement *Rarely* – *Sometimes* – or *Always*:

**R S A** I allow speakers to complete sentences.

**R S A** I make sure I understand the other person's point of view before responding.

**R S A** I listen for the important points.

**R S A** I try to understand the speaker's feelings.

**R S A** I visualize the solution before speaking.

**R S A** I visualize my response before speaking.

**R S A** I am in control, relaxed, and calm when listening.

**R S A** I use listening noises ("um," "gee," "I see," "oh").

**R S A** I take notes when someone else is speaking.

**R S A** I listen with an open mind.

**R S A** I listen even if the other person is not interesting.

**R S A** I listen even if the other person is a jerk.

**R S A** I look at the person I'm listening to.

**R S A** I am patient when I listen.

**R S A** I ask questions to be sure I understand.

**R S A** I have no distractions when I listen.

How you rate as an Effective Listener. How many *Always* did you get?

14-16 You're excellent.

11-13 You're good, but need help in a few areas.

7-10 You're fair, probably think you know it all, and could increase your income significantly with skill-building help.

4-6 You're poor, not listening at all.

1-3 You're ear dead or brain dead or in need of a hearing aid.

### Turn any of the above listening weaknesses into listening goals by substituting "I will" for "I," or "I will be" for "I am."

For example: If you answered *Sometimes* for "I allow speakers to complete sentences," you can make that a goal by writing "I *will* allow speakers to complete all sentences for the next 30 days" on a Post-It Note and putting it up on your bathroom mirror.

### *Effective listening requires regularly practiced skill-building techniques. Here are 17.5 you can practice ... Shhh ...*

1. Look right at the person you're listening to.

2. Focus your attention on the words and their meaning.

3. Limit distractions (even change locations to listen better).

4. Visualize the situation being described to you.

5. Visualize your response or solution before responding.

6. Listen with an open mind. No prelistening prejudice.

7. Listen to the content – not necessarily how it's being delivered.

8. Use occasional listening noises ... "Wow," ... "Gosh," ... "Then what?" ... "Really," ... "That's horrible," ... "Great," ... "That's too bad," ... "I didn't know that," ... "I see."

9. Write things down as others are speaking. Jot down a word rather than interrupt the other person's thought ...
   - To keep the thought.
   - To impress the other person.
   - To be polite.
   - To keep listening instead of interrupting.

10. Verify the situation (sometimes) before giving feedback.

11. Qualify the situation with questions before giving feedback or responding.

12. Don't interrupt the next time you think you know the answer.

13. Go for an hour without speaking.

14. Next time you eat with a group, don't talk for the first half hour.

15. Ask questions to clarify.

16. Ask questions to show interest or concern.

17. Ask questions to get more information or learn.

17.5 Ask yourself, "Are you listening to the other person the same way you want to be listened to?"

## Look out for poor listeners ...

☆ A person who seems to have all the answers usually isn't listening.

☆ A person who interrupts isn't listening (or at least is not a good listener).

How hard is it to listen? For some, it's impossible.
*Test your listening self-discipline ...*

• Try being silent for 1 hour.

• Try not talking in a group of people.

• Try not talking at a party.

## Listen with the intent to understand ... before you listen with the intent to respond.

Listening is my toughest lesson to give. First, because I'm often a poor listener myself. Almost every sale I ever lost I can attribute to poor listening or poor questioning. Second, because I can't change in one or two chapters what took you 20 years to create. If you have any thoughts on the subject, call me. I'd love to listen.

*There are no such things as buyer types,*
*only buyer characteristics.*
*No two buyers are alike.*

# There are 100 billion buyer types. Go figure.

Selling is not about defining the type of buyer you're facing; there are billions of types of buyers. Ever see those four types of buyer things? The Driver, The Amiable, The Idiot, and The Big Idiot. The Big Idiot is someone who thinks there are four types of people and you can somehow pigeonhole them into characteristic categories that will make them buy. Bogus.

I'll give you three words that will let you absolutely identify every type of buyer in the world in 5 minutes …

> **1. Look** (around the office)
> **2. Question** (the right questions)
> **3. Listen** (with the intent to understand)

There. The *Gitomer Method* of identifying more than 100 billion buyer types reduced to three words. These are the methods used in determining customer characteristics. Oh yeah – there's one more thing you need to do to get it right every time …

# Practice!

Selling is knowledge combined with experience. The knowledge you gain about your product, your selling skills, and your attitude. Experience teaches you how to implement the knowledge you've gained. It's a science, remember? Trial and error. Of course there are some absolute rules that can never be broken: Don't argue. Don't lie. But most are shades of gray …

How much pressure do you apply? Someone will say none; someone else wrote a book about hardball selling – it comes with a bat. The amount of pressure is up to you!

There are no *buyer types* – there are *buyer characteristics*. Individual traits that make up a personality. **Don't categorize them; understand them.**

I'm way more interested in buyers' philosophies than their characteristics. But I can only get to their philosophy if I recognize (and understand) their traits. If you've uncovered their "type," but you've said something that they're philosophically opposed to, you're dead.

## Why do customers buy?

- To solve a problem.
- They need it.
- They think they need it.
- To get a competitive edge.
- To save money or produce faster.
- To eliminate mistakes or people.
- To feel good.
- To show off.
- To change a mood.
- To solidify a relationship.
- They were talked into it.
- It sounded too good to refuse.
- They got a great deal (or thought they did).

## How many of these characteristics apply to the buyers you face?

- The tire kicker
- The liar
- The logical
- The indecisive
- The unfriendly
- The impulsive
- The know-it-all
- The Yankee
- The faithful
- The unqualified
- The talker
- The hidden objection
- The procrastinator
- The friendly – won't commit
- The impolite
- The ounce of power
- The price-only buyer
- The bragger
- The arguer
- The no-talker
- The emotional
- The "think it over"
- The rude
- The cheapskate
- The good ole boy
- The corpse

**These characteristics are identified one by one -- BUT your buyer is a combination of several of these and other traits.**
For example, the good ole boy-tire kicker-price buyer-think it over –
there's a prospect who can make a Yankee salesperson go looking for that
U-Haul trailer for a move back north. Or how about the Yankee-know-it-
all-unfriendly-liar? – It's enough to make a Southern salesperson want to go
rent him one.

*Here are a few guidelines that will work on any type of buyer:*

1. Never argue.
2. Never offend.
3. Never think or act like you're defeated.
4. Try to make a friend at all costs.
5. Try to get on the same side of the fence (harmonize).
6. Never tell a lie.

There's a theme here. A common thread that connects all these situations.
One word makes all these types conquerable: HARMONIZE. If you listen to
buyers and watch their actions, they will tell you how to react. They will
tell you what to say and what not to say. They will lead you to the sale. As a
SalesMaster, your job is to take the characteristics of the prospect, and
blend them with the reason the prospect is buying so that it motivates the
prospect to act, and gives the prospect enough confidence to buy. Simple.

There are billions of "customer types." Want to sell them all?
You can do it in five words --

# Look,
# Question,
# Listen,
# Harmonize,
# Practice.

# Toward error-free positive communication.

*When someone talks to you, updates you on a project,
asks you to do something, assigns you a task,
has a business communication of any kind
or just needs a favor ...
here is a method that eliminates
misunderstandings and errors.*

**1. Focus on the communicator.**

*Stop* – whatever else you're doing. Distractions cause errors.

*Look* – at the person who is talking. People communicate both verbally and nonverbally.

*Listen* – with your eyes and ears. Using eye contact increases listening intensity.

**2. Write the communication down.**

Writing the message or task reduces error by 90%.

**3. Repeat it back.**

Repeating gives the communicator peace of mind that the message has been received and understood. Repeat all dates and numbers twice.

**4. Get confirmation.**

The communicator will appreciate acknowledging that you are correct in receiving and understanding the communication.

**5. Deliver what you promised.**

Delivering is as important as listening, writing, and confirming – combined.

## Error-free communication is up to you.

# The Book of Exhibitions

8.2

# Showing Off

Exhibitions …

Remember
"Show and Tell"?
This is the adult version
of the game.

It's called "Show and Sell."

Where else can you be
face-to-face with thousands
of prospects over the
course of a few days?

Everyone is there
to do business.

Fish in a barrel.
Thousands of them.

All you need is a hook.

I'll supply the bait …

*Your annual convention ...*
*You can see a concentration of people in your industry.*
*Nowhere else can you see this many*
*customers and prospects at once.*
**You have no time to waste.**

# 35.5 trade show success rules.

It's time for your annual business fair, trade show, or convention. Hundreds of your customers, prospects, suppliers, and competitors will be in town for 2 days. Nowhere else can you see such a concentration of people in your industry. It's about opportunity – selling, prospecting, and relationship building. How will you take advantage of it?

It's also about time, and the proper use of it. If 7,500 people will attend over a 2-day, 20-hour span, what does that mean to you? And what should you do about it? How do you capitalize on this event? Nowhere else can you see as many customers and prospects at one time. You have no time to waste from the second you get on the plane until you wearily make your way back home from the airport.

Some people go to conventions because it's a chance to get away from the office, get out of town, or have a good time. If you want to be successful, steer clear of these people.

*Here are 35.5 points to help you plan for and maximize your benefit from the next convention you attend. These success rules and observations will help you work the show and understand its power:*

**1. Think. How long does it take you to make 7,500 sales calls anyplace other than a trade show?** At 20 a day – which is a lot of (outside) calls – it would take you 375 days (1.5 work years) to make 7,500 sales calls. Wow. If you telemarketed 125 calls a day, it would take you 60 days to make 7,500 calls. Wow.

**2. Taking advantage of a trade show, the most cost-effective sales opportunity of the year, requires preparation. Lots of it.** You better be ready to win if you expect to win. Be ready with your exhibit, your stuff, your staff. Be prepared with your pitch; have your information at your command. **Have your presentation material ready and rehearsed.** Have Power Questions and Power Statements ready. Your opening line and presentation statements must be perfect.

**3. Develop your game plan before you leave your office.** Have a set of goals and objectives for the number of prospects you want to secure, customers you want to visit, sales you want to make, and how you intend to accomplish the tasks.

**4. Stay at the main/best hotel.** Be in the middle of what's happening. It costs a few bucks more, but it's worth it.

**5. Get there a day early.** You will have the advantage of being relaxed and up to the minute on things of importance. Many convention exhibitors and attendees will be flying in on your plane. Try to find them.

**6. Work the trade show during setup.** If you're not an exhibitor, somehow get in. Go to the truck entrance; tell them you're delivering an important part or paper, but get in. Walking the trade show early gives you a tactical advantage and may net you some valuable contacts. Many company CEOs like to be there when the booth is being set up. It's a relaxed time to get in some valuable contact time without being rushed.

**7. Target five important people** in your industry you want to get to know, and make it your business to seek them out and talk to them. Be memorable.

**8. Target 10 customers.** Connect. Build relationships. Take them to dinner. Solidify your position as a vendor.

**9. Target 10 prospects.** Connect. Build rapport for a sale later.

**10. Find out about every hospitality suite and after-hours party being given.** Target the ones where your prospects are most likely to be. Go there.

**11. Be the first to arrive and the last to leave every day.** This has been most successful for me. It gives me an edge on the people who get there late and leave early. One or two extra hours can mean another 100 contacts.

**12. Be a team ... split responsibilities.** If more than one person is attending from your company, split up and assign responsibilities.

**13. Attend seminars and lectures where you can network with your customers and prospects.** Sitting next to the right person in a seminar can be very beneficial. If you meet a prospect or customer, ask what seminars they plan to attend. Be there.

**14. Be a presenter.** Give a talk or seminar that will establish your expertise and position you or your company as a leader in your field. Pick a topic that your customer or prospect is likely to attend.

**15. Stay focused. Look for opportunities where you least expect them.** In the lobby, in the elevator, in the rest room, in the restaurant – be alert for opportunity. You're going to be face-to-face with decision makers and people who influence them.

**16. Sell everywhere. No place is off-limits.** Aisles, other booths, bathrooms, food stands – be on alert for the people you're looking to meet. Read badges. Talk and look (without being rude). You never know when you'll bump into a major prospect (or miss one if you're not paying attention).

**17. If you want to say hello to everyone, do it fast;** you've got about 7.5 seconds per person. You'd better be able to qualify fast. BUT (and this is a big but), when a person seems to be a good prospect, spend a little extra time building some rapport for the follow-up. Don't waste time doing nonproductive things. Every second is important. If you have 2 days and 5,000 people are there … you get my point.

**18. Don't prejudge anybody.** You never know what boss may decide to come in casual clothing or wear someone else's badge so that he won't be bugged.

**19. Read badges fast.** Stay alert for your target badges (prospects you have selected, customers you've never met, types of businesses likely to need you) … in the booth, in the aisles, while eating.

**20. Be brief.** Your remarks (other than questions) should be no more than 60 seconds.

**21. Be to the point.** Say something that tells prospects exactly what you do in terms of *their* needs.

**22. Have fun and be funny.** Enthusiasm and humor are contagious. People like to do business with winners, not whiners.

**23. Shake firmly.** Your handshake reflects your attitude. No one wants to shake hands with a dead fish.

**24. Fight the urge to talk with fellow employees and friends.** It's a disadvantage to both of you and a huge waste of time.

**25. Establish buyer need.** How can you sell anyone anywhere if you don't know what they need?

**26. Get the information you need by probing first. Don't say too much too soon.** Ask Power and follow-up questions that generate information, establish interest, determine need, and allow you to give your information in a meaningful way. Ask your best questions and have your most concise message ready to deliver when the timing is right. Before you deliver your problem-solving capabilities, know enough about the other person so that your information has impact. ***Know when to say what.***

**27. Show (tell) how you solve problems.** He is bored to know what you do, unless you tell him in a way that serves him, or you have something the prospect thinks he needs. The prospect doesn't care what you do, unless what you do helps him.

**28. Determine level of interest.** If they need what you sell, how hot do they seem to buy? Note their interest level on their business card.

**29. Pin the prospect down to the next action.** Don't let a good prospect go without some agreement of what's next.

**30. Write notes on the back of business cards immediately.** If you make a lot of contacts, you'll never remember everything. Write information on the back of them as you speak and immediately after they depart. If you get 250 cards and have no notes on the back of them to follow up after the show, your effectiveness is reduced by 50% or more. (Use prospects' business cards as sales tools.) You can even write tentative appointment times on the backs of both yours and hers, to be confirmed after the show. Be sure to write down the personal (rapport) items – golf, children, sports, theater – to reference later when following up.

**31. Be remembered.** Say, give, or do something that will stay in the prospect's mind (in a positive, creative way).

**32. Time's up.** When you have delivered your message, made your contact, and secured the next meeting or action, move on.

**33. Have a memorable handout or ad specialty.** Something that will create long-term goodwill with your customer and prospect. Something to talk about when you follow up after the event.

**34. Regroup at night and plan or replan for the next day.** Things happen fast at a convention. You meet new people, deals are in the offing, and influential people in your industry are accessible. The only way to achieve the maximum benefit is to have a written game plan to start, and be flexible to change it as events unfold.

**35. Stay sober all the time.** It's a distinct advantage. If you get drunk and make an ass of yourself, you could do irreparable harm. Party, but party smart.

**35.5 Have a great time!** Don't press or be pressured; it will show. Trade shows are like life: The better attitude you have, the more successful you'll be.

Maximize your base of contacts and leads. **Get the list of attendees from the association host** after the show. This list will be useful to add to your database, to use for follow-up, and to contact the people you missed.

Conventions, trade shows, and business fairs are the best contact opportunity and the most fun a salesperson can have – with the right preparation, focus, and effort.

*When you have an opportunity to*
*see 7,500 prospects in two days,*
*capitalize on every second.*

# Business fair/trade show game plan.

## *Opportunity ...*

A business fair or trade show is one of the most cost-effective marketing methods there is – either as an attendee or exhibitor. How are you going to maximize the benefit and capitalize on the opportunity?

*Your prime objective*
*at a trade show or business fair is*
*to qualify the needs of a target/prospect*
*in a way that you can effectively follow up*
*after the show with a call, letter, or offer*
*that leads a qualified prospect*
*to an appointment and a sale.*

*If you're exhibiting at a business fair or trade show and you're making your game plan, ask yourself ...*

• **What do I expect to accomplish as a result of exhibiting?** *Do I have a clearly defined and written set of goals that include the number of prospects I expect and the number of sales that will result from the show?*

• **When prospects come up to my exhibit booth, what do I want their first impression of me to be? How will I make this happen?**

• **What Power Questions will I ask prospects to immediately qualify them and generate interest in what I do?** *Do I have these questions written down and rehearsed? Are they questions that make a prospect answer with information that leads to an appointment or sale?*

• **What information do I want to get from asking this question?** *Can I tell how qualified my prospect is as a result of the question? Does it take more than one question to find out the information I need?*

• **What powerful statements can I make that will establish credibility and motivate the prospect to act?** *Do I have these statements written down and rehearsed? Is it a statement about what I do in terms of what my prospect needs? Is it a statement that is memorable?*

• **Am I doing anything memorable, is my exhibit memorable, and am I saying anything memorable?** *What can I do that will be remembered and talked about after the show?*

• **Am I doing anything that will differentiate me or distinguish me from the competition?** *When I follow up after the show, what will separate me from my competition in the eyes of the prospect?*

• **What are the tools I'll need to accomplish these tasks?** *What literature, ad specialties, signs, show specials, and people do I need to make this show a success (meet or exceed my goals)?*

• **Am I going to try to sell other exhibitors? Of course I am!**

➤ Let them know you are an exhibitor, too!

➤ The best-selling situation is CEO to CEO.

➤ Use a well-thought-out, rehearsed, short statement about who you are and what you do.

➤ Try to establish quick rapport and confidence, either through mutual friends, known customers, their competition that buys from you, or your ability to explain how your service can benefit the exhibitor.

YOU HAVE LESS THAN 1 MINUTE TO DO THIS.

➤ Remember, the exhibitor is there to sell, not buy.

➤ Don't interrupt a conversation taking place. Ever.

➤ Conversation should carry on 1 to 3 minutes, *not longer*.

➤ Get card, write information, and firm up a get-together.

➤ *GET MOVING*.

- **If you are an exhibiting CEO, walk around 50% of the time** (like I have to tell you that).
- **If you exhibit, start early.** Walk the show on setup night and select targets. There will be other CEOs there to network with as well.
- **When the show starts, be aware of time.** If you see a prospect every 3 minutes for 9 hours, that's only 180 prospects per day. If 3,500 people per day attend, that's less than 6% of the audience.

## Every second is valuable.

*If you're attending a business fair and you're making your game plan, ask yourself …*

- **Am I going as a buyer, seller, or some of each?** *Almost everyone going is trying to sell, planning for sales, or learning how to sell.*
- **If I'm going to sell or get sales information from exhibitors, how can I best accomplish this delicate mission?** *Be discreet and be brief. They are there to sell, not buy. They will form an impression of you that will carry over to the follow-up you attempt after the show. Best way to sell to exhibitors at the show? Be an exhibitor yourself – it's an unwritten law that it's OK to solicit other exhibitors.*
- **As an attendee, should I take more than my business cards?** *Probably not. Get others' cards and mail your information after the show.*
- **How do I find the prospects I'm looking for?** *Target them, look for them, hunt for them, wait for them, and track them down. And when you find them … be prepared for them.*
- **How can I maximize my exposure?** *By being there every second, by being prepared, by saying things that make people think and that make them remember you.*

*RECAP* … As a show attendee or an exhibitor, **qualify**, **qualify**, **qualify**. Use a well-thought-out, rehearsed, BRIEF statement about who you are, what you do, and why you're better than anyone else. Rapport must be established in 1 or 2 minutes. Try to establish needs and confirm to prospects that a callback or mailout will take place. Immediately write on the back of their business cards all the information you will need when the return calls are made. Spend between 1 and 3 minutes per prospect if the floor is crowded.

### *Some guidelines for working the exhibit booth ...*

1. Don't use a fishbowl unless you give a prize that will get qualified leads.
2. Give ad specialties out personally; don't leave them in a pile for anyone to grab.
3. Stand up the entire time.
4. If more than one person is attending from your company, assign coverage responsibilities.
5. Pay attention to customers immediately.
6. Have the booth covered 100% of the time.
7. Qualify each prospect quickly with an open-ended question.
8. Use the four qualifying rules to get leads and make sales:
   1. Establish rapport.
   2. Establish need/qualify.
   3. Establish interest.
   4. Establish next action (mail, call, appointment).
9. Have lead sheets (and a stapler) if you need information beyond a business card.
10. Determine if you have a friend or customer in common with the prospect.
11. Write notes on business cards or lead sheets immediately.

*Exhibiting also gives you the unspoken/unwritten right to solicit at other booths. This doesn't mean you can't sell to exhibitors as a trade show attendee, but if you do, you'd better be fast, accurate, and discreet.*

A business fair is a high-power sales opportunity. Without a doubt, it is the best selling opportunity, until the next business fair. Take advantage of it.

*If you haven't done your follow-up within
2 days of the show, your competition has.*

# After the trade show is over,
# how do I follow up?

Fast.

I was at the Book Expo in Chicago last week. Customers and prospects
everywhere. A real selling bonanza. There were companies that were e-
mailing quotes, confirmations, and copies of orders directly from their
exhibit booths to the office of the prospect or customer. That's real fast.

As competition grows fiercer (and it will), speed becomes a lethal weapon.
Better put – the lack of speed can be fatal in the selling process. How fast
you respond to your trade show or business leads will be the measure of
your success. Get wireless. If you're not sending follow-up e-mails from the
trade show floor, your competitor has beat you to the punch (and sale).

If you got 200 leads from a trade show (or 10 leads from a networking
event), here are some ideas on how to convert them into sales. Many of the
methods and techniques listed here are things you could have (should
have) done weeks before the event took place.

If you find yourself in the large group of people who didn't make follow-
up plans BEFORE the show or event, make follow-up an integral part of
preshow planning the next time you exhibit. Not only will preplanned
follow-up increase your results, it will help you improve the way you
generate leads on the trade show floor.

*If you have difficulty following up, the answers to these questions will tell you why:*

- Do you have a game plan that was finished before the trade show started?
- Do you have blank business cards? Turn your business card "leads" over – if there's nothing written on them, your ability to effectively follow up is diminished.
- Do you have a lead sheet or questionnaire that was filled out at the show?
- Do you have scripts or actions ready for your follow-up contact with prospects?

*Here's how to succeed at trade show or business fair follow-up:*

- Define your follow-up program **before** the show. Make sure the information you're gathering matches the information needed for effective follow-up.
- Meet immediately after the show and review every lead.
- Organize leads by type of follow-up and heat (interest level) of prospect.
- Draft a nice, short, creative, nonvomit follow-up letter.
- E-mail or call every contact within 2 days.
- Have separate contact sheets or data files for each prospect.
- Have a scripted *first contact* that is creative, and ties back to the information given or gained from the show.

*Try these opening lines if you send an e-mail:*

- The Expo presented me an opportunity to meet you. I'd like to get to know you better ...
- We can help! (bold 24-point type). From the information you provided us in the questionnaire, we can ...

*Write a letter that gets attention and creates response.*

*Try these opening lines on the phone:*

- Jim, I had an idea about your business after we spoke, but couldn't find you again at the fair. What have you thought about ... (or how is your company currently using ...)?
- Bill, I couldn't wait until the Carolina Business Fair was over to get back to you. I've been thinking about ...
- Mary, I went to your Web site and I got an idea about ...
- I wanted to get together with you a few minutes to show you some things about (_____) that I didn't get a chance to address at the business fair. I could do it in under 5 minutes. When is good for you?

*Create your own lines. Find one or two that work and use them on everyone.*

## Your entire objective is to get to the next step in your selling cycle. That MAY mean making the sale, but probably NOT. Most of the time it's an appointment that you're selling. Whatever it is, focus on completing that step *only*. Salespeople tend to overshoot the situation and sell too much, or send too much, too quickly. This makes the prospect nervous and defensive. You know my philosophy – send ONE potato chip and make them hungry for another.

*Monitor and measure your results. Evaluate your weekly results for 2 months.* This will help you determine the cost per sale and whether you will be going back to exhibit next year.

After the trade show is over, it's a horse race to the sale. How well you train, how well you're bred, who's riding you, and your speed in the straightaway and the curves will determine the winner of the race.

Here's hoping you're a thoroughbred.

# The Book of Networking

9.1

# We've got to start meeting like this.

Networking …

"Don't talk to strangers,"
your mother said.
(The opening philosophy of
Susan RoAne's bestselling book
*How to Work a Room*.)

I've got nothing against
motherhood, but if you
want to succeed at
networking, you'd better
start talking to strangers.

How do you place a value on
a solid, well-established
business connection, a
friend who is in a position to
help you and your business?

These connections
make careers.

You can never have
too many friends.

So, how do you capture this
opportunity? You network.

Just say, "Hello."
Here's how …

*A wise man knows everything,*
*a shrewd man knows everyone.*
-- Chinese proverb from a fortune cookie

# Networking ... The challenge of making success contacts.

How are you using networking to help build your career?
*Make a networking plan. Today.*

How many hours a week do you spend networking?
*To get ahead it must be at least 5 (nonbusiness) hours a week.*

How many of those hours are spent at optimum productivity?
*It's easy to measure – you should get 20 new contacts per week.*

*This is your career. Your opportunity.*
*Will you take advantage of the power of networking? If not now, when?*
*You're working anyway. You may as well have some fun.*

- Networking is getting known by those
  who can help build your business.
- Networking is creating momentum toward
  business and career success.
- Networking is getting together with
  business contacts and turning them into
  customers, friends.
- Networking is building and nurturing
  long-term relationships.
- Networking is building a people resource
  bank that pays interest and dividends that
  compound annually for as long as you're alive.

## Secret ...
*Networking only works if you have a positive attitude.*

Your goal is to successfully combine effective networking skills with a 5-year networking plan of involvement, the results of which will achieve your objectives of ...

&#9734; More business contacts.

&#9734; More sales.

&#9734; More business education.

&#9734; More community involvement.

*Networker's Credo ...*

**I know if I get involved,
budget my time, attend regularly,
network my butt off, and do it right,
the results will exceed my expectations
of joining any organization.**

**To succeed at networking, you must make a plan.**

*Here is a questionnaire to help you formulate a game plan. Use it.*

- Where do I network now?
- Where should I network?
- Where do my best customers network?
- What are three organizations I should investigate and possibly join?
- How many hours a week should I network?
- Who are five prime people I want to meet?
- What are my first-year networking goals?
- Do I have the networking skills I need?
- Do I have networking tools?
- Who is great at networking so that I can call and get help?

Answer the questions above. They will help direct you toward a perfect networking game plan. The only thing missing from the plan is your commitment. Only you can supply that.

*If you attend a business networking event*
*with a friend or associate, split up!*
*It's a waste of time to walk,*
*talk, or sit together.*

# Networking 101 ...
# How to work a room.
## *The Fundamentals of Networking Success*

*Networking*, the current word for prospecting, has become a vital business tool. It's inexpensive (often free), time-effective/productive (you can usually make 20 to 30 contacts in a couple of hours), and has more of a social overtone (it's easier to do business socially – and it's fun).

If you question the value of networking, consider this: If there are 100 people in a room and you have 2 hours to network, you can speak to at least 50% of them and probably make 30 contacts. How long would it take you to make 50 sales calls in any other environment? Probably a week.

*Many people go to networking events; very few actually know how to network effectively. Below are some techniques and tools you can use to be a more effective and productive networker.*

## 16.5 Fundamental Rules of Networking

**1. Preplan the event.** Figure out who will be there, what you need to bring, what your objectives are, and if anyone else from your company should attend.

**2. Show up early**, ready to move, looking professional, full of cards.

**3. If you attend a business event with a friend or associate, split up.** It's a waste of time to walk, talk, or sit together.

**4. Walk the crowd at least twice.** Get familiar with the people and the room.

**5. Target your prospects.** Get a feel for who you'd like to meet.

**6. Shake hands firmly.** No one wants to shake hands with a dead fish.

**7. Have your 30-second personal commercial down pat.**

**8. Keep your commercial to 30 seconds OR LESS.**

**9. Be happy, enthusiastic, and positive.** Don't be grumbling or lamenting your tough day. People want to do business with a winner, not a whiner.

**10. Don't waste time** if the person isn't a good prospect, but be polite when making your exit.

**11. Say the other person's name at least twice.** First to help you remember it, second because it's the most pleasing word to their ears.

**12. Don't butt in.** Interrupting can create a bad first impression. Stand close by, and when a pause or opening appears … jump in.

**13. Eat early.** It's hard to eat and mingle. Get your fill when you first arrive so that you are free to shake hands, talk without spitting food, and work the crowd effectively.

**14. Don't drink.** If everyone else is a bit loose, you'll have a distinct advantage by being sober. (Have a few beers afterward to celebrate all your new contacts.)

**15. Don't smoke or smell like a cigarette.**

**16. Stay until the end.** The longer you stay, the more contacts you'll make.

**16.5 IMPORTANT NOTE … Have fun and be funny.** It's not a brain cancer operation; it's a great time to get to know others and establish valuable relationships. **People like to be with people who are happy.**

## Where to Go …

If you say,"I go to networking events, but I don't get many prospects," it means you're not following the fundamentals, OR you're not networking where your prime prospects might be.

Event selection is as important as networking itself. Ask your five top customers where they go for their monthly meetings. Start by going there.

Each week the *Business Journal* and the business sections of daily papers publish a list of business events, and the chamber of commerce in your city publishes a monthly calendar. Don't overlook social and cultural events as networking possibilities. Select those events that may attract your prospects or people you want to get to know. Go for it.

> *To make the most of a networking event,*
> *spend 75% of your time*
> *with people you don't know.*

# Networking 102 ...
# How to milk a room.
## *The Secrets of Networking Success*

"I wish I could get more leads when I network." If you have said this to yourself more than once, and you're willing to get serious about the science of networking, I have listed some techniques and tactics that will help you succeed in getting solid prospects.

If you're not following the fundamental rules of networking (see the previous section), don't even try the subtle ones – they won't work.

### 10.5 Subtleties of Networking Success

**1. Early in the event and near the end of the event, stand by the entrance if possible.** At the start you can see everyone and establish your targets, and at the end you can catch anyone you missed.

**2. Spend 75% of your time with people you don't know.** Hanging around with fellow employees and friends is fun but won't put any prospect cards in your pocket or make any valuable contacts.

**3. Spend 25% of your time building existing relationships.** Talk to your customers. The better you get to know them, the stronger their loyalty to you and your company.

**4. Don't give your information out too soon.** After you give your 5- to 10-second introduction, ask the other person what they do BEFORE YOU START TALKING IN DEPTH ABOUT WHAT YOU DO. (See *The Book of Introductions*.)

**5. After your prospect has told you about himself, your next move is a choice between establishing rapport (finding common interests) and an opportunity to arouse interest in your product/service.**
(What the prospect said in his introduction will be your guide.)

**6.** If the person seems to be a good prospect, **you must establish some common ground** besides business if you want to ensure an easier path to doing business. Find one thing you both like or know about.

**7. TRY TO APPOINT THE PROSPECT NOW.** If you want to get the prospect's card, offer your card first, or give a reason you need the card ("Give me your card and I'll mail you some information"). If the prospect is reluctant to give you a card, he/she is likely to be hard to appoint later.

**8. Write all pertinent info on the back of the prospect's card immediately.** You will need this to refer to when following up.

**9. Don't sell your product/service.** Just establish some rapport, some confidence, and *SELL AN APPOINTMENT.*

**10. Be aware of time.** After you have established the contact, gotten the business card, established rapport, and confirmed your next action (mail, call, appointment), **MOVE ON TO THE NEXT PROSPECT.**

**10.5 Play a game with a co-worker.** If you go with someone from your company, bet who gets more (qualified) cards. The more you bet, the less likely you'll spend a second together.

## More Networking Ideas ...

You've got the fundamentals down. Now let's capitalize on your new knowledge. To facilitate implementing your networking plan, you need a few more guidelines. Networking is a powerful, cost-effective marketing weapon. If utilized properly, it can provide the basis for your business growth. It did for me. *Below are 12.5 of my personal networking secret rules for success*:

**1.** Our office has **a yearly wall calendar with all networking events posted** and a small bulletin board next to it to post the event's promotional pieces or invitations. It is updated religiously every week.

**2. I follow the 50-butt rule.** If there are more than 50 butts in one room, my butt is there too.

**3. Learn how to make small talk important talk.** Be brief and to the point. If someone asks what you do, say it quickly and succinctly.

**4. Don't flap your gums just to be talking.** When you engage your mouth, make it count.

**5. Know the kinds of problems you can solve rather than a bunch of boring facts about your product or service.** Talk in terms of how you solve problems rather than the product or service you offer.

**6. Avoid negatives at all cost.** Don't complain or speak poorly about a person or business. You never know if the prospect you're talking to has some connection, interest, or affiliation with the people, company, or product you're slamming.

**7. Be polite.** *Please* and *thanks* go a long way toward creating an impression, whether they are present or absent.

**8. Don't spend too much time with one person** or you defeat the purpose of networking. If you find a good connection or lead, spend a LITTLE extra time. Know when you've said and heard enough. Be smart enough to make an appointment, pique interest, and MOVE ON.

**9. Your objective is to take advantage of the entire room.** If you spend 3 minutes with a prospect, that gives you a possibility of 20 contacts per hour. Every second is valuable. The size of the event dictates the amount of time you should spend with each person. The larger the event, the shorter time per contact, and the less time you should spend with people you know.

**10. Get involved** in the organizations where you network.

**11. People identify with and do business with leaders!**

**12. Have a great time. Lead with your positive attitude and your enthusiasm. Business is sure to follow.**

**12.5 Remember, at a networking event everyone wants to sell!** You may have to play a *buyer* in order to get a chance to be a *seller*. You must be able to wear either hat. Learning the skills of networking will provide you the opportunity to be either … and in complete control of the situation.

*If you are able to establish rapport when networking,
you will have a perfect conversation starter
when you follow-up to make an appointment.*

# Establishing rapport when working a room.

Webster defines *rapport* with several words: relation, connection, accord, harmony, and agreement. **Rapport is a subtle yet vital aspect of the selling process.** Establishing rapport with a prospect at a networking event enhances your ability to appoint (and sell) in the ensuing follow-up.

*Follow these guidelines to maximize your productivity at (and after) a networking event …*

***If you already know the person*** … If you have a business agenda, discuss it within 2 minutes. If this person is your customer, spend a couple of minutes building the personal relationship by establishing mutual interests. If he or she is talking to someone you don't know, get introduced and see if there is a fit for you. If you make a promise or commitment, get another card from the person and IMMEDIATELY write it down on the back. No matter what, after 5 minutes … MOVE ON.

***If you don't know the person*** … Get information before you give your 30-second commercial. Don't elaborate or try to sell until the other person has talked about themselves AND you have tried to establish mutual interest. Ask an open-ended question about how they now use your type of product or service (Where are you presently getting _____?
… How are you using _____? … Who are you buying _____ from?
… What do you know about using _____?). Questions that will engage prospects, make them talk about themselves, and make them begin to open up and reveal themselves are the type of questions you need to ask. **As soon as they broach a personal issue, grab it and expand on it.**

When you engage a prospect, try to find out his personal interests. After the traditional exchange of business information, try to find out what the prospect does after work, or what he's doing next weekend. You might even try out a couple of interest items if an event is near or just passed, like a ball game, car race, concert, play, or business function.

After you have gotten to know a little about this person, you can begin the "let's get together later to finish this discussion" part that will solidify the all-important appointment.

Be careful not to spend too much time on subjects of mutual interest. It's tempting to spend 30 minutes talking about things you like. Don't. Your opportunity to meet others awaits you. You can expand the conversation at a lunch next week. Move on to other prospects.

*NOTE:* **Write furiously on the back of their business cards. Be sure to include anything personal you spoke about so that you can begin the appointment where you left off at the networking event.**

*Building solid relationships*
*through networking takes time.*
*But … mature relationships breed sales.*

# Success rules for joining a networking organization.

How long does it take to establish a networking relationship? There is no set answer. It takes time. How much time does it take to show a prospect you are credible, honorable, have a good company, and can deliver consistently? It takes time.

*How much time are you willing to invest in your network?*
*Therein lies the answer to how*
*successful networking will be for you.*

I belong to the Charlotte Chamber, Early Risers Leads Club, Business Growth Network, Metrolina Business Council, PenWork, and five other groups. I regularly attend meetings, give my time to make the groups better, strive for leadership positions, and work hard to establish and maintain relationships. I am also involved in four community and civic organizations. That's how I network. I spend 60 hours a month doing it. I've spent the last 15 years building my network.

## *My findings are summed up in two words --*
# *It works!*

How and where do you network? Do you just attend functions or are you involved in the group? Are you just a taker, or are you willing to get involved and help the group succeed with your hard work and dedication?

PenWork is a new group of CEOs and principals whose purpose is to exchange clients and do business with one another. At a PenWork meeting last week, we tried to define what makes networking succeed. Here are the combined findings of 25 driving CEOs.

# 14.5 Guidelines for Joining an Organization ...
## *and Succeeding at Networking*

**1. Go where your prospects are.** Try to select groups and organizations that have the best chance of bearing fruit. One good indication is if one or some of your present customers belong.

**2. Don't wait for your success package to arrive from an organization after you join it.** To identify your best resource for networking and success, just look in the mirror the next chance you get (pretty good-looking, huh?).

**3.** To benefit, **you must commit to be involved**, then get involved.

**4. It takes time to build trust and get to understanding.** For the first few meetings, just listen and observe. Pushing too quickly gives others a wary feeling. See where and how you can best fit into the group. Just get to know and help quality people. The rest will take care of itself.

**5. When you commit, be there consistently and perform.** By attending regularly, you will be seen and known as consistent.

**6. A 5-year game plan is essential.** Ask yourself ...

- Where do my prospects/customers participate?
- Who do I want to develop relationships with?
- What are my expected results?
- How much time must I commit?
- Who are the important people involved that I must contact?
- Who else from my company should be involved?

**7. Give first.** This is a key to any relationship, not just business. The classic Zig Ziglar line, *"You can get whatever you want if you help enough people get whatever they want,"* is the best way to describe "give first."

**8. Don't measure.** If you count who owes who what favor, forget it. Just get to know and help quality people. The rest will take care of itself. (Are you getting the idea?)

**9. Don't push.** If you are sincere about establishing long-term relationships, don't put pressure on someone to deliver immediate business. I'm not saying don't do business if the opportunity presents itself. I am saying don't push business.

**10. Be prepared when you get there.** Having the tools to make contacts, cards, and your appointment book are essential in confidence building.

**11. After you meet a prospect in a group, get one-on-one.** You can get to know someone quite well in an hour if you talk about real issues and avoid weather and politics.

**12. Every networking contact need not be a sale.** Often one breeds the other. Get to know and help quality people. The rest will take care of itself.

**13. Be seen (get known) as a leader.** By getting involved, you will be observed by your prospect. He or she will get to know you as a performer, a doer, a leader.

**14. People will do business with you once they get to know you and see you perform.** Your customers and prospects are here! All you have to do is identify them and work (network) with them side by side.

**14.5 Mature relationships breed sales.** If you build a solid relationship with someone, he will go out of his way to find you business. And the recurring universal networking rule applies here too: *Just get to know and help quality people. The rest will take care of itself.*

Your ability to build a successful network is tied to your determination and dedication to take whatever time is necessary to build quality relationships. And you're lucky – the outcome of your success is totally self-determined.

# The acid test of commitment ...
## Mark your calendar 1 year in advance.
### *Don't miss meetings and events.*

*What would you do if you knew you couldn't fail?*
*-- Robert Schuller*

*You'd take a few more chances, wouldn't you?*
*-- Jeffrey Gitomer*

# Networking is getting known by those who count.

Anne Boe was one of America's foremost networkers. She worked hundreds of rooms as a speaker and author (*Is Your "NET" Working?*). Boe turned an idea she had years ago into a career as a keynote speaker – all by networking.

I was present when she spoke to 90 members of the Women's Business Owners in Charlotte. She was great. Her talk provided pragmatic insight into the career and financial rewards of building a solid network.

Boe, a brilliant award-winning speaker, led the audience through the psychological barriers of networking avoidance, and empowered the audience with thought-provoking statements that had people leaning into her words. And her humor had people laughing to the point of applause.

Her call to action *"If not now, when?"* was followed with a wall-sized projection slide of Ziggy saying, "Procrastination is the only thing I have time to do." And the classic Woody Allen quote, "80% of life is showing up." It worked.

*Some of Boe's wisdom included ...*

1. You're working anyway. You may as well have fun.
2. Networking is creating momentum toward what you want.
3. Networking is getting together to get ahead.
4. Networking is getting known by those who count.
5. Build and nurture long-term win-win relationships with networking.

In the middle of her talk, she popped a slide on the screen that said, **"What would you do if you knew you couldn't fail?"** The audience was moved. Two minutes of table murmur ensued. Boe had made her point.

Boe asked, "Do you say, *'I wish I would have,'* after a networking event? If so, you must take risks. Networking involves risk. You must take people risks. *Just introduce yourself.*"

Boe challenges the group to be positive. It won't work if you aren't. Take your fears and negative thoughts and turn them in your favor. Turn them into assets. Since it takes twice as much energy to be negative as it does to be positive, why not increase your energy reserve and just be positive?

By turning negative energy into positive energy, you will learn to trust yourself. It will turn your heavy work into light work. Boe recommended two action steps: (1) Turn worries into goals. (2) Turn fears into goals.

Here is a capsule of Boe's formula for making your "NET" Work:
• Take action every day – one small dose at a time.
• Call at least two people per day (that's more than 500 contacts per year).
• Go to at least one networking event per week.
• It takes time – 6 months – to begin to establish a relationship.
• Make friends when you don't need them.
• Make your customers and clients your friends.
• If you add value out, you'll bring value in.
• Learn to go with the flow. Don't be afraid to trust your judgment.

She gave everyone plenty to think about and plenty to do. With statements like "Networking is getting known by those who count," you became self-motivated to act in your best interest.

At the end of the meeting and seminar, I was hanging around (invoking the *Gitomer Networking Rule #16* – **Be among the first to arrive and the last to leave**). Sure enough, Anne Boe had a box of books that she needed taken to her room and asked if I minded carrying it. As we got on the elevator, I told her I thought of myself as a superior networker. "What makes you think that?" Boe challenged. I said, "Well, there were 90 people at your talk tonight and only one of them is going up to your room."

Anne Boe made me think and made me laugh. The perfect combination to make a meaningful, productive communication. Anne passed away a few years ago. She was a lovely person and her ability to network and make people comfortable was inspiring. She was loved by thousands and will be missed by thousands.

*The object in elevator networking is to engage the other*
*passenger before the doors close*
*and get a card before the ride is over.*

# Elevator selling.
# New heights in networking.

Going up? More than 10 floors? I challenge you to try to get a business
card or lead on your next elevator trip.

Thousands of people take elevators every day ... usually in dead silence.
Company presidents and salespeople in the same elevator and no one is
speaking. That's no fun. I have taken a new approach to elevator riding.
I try to meet someone new and get a card or a lead every time I go up or
down (and there's someone else in the car).

*Here's how it works ...*

1. I watch who enters or see who is on when I enter. I try to select the
best prospect from among the passengers. If there's only one other
passenger, the choice becomes infinitely clear.
2. I immediately engage him or her with a statement or question –
usually humorous.
3. If they laugh or smile, I say, "What do you do?" That is the operative line
in this process. With four words you have struck the target in the bullseye.
It's quick, to the point, and nonthreatening.
4. They will immediately tell you what they do. (People love to talk about
the subject that interests them the most – themselves.)
5. If they seem to be a prospect, you close with "Give me your card and
I'll send you some information I think you can use."
6. He or she gives you the card before the door opens, and you win the game.
7. Give him/her your card. Shake hands firmly.
8. Follow up within 24 hours.

Your opening line on the follow-up call is easy. "I'm the guy in the elevator.
I finally got off and thought I'd give you a call." Both of you will laugh.

***Personal experience:*** On my way up the elevator to the *Charlotte Business Journal* one morning, I engaged a clean-cut, good-looking young man and learned he had just started selling life insurance. A great prospect for my list service. We exchanged cards. That night HE CALLED ME to be sure I sent the information and to try to sell me insurance. He didn't, but he became a subscriber to our lead-list service the next day. I guess it works both ways. But it works!

And remember, every CEO and bigwig in your city gets on an elevator. Want a chance to meet him or her? Just start talking anytime you're in an elevator. It will work.

*Here are some additional guidelines for successful elevator networking:*
• You ain't got much time. Start talking immediately upon entering the elevator. Say the line, "What do you do?" before the elevator begins to move.
• Have your cards in your shirt or jacket pocket so that you can get to them in a second.
• Don't press. If the person chooses not to talk, let it be.
• Men will be more receptive than women.
• If it's a hot one, get off the elevator on the prospect's floor if you haven't completed the deal.
• Be careful if you follow someone off the elevator – these days people may feel you have the wrong intentions.
• If you didn't get all the info, watch which way the person turns and follow up with a cold call.
• It's awkward the first few times. Practice until you can get the person to smile and respond to your opening remark before the elevator door closes.

Try this approach: Get on the elevator at the top floor, tell the person you have a deal for him and you can get him in on the ground floor ... in fact, we'll be on the ground floor in 30 seconds! If he laughs, you've got 'em.

It's fun, you get to build communication skills, you become a bit bolder, you meet new people, and you'll make a few sales. Try it.

After this chapter first appeared as an article in my column in Charlotte, I got a letter from my friend, John Huson. He related a story of getting on an elevator several years ago. Someone asked him, "What do you do?" Being from Brooklyn, his natural reply was, "What do you need done?"

Bravo.

*You must develop a game plan and
purchase some form of computer software for
contacting, following up, and appointing
the people you have connected with.*

# Documenting, tracking, and using your networking contacts for maximum benefit.

To make the most of all those networking contacts you worked so long and hard to get, you need to organize and compile them in some sort of computerized ...

# ROLODEX

**(Or some 21st-century device besides
the dumb card file/box on your desk,
which is as obsolete as the typewriter)**

The ROLODEX is a euphemism for a listing of contacts. Where you list them is superfluous to the fact that you must have them. Whether you choose to keep them in a shoebox, laptop, or a PDA, you're a million miles ahead of the person that does not.

## *Minimum essential information to make contacts valuable ...*

➤ Name

➤ Company name

➤ Title

➤ Company address

➤ Phone (including area code)

➤ Cell phone (if you're good enough to get it)

➤ Fax (including area code)

➤ E-mail address

➤ Company's Web site

➤ What company does

➤ What contact does at company

➤ Who decides or others of importance at company (once you meet others, give them their own file)

➤ Where I met the contact

➤ What I hope to gain/how they can benefit me

➤ Personal things about my contact (wife's name, kids' names)

➤ Special information about other important players (boss, secretary, partner)

➤ Strategy to get what I want

➤ Action sheet (including dates for contact and follow up)

**Keeping contacts, and keeping in contact with your contacts, will build relationships and will help you make more sales more often.**

*An easy way to see how*
*your network is growing.*

# Networking ...
# The Official Game™.

*When you go to a sporting event, concert, mall, flea market, restaurant,*
*and the like, play Networking. The object of the game is*
*to know more people than the person you're with.*
*Here are the official rules of the game ...*

**1 point** if you know someone.

**2 points** if the person sees you (and
acknowledges you) first.

**3 points** if you see a minor celebrity
(sports figure, DJ).

**5 points** if you kiss someone of the
opposite sex.

**5 points** if a celebrity acknowledges
you first.

**It's best to agree on when the game starts and ends.** For example,
at a Hornets game it starts as you enter the rotunda at halftime – you
walk around once back to your section and the game is over. (A scoring
variation at the Hornets game: Spotting someone upstairs when you're
downstairs is worth 2 points.)

Two words that are music to my ears when playing the networking game
... "Hey, Gitomer!" (*2 points*).

# The
# Book of
# Leadership

## Take me to your leader.

Leadership ...

Take leadership positions if you want to take your sales career to the next level.

Lead by example.
Lead so others will follow.
Lead to succeed.

Here are some directions for taking proactive leadership roles ...

## 10.1

*If you're having a hard time following,
you might try leading.*

# 8.5 qualities of a leader.

*Here are a few leadership challenges to ponder ...*

- If you want to lead, where do you start?
- Are leaders born or made?
- What are the leadership skills you need to develop?
- Are you tired of being a follower?

*Want to be a leader? Here's what it takes ...*

**1. Maintain a positive attitude** ... solution oriented, action oriented, people oriented. Enthusiasm begets success.

**2. Embrace change** ... Change is certain. Followers tend to resist change. It is the mark of a leader to embrace change and take advantage of the opportunity it presents.

**3. Deploy courage** ... Douglas MacArthur said, "Courage is just fear that holds out a little longer." Good advice. George Patton said, "I don't take counsel from my fears." Good advice. Leaders choose courage.

**4. Take a risk** ... The biggest risk is to never take one. Leaders are determined to win or try again.

**5. Listen** ... Leaders listen to learn. Your prospects know their needs and they know what's happening on the front lines of their business. Just listen.

**6. Communicate** ... Leaders set the example for open communication. Use their heads. Say what they feel. Speak from their heart.

**7. Delegate and empower** ... Leaders share responsibility. They don't dictate, they set examples for others to follow. Leaders encourage growth in others by challenging them to take new responsibility, encouraging them to succeed, and supporting them if they fail. Leaders understand that mistakes are lessons on the way to success.

## 8. Understand others, yourself, and your situation ... Leaders

understand the importance of an open, inquisitive mind. A constant quest for knowledge brings greater understanding.

## 8.5 Commitment ... Commitment is the catalyst that makes all the other

leadership qualities a reality. Daily rededication to commitment is the difference between leaders and would-be leaders.

Start small. Lead a group or committee. Do whatever is necessary to make it a winner. Do it again until it begins to feel natural. Respect the power of leadership and the power of the people you seek to lead.

*Stop managing. Start leading.*
*If you think about it,*
*there are great world leaders,*
*but no great world managers.*

# Sales manager success requirements.

Stop managing, start leading. Sales managers, beware. No one wants a manager, but everyone wants a leader. If you think about it, there are great world leaders, but no great world managers.

There is one universal misconception among bad sales managers – they all think they're doing a great job! There are thousands of sales managers (and bosses) who do a great job – and unfortunately at least an equal amount who don't.

Many sales managers have risen through the ranks by superior sales performance and are made managers without any (or minimal) training. Most of these "managers" will fail their company twice. Once because they are unprepared for the job, and once because they have left their former position of superstar salesperson, creating a sales volume void.

*Here are seven areas of expertise a manager must perfect to be a leader:*

**1. Administrating** – setting policy, dealing with reports, making sure the flow of paper (from orders in to commissions out) is error-free, and coordinating the selling, delivering, and servicing process.

**2. Recruiting** – going out to find (and solicit) people who may be qualified to sell for the company.

**3. Hiring** – determining by questions, responses, and gut feeling who is a great candidate for, and most likely to succeed at, a sales position. When a person is selected, an integral part of the hiring process is to fully explain all expectations of the job; to set and agree upon sales goals (a nicer word for quotas); and to get and give commitments of specific performance. The best way to do this is to draft a commitment document that has listed what the company will do and what the salesperson will do. Be specific as to sales goals to be met. Have both parties sign the document. It should be reviewed in every performance evaluation.

**4. Training** – If you want to win, win, win, you'd better train, train, train. Sales managers should lead weekly training meetings, do on-the-job training with the staff, attend every seminar possible, listen to sales and management tapes in the car every day, and read six books a year on management, sales, and attitude.

**5. Motivating** – If you want success, you must create an atmosphere in which success can occur. This means a continuous (every minute) positive attitude and atmosphere must exist. It means recognizing and rewarding great performance. Managers create this atmosphere. What kind of atmosphere, recognition, and attitude comes from your manager? If the atmosphere is lacking, or if a manager is using his or her ounce of power to show "who's boss," I guarantee three things will happen: (1) There will be a high turnover of salespeople. (2) The manager will blame everyone but himself. (3) The manager will eventually get the deserved "ax" after doing thousands of dollars in damage.

*Interestingly, it's not the manager's fault. It's the fault of the company president for not providing adequate training or not selecting the right person for the job, or both.*

**6. Selling** – Managers (and trainers) who don't sell every day lose touch with reality. How can you lead your sales force if you don't know what the customer needs? There should be a regular pattern of selling both with reps and alone in a leadership position. The rule is simple: *If you aren't selling, you can't lead.*

**7. Leading by example** – This applies to all aspects of the six areas above. Don't tell someone to do something. Show someone how to do something and provide the support and training to get it done. As a manager, you want your sales team to succeed. The best way to do this is to lead the way. Remember, in order for them to succeed, it's up to you to provide the atmosphere, encouragement, tools, and training.

Tom Hopkins gives a great seminar on sales management. When he was asked to join a management team after an incredibly successful stint as a salesperson, he said yes on one condition. He wanted 6 months of intensive hands-on management training before he accepted the position. That is how he succeeded.

How many months (weeks, days – OK, *hours*) of management and leadership training has your manager had? The unfortunate answer for most is: *Not enough.*

*To be a great leader of salespeople,*
*make them follow you, not your rules.*

# Sales managers can help or hurt. It's up to them.

More sales are lost through poor sales management than through poor salesmanship. **Managers/owners can encourage or discourage sales with their policies and actions.** What makes a great sales manager? Often if you ask a manager, then ask a salesperson who works for him, you will get two completely different answers.

Here is a list of sales leadership traits compiled from three sources: my personal experience, interviewing more than 50 sales managers, and asking more than 100 salespeople *"What makes an ideal manager?"* The compiled results provide some excellent guidelines. How many of these attributes can you say apply to you and describe the way you manage/lead? And if you're a salesperson reading this, **how many of these traits do you wish your boss or manager had?**

• **Lead (manage) by example** – Don't preach things you don't follow or do yourself. You're not above it. Lead by doing, not telling.

• **Get and maintain a positive attitude** – the single biggest step you can take toward your success and the success of your people. Keep your sales team happy by setting a happy example.

• **Set and achieve goals together** – Don't set quotas, set goals. Review their progress weekly. (See *"Post-it Note™ your way to achievement,"* in *Genesis*.)

• **Take sales inquiry calls** – Stay on top by knowing what the customer wants and by sharpening your ability to sell.

• **Make cold calls with your staff** – Walk in their shoes on a regular basis.

• **Make some follow-ups on the phone** – Keep in touch with prospects to find out what it takes to make them customers.

- **Take some customer complaint calls** – Find out what the problems of your customer, your company, and your sales force really are. Make calls to dissatisfied customers to follow up on actions taken.

- **Make calls to lost sales** – Find out why you lost the sale.

- **Make customer thank-you calls after a sale** – A personal call from management makes a great beginning to a relationship.

- **Visit your key accounts with your reps** – Go on at least 10 sales calls per month.

- **Call satisfied customers** – Find out what makes your customers happy and what kind of job your reps are doing.

- **Use sales reports that are by prospect rather than day by day** – Have activity by date by customer or prospect so that you can see the sales cycle on one sheet. It's a total waste of time to know what someone did on a Monday or Tuesday. If you need to know that, get your salespeople to photocopy their schedules and hand them in with their reports so that you can see how busy, organized, or close to meeting their numbers they are.

- **Check on sales reports periodically** – Make sure your people aren't just filling spaces to make it look good.

- **Ask for feedback** – from salespeople, upper management, and customers.

- **Put feedback into action** – Show the staff you're listening. It will encourage more productive suggestions and boost morale big time. Show you have the ability to change and grow.

- **Back your staff** – When a customer has a problem, defend and believe in the capability of your people. Don't judge until you've heard both sides.

- **Say nice things to your staff on a regular basis** – Have 10 times as many nice things to say as bad things. Encourage success with support.

- **Encourage; don't reprimand** – Everyone makes mistakes, even you. Encouragement and positive reinforcement will prevent many more mistakes from being made than a reprimand will. Be a coach; offer support.

- **If you must reprimand, do it in private** – and don't tell anyone else about it.

- **Don't play favorites** – It will kill you, morale, and your most favored.

- **Be inspirational** – Send inspirational messages. Look around your office. Are there inspirational things on the wall? Do you follow those messages, or are they just a hollow reminder of what you should be doing too?

- **Offer rewards and give awards for exceptional work** – Incentives work. Offer incentives that anyone can win.
- **Make your office a fun place to go** – Do reps say "uh oh" when asked in?
- **Be known as the person who follows through and gets the job done** – or else you will die on the job.
- **Keep your eyes open for the opportunity to improve or sell** – When you're sharp, alert, and getting results, it will inspire your staff.
- **Train, train, train** – Train weekly, attend every seminar possible, absorb audiocassette programs daily, and read books having anything to do with sales and positive attitude. And don't just give training; take it too.
- **High turnover?** – If you continue to lose people, you may want to take a closer look in the mirror. It may not be them.

*The most important
of all the guidelines …*
**Don't manage anyone
except yourself --
be a leader.**

# What's New?

Trends ...

Read about people
who are taking
the personal responsibility
for going the extra mile
for their customers,
for their company,
and for themselves.

Take what you learn ...
and start a trend
of your own.

Here's how ...

# The Book of Trends

*The new breed of salespeople …*
*they rely on truth*
*and product knowledge,*
*with a minor in sales skills.*

# The new breed of salesperson.
# A non-salesperson.

Jeff Chadwick is a new breed of salesman – or should I say non-salesman.
For years he worked for Classic Graphics, one of Charlotte's premier
printers. Chadwick was in production, and he had about reached the top of
his earnings potential at the plant position he was in. He gave all the shop
tours. He loved it. People would say, "He's the best salesman you've got."
One day Chadwick sold a surplus printing press. His boss, Bill Gardner, told
him he should go into sales. So Chadwick decided to go into sales.
Commission sales.

"If you ask me what the alternative-of-choice close or the sharp-angle close is, I
don't have a clue," Chadwick says. "But if you ask me can you gatefold (double
fold) this piece of paper, I can sure tell you that – and that's what the customer
wants to know. I love sales. It's a lot of work. Fast paced – no one who needs
printing ever says, 'Take your time.' Everyone needs it yesterday."

I asked Chadwick to define his sales assets and attributes. "Enthusiasm.
Persistence. Pride. Personal pride. I have Classic Graphics posters on my
walls at home. I love being around my peers so I can tell them who I work
for," he said. "I find my best sales asset is my ability to help the customer
select things that will work. I rely heavily on my product knowledge."

Product knowledge is also the sales foundation for Clarkson Jones. The
company he works for, Carolina Asphalt, is a firm specializing in quality
parking lot repair and maintenance. Jones spent 7 years supervising jobs
and heavy equipment operation. During that time he gained incredible
product knowledge. He began developing great relationships with
customers because he had the ability to solve problems and he always gave
straight answers (a characteristic shared by 99% of the new breed).

A few years ago, Jones realized that people were calling him to place orders rather than going through the company's salespeople. Why? "I guess I was nonthreatening to them," Jones said. "I was the guy who got the job done, gave great service, and knew how to solve their problems. Customers just naturally gravitated to me." Life as a salesperson is different for Jones. "I don't miss my old day-to-day grind in the field," he said. "But I could not be in the position I am today without that hands-on experience."

Last year was a banner year for Carolina Asphalt. This year Jones's personal sales are on track to exceed the sales of the company's best salesman.

Sales volume will also be important for Nelson McSwain. He works for Wireway Husky, a leading pallet rack and wire cage manufacturer in Denver, NC. For years Nelson worked in the factory supervising production and was later promoted to head of purchasing. He saw a parade of salesmen come into his office every day. Now he is going out on the road to sell for his company.

"I'm perfecting my sales call based on the hundreds of salespeople who have called on me over the years. Some did it right, but the vast majority had it all wrong," said McSwain. "My sales presentation will be just what the buyer wants to hear. I know because I used to listen for it when I bought. The company has also hired a personal trainer for me and he is incredible. He is helping me gain the sales knowledge I need to complement my product knowledge."

*Chadwick, Jones, McSwain, and thousands like them
are beginning to emerge as a new type of salesperson –
steeped in product knowledge
and practical problem-solving capability.*

*Here are some of the characteristics that are prevalent in the new breed:*

- **Non-manipulative selling at its purest** – They get to the sale by being truthful.
- **Nonthreatening** – They are not perceived as salespeople; therefore, the customer isn't as on-guard.
- **Helpful** – They are not pushy.
- **Consultative** – They can make meaningful recommendations and suggestions based on knowledge of what actually works from their personal experience.
- **Total product knowledge** – They have the information a customer needs to make an informed decision or solve a problem.

• **Error prevention** – Their experience can spot a POTENTIAL error and prevent it.

• **On top of the job** – The job goes smoother because they start it right and are on top of it all the way – just like they were in the shop.

Do you work in the office or factory and wonder if sales is for you? If you answer *yes* to these questions, report to your sales manager in the morning:

> • Do you have great technical or product knowledge?
> • Have you hit the pay ceiling?
> • Do you get along well with customers or have good people skills?

If you think you can do it, you are probably right. But you must be willing to take risks.

And, hey, salesperson without hands-on inside experience – Get some! Devote some time to working in every area of your business. Your inside team will respect you more, you will have a better understanding of your product and co-workers, and your customers will benefit from your newfound product knowledge. So will your wallet.

*I learn how to win*
*by networking and developing*
*relationships with winners.*
*-- Bob Salvin*

# What's Bob Salvin got to do with it? Lots!

"You don't take a chance when you bet on yourself," says Bob Salvin, an international distributor of medical products adapted for implant dentistry. He has customers in all 50 states and in 27 countries. How does he get them?

"I think of myself as humbly assertive. I give first. If I start to think what I'll get back or start to count my orders before I get them, I always lose. My philosophy is to give as much as I can. Eventually it comes back much greater than the original gift, and from the most unexpected places."

"My definition of marketing is getting your telephone to ring with *qualified* buyers."

"How do I do that? By ...

- Giving out thousands of catalogs to the right people at a trade show.
- Mailing catalogs after a trade show.
- Mailing the catalog to qualified lists.
- Mailing catalogs to preregistered meeting lists – buyers put us on their list of 'Must Visit.'
- Mailing quantities of catalogs to dentists.
- Offering clinical courses in their offices.
- Asking lecturing doctors to recommend us.
- Talking to a qualified customer at a meeting or trade show."

*"I have developed a 'cross-mentoring' network locally, nationally, and internationally. I talk to other people who do part of what I do and try to help them as they help me.*
*Sometimes I call them – sometimes they call me.*
*Not direct competitors, but businesses who have the same marketing components."*

- I talk to others who do catalogs.
- I talk to others who do trade shows.
- I talk to others who run distribution centers.
- I learn from them. They learn from me.

## *"I learn how to win by networking and developing relationships with winners."*

"We do a tremendous amount of direct mail and trade show marketing. I know that to be successful I have to capitalize on these leads. I also know that to turn those leads into sales, I'd better be extraordinary.

"Everyone we meet and talk to at a trade show gets a personalized letter with another catalog. We highlight the products they showed interest in – and we do it within 36 hours after the show." Says Salvin, "We want to prepare the customer up front that they are about to receive excellent service." WOW.

"People love to buy," says Salvin, "but customers tend to buy from people they know and trust.

"Every dentist has a closet full of stuff he thought he would like, thought he needed but didn't," says Salvin. "My objective is to never have any Salvin products in that closet.

"A doctor's time is short. I've got to get their attention fast and gain interest so I can gain more time."

- **I don't sell. I make it easy to buy.** My prospects and customers get multiple personal exposures to Salvin – and toll-free communication.
- **I provide multiple choices at multiple levels.** All kinds of options with every product we sell. For example:
    1. Technical literature.
    2. Technical literature plus a video demonstrating the product.
    3. Literature, the video, plus a 30-day trial.

- **I make it easy to decide.** "Evaluate at your leisure. Test it in your environment for 3 weeks."
- **I make it easy to return.** But very few choose that option.

"I'm a puppy dog marketer. I offer our highly technical products on 3-week or 30-day trials," says Salvin. "Less than 1 of 30 return these products, but that's a misleading figure. Our referrals from those who keep the products far exceed the number of products returned. We have added videotape training to enhance the sales ratio. And even those who do return continue to purchase our other products."

*We create multiple ways to win ...*
- Create different benefits.
- Create different terms.
- Create different perceived values. (*Example:* Lifetime warranties might be important to some, not to others.)
- The comfort level of my prospect is paramount to their deciding to buy my product. We create multiple opportunities to win by offering the prospect comfortable choices.
- My objective is to create enough confidence to make the initial sale, then deliver in a manner that creates long-term opportunities.
- I explore how many ways I can develop communications so that the customer gets my message in a way he or she finds comfortable.

Bob Salvin does not always have the lowest the price, and he's proud of it. He tells a customer, "First let me tell you the price, but price is not why most of my customers (94% of whom are repeat) buy. They buy the value, the extended warranty, the extended terms, the help to finance, and the technical support. They buy the product, the support, and the organization – then they buy the price." WOW.

> *"I create winning situations.*
> *I train my customers how to understand,*
> *use, and profit from the equipment I sell," said Salvin.*
> *"It's not what it costs, it's what it produces.*
> *I tell my customers we usually have the best price –*
> *but we always have the best value."*

"I make sales in the most unorthodox ways I've ever seen," Salvin says. "I'll invite a prospect 1,000 miles away to have lunch with me." I say, "Let's have lunch together at our desks, over the phone. I send my product ($1,000 to $5,000 value), we discuss the possibilities, and I do a demo over the phone while we eat a sandwich. The products we sell are technique sensitive, and a big part of our value is to convey proper use."

How many ways do you have for your customers to buy or get to know about and buy your product? *Here are 10 more of Salvin's multiple ways to win:*

1. Literature and technical manuals.
2. Training video.
3. Third-party referral.
4. Extended warranty (beyond factory).
5. Lifetime warranty.
6. Return it if not satisfied.
7. Training.
8. Support before and after the sale.
9. Sample of product or free trial.
10. Loaned equipment during repair.

*"By eliminating ways to fail, you give the prospect comfort to buy, and buy now. In my marketing plan I have ostensibly eliminated the risk of my prospect making a poor choice."*

*Bob Salvin is not just smart, he's wise. Here are a few of his philosophies of marketing that we can all benefit from:*

• Try to personalize everything you do.
• Look for ways to go beyond what's expected, then do them without being asked.
• Make prospects or customers think about you, even if they don't buy.
• Make your prospect excited to get your stuff.
• Make your prospect feel comfortable enough to do business with you.
• Make them laugh.
• Learn what is important to them.
• Give prospects choices they can't refuse.
• Create new ways to say, "Thank you for your business."

"I'm Southern polite when I sell. I ask permission to do everything," says Salvin. I ask, "Is that OK?"

Evidently it is, because Salvin's phone rings off the hook.

# The Book
## of
# Prophets

**10.3**

# Crystal Balls

Prophets ...

There are two aspects of
prophecy.

One is to see into the
future. The other is to see
deeply into the present.

Here is a group of
individuals who have done
both.

They are excellent role
models for leadership.
Individuals who have done
what all great leaders must
do ... put themselves on
the cutting edge.

They've inspired me.
They'll inspire you.

*Harvey Mackay and Ken Blanchard*
*have written benchmark business books*
*that, if read and followed,*
*will help you reach your goals.*

# Ken Blanchard and Harvey Mackay gave a seminar to remember … and information to use.

Harvey Mackay and Ken Blanchard gave an all-day seminar in Charlotte recently. Fantastic is an understatement. Mackay is the consummate showman, storyteller, and presenter. His *Swim with the Sharks Without Being Eaten Alive* made it to #1 on the *New York Times* Best Seller List. The book is a classic piece of business literature, written in short-lesson format … easy to understand, and quickly assimilated. In his book and seminar he shares practical concepts that have worked for him personally.

His talk focused on the value of contacts and the word *ROLODEX* as an important method of cataloguing valuable contacts. He also spent time on the famous *"Mackay 66"* customer questionnaire, which asks everything you need to know about your prospect, from birthday to special interests. It asks questions that reveal facts and insights about the prospect. Things like significant achievements the prospect has made, names and ages of children, business background, family, education, lifestyles, and relationship potentials.

To prove its impact, Harvey did the *Mackay 66* on me, without my knowledge. He knew my birthday, my kids' names, where I went to high school and college, that I like karaoke, that I collect rubber stamps, and about 10 other personal facts. It blew me away.

Mackay's point is that if you know all the important customer information and your competition does not, you have a significant advantage and are more likely to make the sale. He is absolutely right. At that point he could have sold me anything.

How much do you know about your customers? How much does your main competitor know about your customers? Gaining and KEEPING the competitive edge is not just delivering a product or service; there is also a huge human factor. Getting information about your prospect/customer may be the most important part of the selling process.

Overkill? Takes too long? Not important? Consider these facts before brushing the concept aside:

1. It helps you understand your prospect.
2. It helps you find areas to establish initial rapport with your prospect.
3. It helps you identify ways to establish a long-term relationship.
4. It helps solidify the sale.
5. It helps ward off the competition.

It might also be worthy to note that Mackay is a multimillionaire. He must have done a few things right along the way. His seminar, like his book, cited excellent real-world answers that made learning fun and memorable.

I always take notes. In the Mackay seminar I noted 73 significant points, ideas, or concepts, ranging from impact statements like, "Dig a well prior to becoming thirsty" and "Agreements prevent disagreements," to helpful information on time management and making a sale. He told everyone to find mentors who will help lead them to entrepreneurial success. Mackay delivered his message eloquently and played to the audience well.

## Ken Blanchard's *One Minute Manager* is legendary. There are
very few people who are able to effect rule changes in a game. It is a sign of greatness. In basketball they widened the foul lanes because of Wilt Chamberlain. Ken Blanchard changed the rules of management. He gives management insight in a manner that has revolutionized the way managers interact with staff. The book focuses on 1-minute goals, 1-minute praisings, and 1-minute reprimands. Blanchard's methods increase productivity, to be sure, but more than that, his philosophy enhances insight and communication. Far too many people dislike and/or disrespect their boss. These methods, if studied and practiced, will bring rewards you can't imagine.

If you're a salesperson, buy two copies – one for yourself, one for your boss. If you're a sales manager or company president, read it and live the principles. You will not only develop and KEEP good salespeople, you will also be liked and respected.

Blanchard's seminar was absolutely brilliant. Down to earth. Humble. He always spoke as "we" when giving advice, including himself as the advice receiver as well as the advice giver. (It is interesting to note he is a mentor to Harvey Mackay.)

Blanchard began his talk offstage on the auditorium floor. It was an intimate communication with the attendees. He stated that even though he has written several books on managerial excellence, he must rededicate himself to those principles every day. Among the 67 ideas, principles, and gems of wisdom he shared that I captured were ...

- Narrow the gap between who we can be and who we are.
- We need each other.
- Prepare your own personal mission statement ... and live it.
- If you want to know if you're on the path you want, write your own obituary. See if it contains what you wanted to accomplish in your lifetime.
- A goal is a dream with a deadline.
- Give up being right all the time. Admit you screw up once in a while.

Ken Blanchard is real. Ken Blanchard is inspiring.

I go to live seminars whenever I can. I always learn something, and they never fail to inspire me. In my years of attending seminars and listening to tapes, Blanchard and Mackay delivered the best dose of practical knowledge I've ever had in a day. This chapter is not a review of what happened. It is a challenge for you to take action and go purchase the works of Mackay and Blanchard. Read them and enact their principles. They will inspire you and help you succeed. **It is also a personal, public *thank you* to Ken Blanchard and Harvey Mackay.**

*You can get whatever you want,*
*if you help enough people get whatever they want.*
*-- Zig Ziglar*

# Zig Ziglar almost failed, almost quit.

"I almost failed as a salesman," said Zig as he stood beside me an hour before delivering his motivational message to 2,700 Ziglar disciples. "I had struggled for 2 1/2 years. I was on a losing streak, but I never saw myself as a loser." What verbal poetry. I was standing with the best motivational speaker of our time.

"I still had the fear of rejection," Zig said. "I didn't understand that prospects weren't rejecting me; they were only rejecting the offer I was making them."

Sales wisdom of the first order. If every salesperson could grasp that philosophy, problems like cold call reluctance and fear of closing would evaporate.

"If it wasn't for some words of encouragement from my company president, P.C. Merrell, I would have probably found another job," said Zig. "Merrell said, 'Ziglar, you have real ability; you're champion caliber, I'm looking at you as a future officer of this company.' Those words inspired me to become the #2 salesman in a company of 7,000 in 1 year," said Zig with an intense yet peaceful look on his face. He says of his mentors, "Bill Cranford [the man credited with training Ziglar] got the salesman ready. P.C. Merrell got the man ready."

That was a long time ago. It's hard to count the years, or the millions of dollars earned since then by this legendary salesman. It's Tuesday, and he will deliver an inspirational message to a Charlotte audience that he has delivered 300 times before. He told me he had rehearsed in his room last night for 3 hours. Talk about practice what you preach! Zig Ziglar is a classic example of focus, dedication, and self-discipline.

Ziglar has been a sales and speaking inspiration to me for the past two decades. Now I'm standing next to him as he greets every one (125) of the VIP breakfast attendees as though they were a long-lost relative. "Hi, I'm Zig Ziglar. Glad you could join us this morning," he said to each person as he shook their hand. People brought books to autograph, had cameras to take photos, and all had something nice to say about this man who walks and talks with grace.

Now we're live on stage. Zig has the entire audience in the palm of his hand. Bouncing across the stage, down on one knee, arms expressing the words he wants to punch, all in total control. A master of the spoken word.

There were over 90 ideas that I took away from Zig's presentation. *Wisdom like ...*

- You can get whatever you want, if you help enough people get whatever they want.
- You were born to win, but you must plan to win, prepare to win, then you can expect to win.
- I wasn't born in Dallas, but I got there as quick as I could.
- It's not where you start, it's where you go.
- Money ... you like the things it can buy, but you love the things it can't buy.
- We hear or say the word *no* over 116,000 times in our lifetime.
- The health club is packed the first few weeks in January from people making New Year's resolutions, but the crowd thins out in less than 30 days.

Zig shared the stage with Peter Lowe, an international sales trainer who speaks with Ziglar about 40 times a year. Peter presented some interesting and innovative sales techniques, and provided a practical training balance to the inspired audience.

After his presentation, I asked Peter what the biggest shortcoming was in today's salesperson. He responded without hesitation, "Improper communication skills and inadequate training in the fundamental science of selling techniques."

I left the hall feeling great.

## *Personal note ...*

My favorite image of Zig Ziglar was one morning several years ago on *The Today Show*. Zig was on to promote his book and was the last guest. He was sort of talked to as a sideshow attraction – a salesman. At the end of the interview – literally the end of the show – Tom Brokaw said, "We've got 30 seconds left, Zig. Sell me some insurance."

Ziglar went into a 25-second pitch that was creative and sharp. Brokaw was somewhat impressed but turned to the audience and said triumphantly, "See, I didn't say *yes*." Ziglar instantly snapped back – "Yes, but you didn't say *no*," and they went off the air.

Positive attitude is not hearing *no*.

*When I fail,
I look at what I did right,
not what I did wrong.*
*-- Tom Hopkins*

# The sales doctor makes a house call.

Tom Hopkins is a master sales trainer and presenter. He has delivered more than 3,200 seminars and helped more than 2 million people strive for greater success in the selling profession.

His first book, *How to Master the Art of Selling*, has sold more than 1 million copies, making it the best-selling book to date on the subject of "how-to" selling techniques. With his audiotapes, hundreds of thousands of salespeople (including me) drive from appointment (Tom prefers to call them "visits") to appointment with Tom Hopkins helping them turn their cars into classrooms.

The first time I saw Tom Hopkins live was at the Sheraton Hotel in Valley Forge, PA, in 1982. I had just read his book and listened to the entire series of cassettes titled *How to Master the Art of Selling Anything* ... and I was pumped. Tom held the standing-room-only audience in the palm of his hand for 6 hours. Every person in the audience will remember that day.

*Everyone in the audience was leaning forward ...
in the buying position. Hopkins literally had them
on the edge of their chairs the entire day.
He is a sales wordsmith of the first order.*

Hopkins delivered meat. Information you could take to the streets and convert to commissions – Tom prefers to call them "fees for services." In fact, there were several words he recommended salespeople change in their jargon to take away the prospect's fear of buying.

*A few examples* ...

> cost or price = *amount* or *total investment*
> down payment = *initial amount* or *initial investment*
> contract = *paperwork, agreement,* or *form*
> buy = *own*
> problem = *situation* or *challenge*
> objection = *area of concern*
> cheaper = *more economical*

He challenged us that to be better salespeople, we must discover our areas of sales weaknesses and strengthen them. A 50-question sales skill evaluation was part of the seminar, and Hopkins promised everyone a computerized diagnosis within a few weeks. He donned a stethoscope to make his point. The sales doctor. The audience loved it.

Hopkins encouraged the audience of 1,000 to learn to accept rejection and failure as a part of the profession. He said, "When I fail, I look at what I did right, not what I did wrong." He challenged everyone to look at these inevitable events in a new way. He said, "I never see failure as failure, only as ...

> 1. A learning experience.
> 2. The negative feedback I need to change course in my direction.
> 3. The opportunity to develop my sense of humor.
> 4. The opportunity to practice my techniques and perfect my performance.
> 5. The game I must play to win."

*The benchmarks of his presentation centered around fundamental issues of sales and life's ethics. They are brilliant. They are simple.*

• Selling is finding the people to sell and selling the people you find.
• Great sales presentations consist of three parts –
> 1. Tell them what you're going to tell them.
> 2. Tell them.
> 3. Tell them what you've told them.
• In sales, the objective is moving people to decisions.
• Failure is an event, not a person.
• Make people feel important.
• Build your business on truth.
• Listening is more important than talking.

- Get your prospect (future client) involved by asking questions.
- Learn the science of asking questions.
- Use tie-down ("Aren't you?" … "Isn't it?" … "Doesn't it?") questions (that command *yes* answers) to confirm your prospect's agreement.
- Learn to recognize buying signals.
- Know when to ask for the sale.
- Take notes during the selling process, especially when the prospect is talking.
- Giving exceptional service will keep the people you serve in your camp forever and get them to recommend their friends and associates.
- Do the most productive thing possible at every given moment.
- Have fun.

*Hopkins also shared his philosophy on enthusiasm:*

♥ Make sales your first love.
♥ Treat sales like your favorite hobby.
♥ People will say yes based more on your conviction and enthusiasm than on your product knowledge.

How do you attain and maintain enthusiasm?

*Here's Hopkins five-step formula:*

1. Maintain your curiosity.
2. Sustain interest in all you do.
3. Have a never-ending thirst for knowledge.
4. Believe in what you do.
5. Your purpose in life must be more than money.
   (I would dare to add a sixth – Don't dwell on problems. Concentrate on solutions.)

His enthusiasm is so real it's contagious. Tom Hopkins burns with the overwhelming desire to increase the effectiveness and the incomes of the people who seek his teaching and want to become highly skilled, professional salespeople. I was fortunate to spend some personal time with Tom, and I can tell you his passion for training is straight from his heart.

I own every book and tape Tom Hopkins has written or recorded. He even has a series for children called *How to Make Your Dreams Come True*. I urge you to make his training material a part of your library.

Tom Hopkins is the sales doctor. A man who has dedicated his life to helping salespeople develop a cure for the common close.

# The Book of Numbers

**11.1**

# Up Your Income!

Numbers don't lie ... and they don't make excuses.

Do you?

If you don't hit your numbers in sales, you're only doing a number on yourself.

The law of numbers is the law of averages combined with your ability to master the science of selling, help other people, and establish long-term relationships.

You got into sales because it had unlimited income potential.

Are you limiting yourself because you failed to commit to the dedication necessary to achieve "unlimited"?

Unlimit yourself!

*Up Your Income!*™
*Double the money you make in just 30 days!*

> *Selling success is a numbers game ...*
> *and a magic game.*
> *You must combine the magic*
> *with your numbers to produce ...*

# The pipeline of success.

*Aren't making enough sales? Your numbers will tell you why.*
*Your numbers can double if you follow this formula! WOW.*

I am about to present you with a formula and a challenge.

If you're looking for a magic formula, go read a book on the life and times of Houdini. *If you're looking for magic, that's different.* You have all the magic needed to double your present income. All you have to do is learn and execute the tricks.

*Here is the theory behind the formula. These questions will provide the answers to your sales earning capacity:*

- How many sales do you want to make per day, per month?
- What is the dollar value of your average sale?
- To make your goal, how many dollars in sales do you have to make per day, per month?
- How many prospects do you need to see to make a sale?
- What is the set of numbers I need to get to these answers?

Want to do it in 30 days? Easy – up your urgency. Get committed.
I can supply the jet plane. It's up to you to provide the jet fuel. When I started out in sales, I used to pick up the paper and read the obituaries until I found someone who was close to my age. It lit a candle under me for weeks.

*Below are the components of the doubling formula.*
*The mastering of each component is discussed*
*in different chapters in this book.*
*Each chapter gives you information and insight.*
*All of the elements (components) are linked.*
*Their combination will create your Pipeline of Success.*

## There are 12.5 elements in the formula ...

**1. Your attitude** – The key to your success. Get tapes now. Listen 2 hours a day for 6 months. Stop doing or listening to negative things.

**2. Your goals** – Set them today. Read the seven steps in the *Post-it Note* section again. Use the Post-it Notes beginning right now.

**3. Your networking** – Find out where your best customers and prospects meet (trade association, chamber, club). Begin attending every meeting you can. It is imperative that you attend regularly.

**4. Your Power Questions** – Write 'em ... learn 'em ... use 'em.

**5. Your Power Statements** – Write 'em ... learn 'em ... use 'em.

**6. Your sales tools** – Figure out what tools you need and get 'em.

**7. Your sales knowledge** – Get tapes and listen to them. Alternate with the attitude tapes. Use the technique as soon as you hear it. Read every chapter in this book twice. One chapter per day.

**8. Your preparedness** – Are you truly ready to sell? If you are, you will. If you're not, you won't. The opposite of preparedness is failure.

**9. Your follow-up** – tenacious, creative persistence that leads to a sale.

**10. Your sales numbers** – making yourself see the numbers you need to build your pipeline and keep it full. Find your formula and use it.

**11. Your prospect pipeline** – Seeing the proper number of people a day who are qualified to buy builds your pipeline. The key to double income is having the right number of prospects ready to buy.

**12. Your commitment** – Write it to yourself. Tell others who will help you. Your commitment is your personal promise to yourself. Keep it at all costs.

**12.5 Your self-discipline** – Your determination and ability to achieve your goals and live up to your commitments.

There is a sales adage that says, "Your chances for success increase in proportion to the number of sales calls you make." It's amazing how the truth can be so simple. **If it's so simple, why don't you do it?**

Good fundamental sales skills and solid product knowledge
are meaningless unless you see and follow up
the proper number of prospects.

Seeing the numbers creates a pipeline ...
the number of prospects at or near the buying point.

*A quick check of your numbers will reveal why your sales
are booming or slumping ...*

If you appoint and present to 10 prospects, 2 will buy no matter what you
do and 2 won't buy no matter what you do. The other 6 are on the fence
and will buy or not buy as a result of what you say or don't say. A sale will
be made either way. Either you sell them on yes, or they sell you on no.

### *Your follow-up habits and skills are responsible for 80% of your sales.*

*It boils down to your self-discipline.* How good is it? How consistent is it?
Without it you should consider an assembly-line job, because you won't
make it in sales. Here is a sample formula to keep your sales pipeline (and
wallet) full:

1. Make 10 new prospect calls per day.
2. Make 10 new appointments per week,
   preferably by Monday.
3. Make 10 follow-up calls per day.
4. Make one strong presentation in the morning
   and one in the afternoon.
5. Take prospects or customers to lunch four
   times a week.
6. Join two business or leads associations.
7. Attend at least two networking functions
   per week (where your best customers or
   prospects go).
8. Keep accurate daily records.

If you don't record what you do each day, your ability to follow up is nil. Your daily sales log (or computerized sales records) should keep and total the following statistics:

- Calls out by type (new, follow-up)
- Number of follow-ups made today
- New appointments made today
- Appointments seen today
- Sales made today
- Dollars contracted for today
- Dollars collected today
- Commissions/dollars earned today

**Important Note:** Keep separate sheets or files for each contact. Your reporting should be by contact status, not by time status (what you did on Tuesday morning). If your manager is still in the Dark Ages about contact management or has that paranoia of needing to know where you are every minute of the day, ask him to read *The Book of Leadership* in this volume.

## Your contact management program will tell you where you are in the selling cycle.

*Answer these questions – they reveal the truth about your potential for sales success:*

- ✔ Do you have a hot prospect list daily?
- ✔ Are you doing (and recording) the numbers it takes to make your sales goals a reality?
- ✔ Is your sales pipeline (prospects you can convert to sales) full?
- ✔ How many prospects are you working on? (Should be 100+.)
- ✔ Are you working on enough prospects to fill your sales goals for the next month? If not, your pipeline isn't full, is it? Go back to the 12.5 elements listed above. They hold the key to your sales backlog (and your success).

*You know what to do. Why don't you do it? Here are some reasons why you don't (the answers are provided in parentheses):*

- You're on your own and don't know how to do it. (*Poor training. Get some good training soon.*)
- You're lazy. (*Find new employment.*)
- You have poor work habits. (*You can change them with 30 days of doing it differently.*)
- Bad boss. (*Don't blame failure on others. This is no reason to fail if you are determined enough to succeed.*)
- No or ineffective reporting system. (*Get a laptop, or make a form and do it yourself.*)
- Low, poor, or unfair compensation package. (*Change jobs.*)

*If you see and call enough prospects per day, per week, per month ... you will build your pipeline. A full pipeline will bring you sales you never imagined.*

Do you floss every day? You know you should, but you don't. Eventually all your teeth will fall out, but you can't see them eroding day by day until it's too late. **Floss every day -- your teeth will be perfect.** The same is true about the fundamentals of sales follow-up. If you don't follow up every day, your sales backlog will rot. **Add to your pipeline every day and do your follow-ups -- your sales will be perfect.**

Want proof? Go back to the best week you ever had and look at the numbers that made it happen. I guarantee if you work those numbers every week, your sales (and earnings) will soar.

**All it takes is self-determination and hard work. That's the magic. Ask any magician.**

# THE SALES BIBLE

**Part 12**
**Can I Get an Amen?!**

# The Book of Exodus

## Let my money go.

Exodus was the road to freedom.

The end of *The Sales Bible* is really the beginning ... the beginning of a revolution in your sales career.

It's a Sales Crusade, and you are your own Sales Crusader.

You're on a journey to personal sales success.

Others won't do it for you, but others will help you, if you help them first.

You have the opportunity to take the wealth of information you've gotten from this book and turn it into a fortune.

I hope you do.

12.1

# Dads teach sales success without knowing it.

My dad set examples for me like yours did for you. Sometimes they were good examples; sometimes they were bad. But every time my dad set one, I paid attention to it, and decided when I grew up whether I would follow that example. Here are a few to ponder.

**Don't let lawyers or greed sway good business judgment.** In 1960, after 15 successful years of operation, my dad's factory burned to the ground. We were stunned. Two days later, the insurance adjuster came to our house with a check for $750,000 to settle the fire loss and let my dad rebuild his business. My dad's lawyer took him aside and told him he thought we could get a million and to reject the offer. My dad went for the million. Three years later, my dad settled for $333,000, one-third of which went to the lawyer. The lessons I learned were: Lawyers are for legal advice, not business advice; and take your losses quickly and move on to rebuild your life. Those lessons helped me when I faced failure.

Provide simple solutions. One night my brother turned over in his single bed and fell onto the floor. He went downstairs and pounded on my parents' door: "Dad, I fell out of bed!" he moaned. "Get back in, son," my father said.

Often the most simple solutions to problems are the best. But they're hard to uncover if you're only concentrating on the problem.

**Anything 10 grand won't cure?** Coming home from college I was sometimes in a bad mood. One day when I was slamming doors and looking glum, my dad asked, "Problems, son?" "A few," I muttered. "Anything 10 grand won't cure?" he asked. My whole mood changed. "No," I said. And realized I didn't really have any problems.

*Anything ten grand won't cure?* Ask yourself that question the next time you're lamenting your woes. If 10 grand (or money) would solve the problem, you really don't have a problem. Do you? Find a child in a wheelchair. That's a problem. You're just whining.

# Write it all down
# at the end of each day.

I'm asleep in 2 minutes or less every night; I wake up refreshed every day;
I don't drink coffee in the morning; I never worry about what I have to do
or what loose ends there are. I'm always prepared for the day and get my
best ideas in the shower.

The secret? Three words: **Write everything down.**
I keep a legal pad by my bedside. Before I go to bed, I write down
everything I need to do or problems I need to solve. Once I write
everything down, my mind is clear.

Mental freedom is a wonderful thing. It creates opportunities not available
to a cluttered mind.

It provides clear channels from the subconscious for solutions and new
ideas, and it lets you sleep like a log.

I've been doing it for 35 years. It works.

# The perspective of sales.

## *In the end ...*

➤ There is only one point of view that matters.

➤ There is only one perspective that matters.

➤ There is only one perception that matters.

# The Customer's

# The end is the beginning.

## As my valued customer ...

You'll read my weekly sales column in a
business paper near you.

I'm coming to see you.
I'm coming to talk to you about sales.
I'm coming with the intent to help you and
establish a long-term relationship with you.

I'm coming to have fun and make people laugh.
*and* ...
I'm coming with the intent to sell you something.

*I hope you feel the same about coming to see me.*

# Commit yourself!

For 35 years I have been on a personal crusade to be the best salesperson in the world. I set that goal (in stone) the first time I ever realized there was a *science* of selling – that selling was a set of learnable, repeatable skills that I could modify to my style and personality. (I was listening to a tape by J. Douglas Edwards on closing the sale.) I knew that if I became the best, I could achieve anything I wanted. When I combined the science of selling with my attitude and sense of humor, I provided myself the gateway for tremendous achievement.

I have written this book (and will continue to write my column every week) to help guide you to the same achievement. Take 30 minutes and read something about *The Crusades*. They were much more than a religious war. *The Crusades* were about people going after what they believed in ... passionately. They did it regardless of the hardship and risk. Do you?

Sales is not a religion, but it is a way of life. It should not consume your life; rather it should be incorporated into your life. It enhances life and embraces the philosophy for living it to its maximum potential.

*Doubling your income isn't pie in the sky.*
*If you are determined to get to the top,*
*here are the principles that will get you there.*

## 11.5 principles to lead your own sales crusade.

**1. Get a positive attitude and keep it.** Most everyone thinks they have a positive attitude, but they don't. Usually not even close. Earl Nightingale, in his legendary tape, *The Strangest Secret*, reveals the secret of a positive attitude: *We become what we think about* ... but it's a dedicated discipline that must be practiced every day. People don't understand that the essence of attitude is not a feeling – it's a state of mind that is self-induced. You are in complete control of it. You determine what your attitude is. It has nothing to do with what happens to you. It's not about money or success. **It's the way you dedicate yourself to the way you think.** But you must rededicate yourself to the principles of it every day.

How do you attain a positive attitude? Begin to surround yourself with positive ideas and positive people. Read and listen to positive writers and speakers. Believe you can achieve it. Don't listen to other people who tell you you're nuts – they're just jealous. Start now and work at it every day.

## 2. Set goals, and make a commitment to achieve them.

✔ **Project yourself** – If your targets are in front of you, it makes it easy to hit them. Being able to hit the targets depends on your focus. The clearer your focus, the more likely you are to hit a bullseye.

✔ **Commit yourself** – Which do you plan for more: your vacation or your life? If you don't emotionally, physically, mentally, and spiritually commit yourself to achievement, it is likely you will fall short.

✔ **Satisfy yourself** – Make a list of the benefits of achieving each goal and carry the list with you. Achieving a goal is incredibly self-satisfying. It gives you a feeling of accomplishment, purpose and the inspiration to set out and achieve the next goal. Big Clue … Figure out the daily dose. An amount you can measure, an amount you can achieve. Determine how much you need to do each day to reach your goal in short steps (pennies per day, ounces per day, pounds per week, calls per day, dollars per sale) and do that daily dose each day.

## 3. Dedicate yourself to mastering the science of selling. *Learn something new about sales or your attitude every day.* Feed your head with new knowledge that will help you make that next sale. If you want to become an expert in sales, learning one new technique per day gives you 220 new techniques per year. If you sell for 5 years, you'll have more than 1,000 techniques at your disposal. Amazing what you can do if you just do something small every day. If you just dedicate 15 to 30 minutes a day to learning something new about sales and achieving a positive attitude, at the end of 5 years you will be a master salesperson and have a great attitude about life.

**4. Design a networking plan and implement it.** Make a 5-year plan to get known and get to know those who can build your business. Networking is the fastest, surest method to increase your sales and stature.

**5. Be a leader.** Look for and strive for leadership positions. Take charge of a committee; speak to a civic group, write an article for a local paper. People love to do business with leaders.

**6. Get involved in your community.** Select a charity or community organization worthy of your time and make a contribution. You'll grow in success and reputation, but more important you'll feel great about living to help others.

**7. Know your prospect and your prospect's business before you make the sales call.** Get the information you need to make every appointment intelligent and impactful. Use this guideline to assure it: *Ask the buyer questions that only he or she knows the answers to.*

**8. Be memorable in all that you do.** Take a creative idea to each sales call. Have the courage to live your dreams and goals. Your work and dedication will inspire others. Your words will be remembered because you backed them up with deeds and delivery. Will they talk about you after you're gone?

**9. Help other people.** When you establish this belief as one of the foundations of your selling process, the attributes that accompany it are the keys to making your customer feel motivated to act and confident enough to buy. There is an offshoot of this philosophy: *Get business for others.* It is as powerful as any sales tool you can imagine.

**10. Stay focused and look for opportunity.** How important is it to be focused? In 1982, after a big imprinted sportswear show, I was at the Dallas airport when I noticed a guy I met from a T-shirt manufacturing company. He was swearing at the American Express money machine. It seems the machine ate his card. He was looking desperate. I walked over, reintroduced myself, found out the problem, and loaned him $100 so that he would have cash for the trip home. Two days later, he sent me a check for $100 and a thank-you note. Turns out he was the president of his company. Two months later, he called me and asked if I was interested in printing garments for the 1984 Olympics. He had the sublicense to manufacture from Levi's. We had a state-of-the-art printing facility. I said, "Of course." He gave me a contract to print every shirt – 1,600,000 garments, $750,000 worth of business – because I was paying attention at the airport. And because I was living my philosophy of "help other people."

**11. Establish long-term relationships with everyone.** If you look to establish a long-term relationship each time you sell, it assures that the integrity, sincerity, honesty, and doing what's best for the customer are a given. Make long-term a prerequisite for selling. Be sure to share this philosophy with your customers.

**11.5 Have fun.** Look at the most successful people in any field. One thing they have in common is that they love what they do. They pursue what they do with a passion and enthusiasm that is admirable (and contagious). How much fun are you having?

# I hope
# all your
# appointments
# are one-call
# closes …
# that lead to
# long-term
# relationships.

-- *Jeffrey Gitomer*

# Afterword ...
# When I grow up.

I always wanted to be a businessman, an entrepreneur, like my dad.
I decided to commute to college so that I could be close to home and
his business.

My mother, Florence, passed away in 1986. My fondest memory is of her
chasing my car as I backed out of the driveway on my first day to register
for college (Temple University): "Take pre-med," she screamed. "You can
always switch." But I wanted to be a businessman, like my dad.

In college I played Scrabble every day with my best friend growing up,
Michael Toll. He usually won. It taught me about words and how to use
them. Michael also provided me with the challenge of winning at games,
both sports and intellectual. He'll tell you he was better than me at
everything. I feel the same about him. That was the fun. We rarely studied.

Six years later, I finally dropped out of college. I traveled in Europe for a
year (and came to the realization that I knew very little compared to what
there was to know, which is funny, because I left for Europe knowing
everything). I came home and started a business (manufacturing beanbag
chairs) and a family (twin girls in 1972).

One day, Jay Plasky and Barton Cohen (college friends) came to my office
and started talking to me about this money-making idea. It seems they had
been involved with this guy named Glenn Turner, and he had this idea to
get people to invest in an opportunity that was not quite clear to me, but
everyone was making money – big money – and they all had these *positive
attitudes*. After a few alterations, Jay, Barton, and I embarked on a multilevel
marketing deal (which was referred to in those days as a pyramid scheme).

Every day from 8 A.M. to noon, we had a sales training meeting. We learned
the science of selling from every available source. Tapes, books, movies, and
lectures. Every sales expert was played and replayed – gleaned for
information. None had all; all had some. Napoleon Hill's *Think and Grow
Rich* was mandatory reading, and we dissected the book line by line.
Attitude and sales skills became my life.

My friends thought I was nuts – some still do. I watched a Glenn Turner movie (no video in those days), *Challenge to America*, 200 times. It was the best sales pitch I'd ever seen. I had the entire presentation and all the stories memorized.

I became a salesman. My first goal was to be the best salesman in the world. I'm still on that journey, every day.

I started a T-shirt factory with Duke Daulton and Bud Massey in Florida. It was so successful that the title of president was vacated, and we were all vying for the titles of emperor and king. We lost that business because everything we did we measured … who did what and how much. I vowed I would never measure or keep score again. And I haven't. Duke and I went on to become consulting legends (in our own minds), and we had a blast.

After thousands of sales presentations to every conceivable prospect, from Fortune 500 company presidents to unemployed job seekers, and after several huge successes and huge failures in business, I somehow landed in Charlotte, N.C., starting over.

My first challenge was to learn how to calm down. I had to adapt the high-speed New York (actually Philadelphia) style to the pace of this genteel Southern city. That took 6 months. During that time, I met Joan Zimmerman, a world-class entrepreneur. She said, "Charlotte is a city that you can affect." WOW – what a powerful statement. I decided to stay.

My weekly column *Sales Moves* has changed my life. It has given me a vehicle to share my sales knowledge and secrets. My mother – in heaven – is bragging to other angels, because in the *Dallas Business Journal* her son's picture is right next to Tom Peters'.

My father, Max – in heaven – taught me to write. He taught me a thousand other things by setting both good and bad examples, but the way he wrote always had my admiration. No wasted words. Absolute clarity of message.

Max was the consummate entrepreneur. Growing up, I used to sneak downstairs and listen to my father's Thursday night pinochle game. Arguments and laughs about business and life. It was the inspiration for my life's pursuits. My pal, Duke Daulton, said, "You know what I hate about your old man? He's never wrong."

I'm grateful to my father for his wisdom – the stuff he accused me of never listening to for 30+ years. Thanks, Pop, I love you. I miss my mother. I miss my father. If your parents are still alive, call them *right now* and tell them you love them.

My brother, Josh, taught me to edit. He has the sensitivity to know how words fit and the gift to teach it. He showed me where unnecessary words made things complicated. His philosophy is: Use as few words as possible. Josh, I've tried.

My wife and friend, Teresa, who I sold a book to in Dallas, and 3 years later, I married.

My children, Erika, Stacey, and Rebecca, taught me patience. They also gave me the inspiration to achieve in the face of failure. Girls, I love you.

My attitude was there with me when everyone else was not.
So was my cat, Lito.

My name is Jeffrey Gitomer.
I'm a salesman.
I'm a dad.
I'm a college dropout.

My objective in life is to help others, establish long-term relationships, and have fun – every day.

# Thank you's.

*Thank you's are only meaningful to the author.* You read a book and you get to the thank-you page, and some guy is thanking someone who was obviously inspirational, but who the reader is clueless about. Here are mine.

I've been blessed with a lifetime of inspiration created from the challenges issued by friends. I want to thank my friends – hundreds of them. My parents, Max and Florence; my brother, Josh; my wife, Teresa; my children, Erika, Stacey, and Rebecca; and their mother, Donna. The people I met and befriended in the city of Charlotte – it's a great place to be an entrepreneur. I hope to stay here forever. My clients and business friends, Jim, Bill, Curtis, Rick, Jody, Bruce and his boss, Milton, Margurette, Nickyo's Rodeo, Belle Acres Country Club, Cindi, George, Jean, David, Jill, Doug, Joe, Steve, Aaron, Tom, Russell, Rich, Kelly, Ron, Greg, Howard, Chris, Jim, and Bucky, who helped me by allowing me to help them. My old friends, Michael, Duke, Jocko, Leslie, Gail, Klause, Frank, Bruce, Richard, Randy, and Walshie. My new friends, Angela, Richard, Laura, Katie, Bob, HA, Chubby, Ward, Barney, Dutch, Art, Lendon, Lawrence, and several guardian angels who showed up along the way – Sherry Bunn, Joann Sumner, Jan Taylor, Bob West, and some who have yet to reveal themselves. I even want to thank the people who I was with when I failed. I learned from them, too.

Bill Lewis for appearing out of the blue; Ty Boyd for special guidance.

The team/staff of great co-workers at BuyGitomer and TrainOne.com. The Charlotte Chamber of Commerce. The *Charlotte Business Journal*. Mark Ethridge and his fine staff. Joanne for edits – needed and otherwise. All the papers that publish *Sales Moves*.

Special book helpers – Rod Smith for criticism, feedback and inspiration; Cliff Glickman for getting "Sales Moves" started; Culp Elliott & Carpenter law firm; Christine Pearson; Jack Marks; Rick Marsh; Tom Dillon; Debbie Tillis; First Citizens Bank – Margaret, Linda and Linda; Interactive Knowledge; Maria, Jeff, and Matthew Davidson. Adrian Zackheim and Larry Norton for believing in me and challenging me. Debbie Mercer for being so helpful I couldn't believe it. Ken Blanchard for wisdom.

A special dedication to the Thompson Children's Home and the people who have dedicated themselves to helping children in the battle against child abuse. To Tom, who got me there, to Bill and Bill who encouraged me there.

My friends at Sunday dinner who read my writing and challenge it – Rick, Debbie, Richard, Mitchell, Connie, and Paula.

To original mentors in faraway places – Mel Green and Earl Pertnoy.

# Thank You!

## A Special Note of Thanks and Gratitude to Rod Smith

Rod Smith spent countless hours with this book. He gave insight and a creative spark to the overall organization of the material. He edited, re-edited, changed graphics, won and lost wording battles, fixed typos, and bulldozed the computer diskette through development. He did a world-class job. We killed each other laughing. We cherished each other's arrogance. (He wrote that line.) I'm appreciative of his help, his dedication, his spirit, and most of all, his friendship.

## A Special Note of Gratitude

Editorettes – the Second Decade. Books need editing and mothering. I have been blessed with two exceptional women who can do both. Laura Rager Miller and Rachel Russotto, two of my GitGirls that are part of *The Sales Bible*'s revisions, you are …

> Short on height
> Tall on talent and brains
> Long on hours and dedication
> Thank you. Thank you.

*Services Available ...*

# More Sales Now!

I am available for speaking engagements and training programs. Hire me.

I will design and deliver a customized program for your sales force that will have them laughing, learning, and ... selling.

I will make my presentation directly applicable to your selling situation. The program is developed for your company, your product, your customers, and the objections you face in your selling environment.

Your team can take my material out to their prospects and use it to make sales the same day they hear it.

**Assess yourself:** Since you bought *The Sales Bible*, you are entitled to your very own Sales Assessment. Go to www.gitomer.com and click on *Sales Bible Assessment.* This 12-question assessment will get you started on your journey to sales success. It's FREE, and it's a THANK YOU to those of you who bought this book. You may want to go to the "full-meal deal" at www.knowsuccess.com. Then again, you may not, because:
• It costs money.
• You may not want to know you're not as good as you think you are.

**Train yourself:** You are also entitled to a free TrainOne sales program. Go to www.trainone.com to view the demo. You need to have high-speed Internet access to view the demo and to become a TrainOne.com subscriber. If you don't, your competition is already beating you.

It's not just cost-effective, it's sales-effective. And it's fun.

A friendly person from my office is standing by ...

Jeffrey Gitomer
BuyGitomer, Inc., 310 Arlington Avenue, Loft 329, Charlotte, N.C. 28203
office 704.333.1112 * fax 704.333.1011
salesman@gitomer.com

**3.5 million readers of "Sales Moves"** – If my column is not in your local business paper, call them up and say, "Hey, get Gitomer. Publish his weekly column, 'Sales Moves.' It's helping salespeople all over the country. Get him now!" You are my field sales force. I need your help to achieve my goal of 10 million readers a week by the end of this decade.

# Jeffrey Gitomer
*Chief Executive Salesman*

**Author** – Jeffrey Gitomer is the author of *The Sales Bible*, now in its 18th printing, and *Customer Satisfaction Is Worthless* – *Customer Loyalty Is Priceless*. Gitomer's latest book, *The Patterson Principles of Selling*, will be released in late 2003. Jeffrey's books have sold more than 350,000 copies worldwide.

**Over 100 presentations a year** – Jeffrey gives seminars, runs annual sales meetings, and conducts training programs on selling and customer service. He has presented an average of 115 seminars a year for the past 10 years.

**Big corporate customers** – Jeffrey's customers include Coca-Cola, Cingular Wireless, Hilton, Choice Hotels, Enterprise Rent-A-Car, Cintas, Milliken, NCR, Financial Times, Turner Broadcasting, Comcast Cable, Time Warner Cable, HBO, Ingram Micro, Wells Fargo Bank, Mercedes Benz, Baptist Health Care, Blue Cross Blue Shield, Hyatt Hotels, Carlsberg Beer, Wausau Insurance, Northwestern Mutual, Sports Authority, GlaxoSmithKline, XEROX, A.C. Nielsen, IBM, AT&T, and hundreds of others.

**In front of millions of readers every week** – His syndicated column "Sales Moves" appears in more than 85 business newspapers and is read by more than 3,500,000 people every week.

**And every month** – Jeffrey's column appears in more than 25 trade publications and newsletters. Jeffrey has also been a contributor and featured expert in *Entrepreneur* and *Selling Power* magazines.

**On the Internet** – His three WOW Web sites – *www.gitomer.com*, *www.trainone.com*, and *www.knowsuccess.com* get as many as 5,000 hits a day from readers and seminar attendees. His state-of-the-art Web presence and e-commerce ability has set the standard among peers, and has won huge praise and acceptance from customers.

**Up Your Sales Web-based sales training** – A weekly streaming video (low cost – high value) sales training lesson is now available on *www.trainone.com*. The content is pure Jeffrey – fun, pragmatic, real world, and immediately implementable. This innovation is leading the way in the field of e-learning.

**Sales Caffeine** – A weekly "e-zine" sales wake-up call delivered every Tuesday morning to more than 65,000 subscribers free of charge. This allows us to communicate valuable sales information, strategies, and answers to sales professionals on a timely basis.

**Sales assessment online** – New for 2003 is the world's first customized sales assessment. Renamed a "successment," this amazing sales tool will not only judge your selling skill level in 12 critical areas of sales knowledge, it will give you a diagnostic report that includes 50 mini-sales lessons as it rates your sales abilities and explains your customized oppotunities for sales knowledge growth. Aptly named KnowSuccess, the company's mission is: You can't know success until you know yourself. Visit *www.knowsuccess.com* to find out more.

**Award for Presentation Excellence** – In 1997, Jeffrey was awarded the designation Certified Speaking Professional (CSP) by the National Speakers Association. The CSP award has been given less than 500 times in the past 25 years.

BuyGitomer, Inc. • 310 Arlington Avenue • Loft 329 • Charlotte, N.C. 28203
www.gitomer.com • 704.333.1112 • salesman@gitomer.com

# Index